THE REDCOATS OF WELLINGTON'S LIGHT DIVISION

THE REDCOATS OF WELLINGTON'S LIGHT DIVISION

UNPUBLISHED & RARE MEMOIRS OF THE 52ND (OXFORDSHIRE) REGIMENT OF FOOT

EDITED BY
GARETH GLOVER & ROBERT BURNHAM

FRONTLINE
BOOKS

First published in Great Britain in 2023 by
FRONTLINE BOOKS
an imprint of Pen & Sword Books Ltd,
47 Church Street, Barnsley, S. Yorkshire, S70 2AS

ISBN: 978-1-39908-496-3

CIP data records for this title are available from the British Library

For more information on our books, please visit
www.frontline-books.com, email info@frontline-books.com
or write to us at the above address.

Printed and bound by CPI Group (UK) Ltd, Croydon, CR0 4YY
Typeset by Concept, Huddersfield, West Yorkshire
Pen & Sword Books Ltd incorporates the imprints of Pen & Sword
Archaeology, Atlas, Aviation, Battleground, Discovery,
Family History, History, Maritime, Military, Naval, Politics,
Social History, Transport, True Crime, Claymore Press,
Frontline Books, Praetorian Press,
Seaforth Publishing and White Owl

For a complete list of Pen and Sword titles please contact
PEN & SWORD LTD
47 Church Street, Barnsley, South Yorkshire, S70 2AS, England
E-mail: enquiries@pen-and-sword.co.uk

Or

PEN AND SWORD BOOKS
1950 Lawrence Rd, Havertown, PA 19083, USA
E-mail: Uspen-and-sword@casematepublishers.com

CONTENTS

FOREWORD

Having spent the last two decades scouring the archives for unpublished letters and journals of soldiers who served in the Napoleonic wars, I have not particularly concentrated on the regiments that formed the Light Division in the *Peninsular War* because I was aware that due to their fame, many memoirs from members of these regiments had already been published and it was therefore highly likely that there was little left to publish.

However, a steady trickle of further memoirs by members of the Light Division have been published in the last twenty years to add to the already impressive total, showing that the mine is far from fully exhausted. These include those of Captain George Miller,[1] Lieutenant James Gairdner[2] and Rifleman George Walton[3] of the 95th Foot, Sergeant Samuel Harrison[4] of the 43rd Foot and Captains George Ulrich Barlow,[5] Charles Kinloch,[6] John Ewart[7] and Lieutenant Charles Holman[8] of the 52nd Foot.

I also received a request from my good friend Robert Burnham, who resides in Hawaii, to help him search the archives for any unpublished

1 Published as *The Making of a Rifles Officer: The Life and Letters of Colonel George Miller CB FRS (1786–1843)*. Elizabeth Laidlaw: Edinburgh: Burngrange, 2019.

2 Published as *The American Sharpe: The Adventures of an American Officer of the 95th Rifles in the Peninsula & Waterloo Campaigns*. Gareth Glover. Barnsley: Frontline, 2017.

3 Published as *George Walton 1796–1874: the Journal & Diary of a Rifleman of the 95th who Fought at Waterloo*. Peter Coleman: Studley: Brewin Books, 2016.

4 Published as *The Peninsular War Journal of Sergeant Samuel Harrison of the 43rd Foot 1796–1812*. Gareth Glover: Godmanchester: Ken Trotman, 2017.

5 Published as *A Hellish Business: the Letters of Captain Charles Kinloch 52nd Light Infantry 1806–1816*. Gareth Glover. Godmanchester: Ken Trotman, 2007.

6 Published as *The Peninsular War Diary of Captain John Frederick Ewart, 52nd Light Infantry, 1811–1812*. Gareth Glover. Godmanchester: Ken Trotman, 2010.

7 Published as *A Light Infantryman with Wellington: The Letters of Captain George Ulrich Barlow, 52nd and 69th Foot, 1808–1815*. Gareth Glover. Solihull: Helion, 2018.

8 Published as *52nd (Light Infantry) Eyewitness accounts of the Waterloo campaign*, Gareth Glover: Godmanchester: Ken Trotman, 2020.

material by members of the Light Division still existing in the British Library, the National Archives at Kew, the National Library of Scotland, the Royal Green Jackets Museum (now held by the Hampshire Record Office in Winchester) or in the Soldiers of Oxfordshire Museum at Woodstock in Oxfordshire, as part of his thorough preparation for his excellent book on the Light Division in 1810[9] and for his further projected volumes. This search unearthed a virtual treasure trove of material that astounded both of us. There was simply more than we could have possibly imagined there, indeed material was discovered that some of the museums didn't even realise that they had themselves.

From this was spawned the idea of producing a book on each of the three regiments that formed the core of the Light Division, publishing the masses of material unearthed, much for the very first time, or at most only previously appearing in obscure and very rare publications. This, the second volume, covers perhaps one of the best known of the three regiments and certainly one with a number of memoirs already published, that is the 52nd (Oxfordshire) Regiment of Foot. Some fifteen individual memoirs have emanated from this regiment to date, whereas the 95th Foot boast no fewer than seventeen.

The three infantry regiments of the Light Division in the *Peninsular War* maintained quite different characteristics from each other. Captain John Cooke of the 43rd Foot explained not only the brotherhood of regiments, but also their subtle differences at the end of the war in 1814:[10]

> Though amongst the regiments which composed it there existed an unanimity which was almost without a parallel in war, yet there was a shade of difference between them, a something peculiar to each corps distinguishing it from the others, which was the more remarkable as amongst them there was a sort of fraternal compact, and it has occurred that three brothers held commissions at the same time in the 43rd, 52nd and Rifle Corps.
>
> The 43rd were a gay set, the dandies of the army; the great encouragers of dramatic performances, dinner parties and balls, of which their headquarters was the pivot.
>
> The 52nd were highly gentlemanly men of a steady aspect; they mixed little with other corps, but attended the theatricals of the 43rd with circumspect good humour and now and then relaxed, but were soon again the 52nd.

---

9 Published as *Wellington's Light Division in the Peninsular War: The formation, campaigns & battles of Wellington's famous fighting force 1810.* Robert Burnham. Barnsley: Frontline, 2020.

10 A Narrative of Events in the South of France, Captain John Cooke, London, 1835.

> The Rifle Corps were skirmishers in every sense of the word; a sort of wild sportsmen and up to every description of fun and good humour. Nothing came amiss: the very trees responded to their merriment and scraps of their sarcastic rhymes passed current through all the camps and bivouacs.
>
> In this way the brothers of the three regiments met together, each being the very type of the corps to which he belonged.

Some of these attitudes are clearly borne out by the memoirs and letters of the men of each regiment.

With so much new material to be studied, it is inevitable that a great deal of new evidence will be discovered that will change our understanding of many aspects of the life of the troops, the military operations and even their thoughts on their fellow officers and seniors at the very time that incidents occurred.

I hope that you the reader will be as intrigued with what we have unearthed as much as we are.

ACKNOWLEDGEMENTS

A work of this kind cannot come to fruition without the help and advice of a large number of people, but before I make the customary thanks, I must mention one person in particular.

I must thank Robert Burnham, whom I am pleased to consider a close friend, for his help in transcribing the numerous accounts from their original handwriting, he has now been bitten by the bug and has been fully ensnared by the dark arts of transcribing, helping me to prepare these volumes for publication. I have to also thank John Grehan and Martin Mace of Frontline Books for believing in this project when others were not perhaps so keen.

I also thank the staff of many of the archives around the country, who have cheerfully and patiently dealt with my incessant requests and queries. I have received every help and courtesy from the National Library of Scotland, the National Army Museum, the Hampshire Record Office and the British Library.

I must particularly thank Peggy Ainsworth, Collections Manager/ Deputy Museum Director, for allowing me to literally ransack her archives at the Soldiers of Oxfordshire Museum in the search for material and her unbelievable helpfulness in arranging for copies to be made of literally thousands of documents.

I must also thank Ron McGuigan, with whom I have only ever corresponded by email, but who is the font of all knowledge and finds information on the most obscure subject or person you can ever imagine and rarely fails.

Gareth Glover
Cardiff

1. HISTORY OF THE 52ND FOOT IN THE PENINSULA AND AT WATERLOO

Raised in 1755, the 52nd (Oxfordshire) Regiment of Foot had originally been the 54th for two years[11] before becoming the 52nd. They served in Ireland initially for some seven years, in Canada, the American War of Independence and in the south-east of England. The regiment embarked for India in 1783, becoming involved in the hostilities with Tippoo Sahib and the capture of Ceylon from the Dutch in 1794. They remained in the East Indies until 1798, when they returned to Britain again as a mere skeleton of 184 officers and men, remaining in Colchester to recruit their numbers. This was so successful that in 1800 a second battalion was inaugurated, both battalions containing about a thousand men.

In June 1800 the first battalion of the regiment participated in an expedition to the Isle of Houat in Quiberon Bay. Both battalions subsequently took part in the abortive landing at Ferrol. In this action, the two battalions only lost one officer and ten rank and file killed and forty-three other ranks wounded, almost all of which occurred in the 1st Battalion. The troops then moved to Lisbon before returning to Kent in 1801. In May of that year Major General Sir John Moore was appointed colonel of the regiment.

In January 1803 the regiment was designated as Light Infantry, but the second battalion were *redesignated* the 96th Foot. This was done by transferring those not deemed ideal for light infantrymen in the first battalion into the 96th and a sizeable number of the second battalion deemed more suited to light infantry training moving

11 Oddly the 43rd Foot had also begun life as the 54th Foot, before being renumbered in 1751. A strange coincidence for two regiments that were to be so inextricably linked throughout their long and distinguished careers.

the other way. Officers were divided by seniority, the most senior in each rank remaining with the 52nd and the most junior joining the 96th.

On 9 July 1803 a brigade under the command of Sir John Moore was formed and encamped at Shorncliffe. The brigade consisted of the 4th, 52nd, 59th, 70th and 95th Foot and the 52nd and 95th along with the light companies of the other regiments began light infantry training. In August 1804 a second battalion was ordered to be formed and the 43rd Foot joined the brigade; the 59th and 70th leaving it.

The brigade remained at Shorncliffe protecting the south coast from the threat of invasion until finally the 1st Battalion 52nd was sent to Sicily on 25 September 1806 and were stationed at Melazza [Milazzo]. The 2nd Battalion joined the force sent against Copenhagen, where they engaged a Danish force at the Battle of Køge and which eventually saw the entire Danish fleet captured. They then returned to Britain.

In October 1807, the 1st Battalion sailed from Sicily and arrived at Canterbury on 19 January 1808. In April 1808 the battalion formed part of a force sent to help defend Sweden, but difficulties with the King of Sweden eventually caused the force to sail back to Britain, where orders sent them directly on to Portugal, landing at Mondego Bay on 19 August.

A large force had been ordered to the peninsula, initially under the command of General Arthur Wellesley to attempt to drive the French forces out of Portugal. The 2nd Battalion of the 52nd was part of this force, landing on 19 July at Vimeiro and were engaged in the *Battle of Vimeiro* two days later, supporting a bayonet charge by the 97th Foot. The 2/52nd lost five men killed and two officers and thirty-four men wounded. The Convention of Cintra saw the fighting come to an end.

In late September, part of the army, including the 1/52nd, began to march into Estremoz, arriving there on 5 October. On 25 October orders were received for the army, now under the command of Sir John Moore, to march to Salamanca, the 1/52nd being allocated to Brigadier General Anstruther's Brigade and the 2/52nd to Major General William Beresford's 1st Flank Brigade. The army finally concentrated in the vicinity of Sahagun in late December 1808.

A force of 10,000 men under Sir David Baird landed at Corunna and marched to join Sir John Moore, which was achieved at Mayorga on 20 December. On 24 December, Moore, learning of the advance of greatly superior numbers of French troops, ordered a retreat for Corunna.

1809

The 2/52nd were in Brigadier General Robert Craufurd's brigade that marched to Vigo, while the 1/52nd were in the Reserve commanded by Major General the Honourable Edward Paget marching with the main body for Corunna. Arriving at Corunna, the army was forced to stand and fight while awaiting the arrival of the fleet to evacuate them. The 1/52nd were engaged in opposing a flanking movement by the French left wing during the Battle of Corunna, the battalion sustaining losses of five men killed, two officers and thirty-one men wounded, with another ninety men missing. The losses of the two battalions during this campaign were quite heavy, the 1/52nd losing ninety-three men on the retreat to Corunna, almost all the deaths being caused by fatigue and sickness and many of the sick being made prisoners of war. Returning to Britain, the two battalions returned to Deal Barracks and rapidly recruited their numbers, but the toll of the campaign is shown in the records, with more than half of the battalion sick in hospital in March 1809 and only one third deemed fit for service. The death of Sir John Moore at Corunna led to the appointment of Major General Sir Hildebrand Oakes as colonel of the 52nd Regiment.

The British effort on the peninsula was reinvigorated by the return of Sir Arthur Wellesley to command the army and the arrival of large reinforcements. The 52nd were represented by a single company in a battalion of detachments in Wellesley's first success in crossing the Douro and defeating Marshal Soult's troops, driving them out of Portugal. In May 350 men were transferred in from the second battalion, while 355 unfit men were sent to the second battalion. The first battalion also received a further 255 volunteers from the Militia.

On 25 May 1809 the first battalion was ordered to embark as part of the major reinforcement in Portugal. Sailing from Dover, they arrived at Lisbon on 29 June. The 1/52nd were formed into a brigade under Robert Craufurd with the 1/43rd and 1/95th, forming the Light Brigade, which also included light cavalry and horse artillery. Hearing that Wellesley's army had marched into Spain and that there was likely to be a battle soon, Craufurd ordered his brigade to force march, but they arrived just after the Battle of Talavera had ended. They joined the difficult retreat that followed and suffered equally from the prevalent fevers, losing a number of men to the epidemic by the time they went into quarters at Campo Maior.

The 2/52nd were sent on the Walcheren expedition, with five companies sailing on 17 July 1809 from Deal. The battalion saw little action but suffered severely from the fever raging through the army. The second battalion then remained in England and sent regular drafts to reinforce the first battalion in the peninsula.

1810

The 1/52nd marched with the Light Brigade to the Portuguese border in January, arriving at Pinhel on 5 January. On 22 February, the Light Brigade was reinforced by two battalions of Portuguese cacadores and the Light Division was officially announced, with Robert Craufurd retaining command, despite his lower rank. In March the division was pushed forward to the River Agueda, where they would act as a corps of observation as the French *Marshal Masséna* brought his troops forward to besiege the fortress of Ciudad Rodrigo. The eventual surrender of Ciudad Rodrigo after a stubborn resistance by its Spanish garrison meant that the French could now contemplate an invasion of Portugal via the Northern corridor. Wellington (Wellesley had gained the title for Talavera) maintained this defensive screen in front of Almeida, but urged extreme caution on Craufurd, his division being deployed with the Coa River in its rear. The advance of the French to besiege Almeida in July forced Craufurd to retire, destroying Fort Concepcion and retiring under the walls of the fortress, but stubbornly maintaining his troops in front of the Coa, with only one narrow bridge in his rear to escape by. Attacked by an overwhelming force from Marshal Ney's corps on the morning of 24 July, the division was forced into a hasty retreat over the bridge and only escaped total destruction by a whisker. The 1/52nd being on the right of the line were not as severely engaged and their losses were one soldier killed, two officers and sixteen men wounded, with three men missing. Soon after the Light Division was formed into two brigades, the 52nd forming part of Lieutenant Colonel Barclay's (52nd Foot) Brigade with the 1st Caçadores and four companies of the 95th Foot.

Wellington had banked on Almeida resisting a French siege for weeks, but one day into the bombardment a lucky shot, or an accident, caused the huge powder magazine to explode, killing dozens of the defenders and destroying a number of guns. Almeida promptly surrendered. The British were forced to continue to retreat towards Lisbon, with a far superior French army in pursuit. To slow their progress Wellington offered battle at Busaco and successfully defended the steep ridge line against all attacks. Craufurd's troops comprehensively defeated Loison's Division, driving them back down the slope in great confusion at the point of the bayonet. This was achieved with the loss of only one officer (Colonel Barclay dying of his wounds) and three men killed and two officers and ten rank and file wounded in the 1/52nd. The French General Simon was captured by two men of the 52nd, Private James Hopkins receiving a pension of £20 per annum, while Private Harris had to wait until 1843 for his pension for his part in the capture.

The following day, the French found a way around the left flank of Wellington's position, forcing him to resume the retreat. At this point, Wellington's army filed into the secretly prepared defensive lines known as the Lines of Torres Vedras, which were a pleasant surprise to his own army and a great shock to the French. *Marshal Masséna* deemed the lines too strong to be attacked and found that much of the resources of the country had been destroyed in a 'scorched earth' policy. The French therefore sat down before the lines, awaiting reinforcements and quietly starved, forcing them eventually to a defensive location at Santarém, desperately holding on until the promised reinforcements arrived.

The 2/52nd was sent from Chatham to London in April 1810 to help quell the riots caused by Sir Francis Burdett's incarceration in the Tower of London for libel. After returning to Chatham it was stationed successively at Ashford, Shorncliffe and Lewes.

1811

With no reinforcements or substantial supplies arriving, *Marshal Masséna* skilfully retired from Santarém on 5 March. The Light Division led the pursuit and they were involved in a number of actions as they harried the French out of Portugal: Pombal on the 11th, Redinha on the 12th, Casal Novo on the 14th and *Foz de Arouce* the following day. The regiment lost during these actions one lieutenant and twelve rank and file killed and six officers and seventy-five men wounded.

On 25 March the 2/52nd joined the Light Division, having embarked at Portsmouth on 26 January and disembarked at Lisbon on 6 March. It joined the 2nd Brigade alongside the 1/52nd.

The French retreat continued with constant harassing by the Light Brigade until Sabugal on 3 April. Here Masséna stood his ground and sought to push his pursuers back. On a foggy morning, an ill co-ordinated advance left the 1/43rd facing heavy attacks, having crossed a bridge without support. Thankfully the eventual arrival of the 2nd Brigade on their right caused the enemy to hastily retire. Despite the severity of the action, the losses of the 1/52nd totalled three men killed and two officers wounded. This drove the French out of Portugal and Almeida was besieged, while the Light Division resumed their old haunts watching Ciudad Rodrigo.

On 3 May Masséna sent his army forward once again in an effort to succour Almeida, but Wellington placed his army in the way at *Fuentes de Oñoro* and a general action took place over three successive days. During this action, the Light Division was obliged to retire in squares across a wide expanse, which offered the French cavalry a superb opportunity to attack. However, their disciplined manoeuvring saw them successfully march across the plain without serious mishap, although their troop of horse artillery was fortunate to escape destruction. The following day the French retired and that night the garrison of Almeida blew up the works and escaped through the British lines to safety, much to Wellington's fury. Further movements of the French caused the light troops to move constantly and in late June they were stationed near Campo Maior. The battalions returned to the banks of the Agueda in early August.

A further French advance to send a supply column into Ciudad Rodrigo in late October caused small affairs at *El Bodón* and Aldea de Ponte, but the 52nd were not seriously engaged at either. This brought this year effectively to a close.

1812

The Light Division were abruptly ordered out of their cantonments and began the investment of Ciudad Rodrigo on 8 January. That night four companies of the regiment participated in the attack on the outwork of St Francisco led by Sir John Colborne, the 52nd only losing a handful of men wounded. The Light Division was one of four allocated to the siege of the fortress and as such they took turns in rotation to man the trenches for twenty-four hours at a time. Two breaches being reported practicable, one hundred volunteers from each regiment of the division led the assault on the lesser breach on 19 January, while the 3rd Division took the heavily defended greater breach. The brigade successfully took the lesser breach and turned to clear the ramparts, the 52nd turning to the left and 43rd to the right, finally allowing the 3rd Division to enter successfully. Losses in the 1/52nd were one captain and eight men killed and four officers and thirty-four men wounded. The 2/52nd suffered only four men killed and one officer and five men wounded. General Craufurd was mortally wounded during the assault and died on 24 January.

In February 1812, the 2/52nd was ordered home; the fit men of the 2nd Battalion, numbering ten sergeants, seven buglers and 487 rank and file transferring into the 1st Battalion, and ten sergeants, five buglers and eighty-five men who were deemed unserviceable transferred from the first into the second battalion. The skeleton 2nd Battalion marched for Lisbon on 25 February.

Having successfully captured the key fortresses commanding the northern access to Portugal, Wellington now turned to the southern access route controlled by the fortresses of Elvas and Badajoz.

Elvas was already in his possession, but Badajoz would be a very tough nut to crack. The bulk of the army marched south and Badajoz was invested on 16 March. By 6 April two practicable breaches had been formed and the orders to storm were issued. The Light Division furnished one hundred volunteers per battalion again but their assault on the breach was to be much harder than at Ciudad Rodrigo. The storming parties being decimated, the Light Division advanced against the breach but could not effect an entry despite all attempts and huge numbers of men were cut down. Luckily 'diversionary' attacks at other points, by the 3rd and 5th Divisions succeeded in gaining a foothold and French resistance eventually collapsed. The loss of the 1/52nd during the entire siege operation amounted to five officers and sixty-four men killed and seventeen officers and 328 men wounded.

While Wellington's troops were engaged at Badajoz, *Marshal Masséna* made an advance into Portugal in his absence, causing the army to march north again without delay. Marmont retired to Salamanca, but the two armies of near equal size now manoeuvred for advantage, the troops of both often marching within cannon shot of each other for days. Marmont over-extended his line of march on 22 July and Wellington pounced, ordering his concentrated force to break the van and centre of the French army. The Battle of Salamanca was a huge victory and made everyone in Europe aware of Wellington's name. The Light Division saw little action in the affair, but was involved in trying to cut off the enemy's retreat over the River Tormes. They were disappointed when the French escaped using a ford that Wellington mistakenly believed was defended by a Spanish force.

The army now marched on Madrid, which they entered on 12 August. Wellington took his main force northwards to besiege the fortress of Burgos and left a covering force in front of Madrid, which included the Light Division. When the attack on Burgos failed and with the threat increasing from other French forces, Wellington ordered a retreat, which included the troops at Madrid, the two forces forming a junction at Alba de Tormes on 8 November. Wellington offered battle on the old Salamanca battlefield but the French troops refused and sought to turn his flanks. The retreat was therefore continued to the Portuguese border, but the commissariat failed and the troops starved on this march. Finally the French left off their pursuit and the 1/52nd settled for the winter at Fuenteguinaldo. During the retreat, the battalion lost one officer and two men killed and four officers and thirty men wounded.

1813

The military situation had altered dramatically following the disastrous retreat of the French army from Moscow, and the subsequent large-scale movement of troops out of Spain meant that Wellington began the campaign with superior numbers. The campaign began in the middle of May with the Light Division advancing on Salamanca as a feint, while General Thomas Graham led the main advance around the French right wing, forcing them to abandon their defensive positions without a fight. On 27 May, the 1/52nd entered Salamanca, having found that the French had retired. The Light Division now marched northwards and joined the main advance near Toro. As the advance continued, the entire army was relieved to witness the French blowing up the fortress of Burgos rather than defending it.

On 18 June the Light Division on the march suddenly stumbled into two brigades of General Maucune's Division also on the march, an action of encounter saw the French scattered and their baggage captured along with a huge quantity of medical supplies. Continuing their march, the army discovered the entire French army drawn up for battle in front of the city of Vitoria. At the Battle of Vitoria, which took place on 21 July 1813, the Light Division was initially placed opposite the French centre awaiting the order to charge over a defended bridge at Villodas, however a local guide advised them that the neighbouring bridge at Trespuentes was not guarded. The division including the 1/52nd soon crossed here and established a bridgehead on the enemy side of the River Zadorra. Within an hour the French line had retired because both wings were under threat and the Light Division advanced to drive the enemy from the village of Ariñez. After some hard fighting, the French resistance evaporated as a flank movement by Sir Thomas Graham threatened to cut off their retreat. The Light Division marched a league beyond Vitoria before halting. The 52nd lost only one officer and three men killed and one officer and eighteen men wounded.

On the following days the division marched past Pamplona towards Vera, skirmishing with the enemy on route. The division eventually encamped on the heights of Santa Barbara overlooking Vera. The Light Division were not involved in countering the attacks made by Marshal Soult with the aim of relieving Pamplona. However, the enemy advance having been halted and driven back with loss during the two battles of the Pyrenees, the Light Division was ordered to advance in an attempt to cut off the retreat of the French. The division resumed its position at Santa Barbara.

The initial storming of the Fortress of San Sebastian having failed, volunteers were sent from the 1st and Light Divisions to bolster the next attempt. The storming took place on 31 August and after very stubborn resistance the attack succeeded; of the detachment of the 52nd numbering two officers and thirty-eight men, three were killed (including one officer) and eighteen wounded.

On 7 October the division took part in the crossing of the Bidassoa River into France. The Light Division attacked the heights above Vera and eventually succeeded in driving the French off after some very bitter fighting. Of the 1/52nd, twelve men were killed and six officers and sixty-six men wounded.

On 9 November, as part of the Battle of the Nivelle, the Light Division was ordered to take the heavily defended summit of La Petite Rhune. The works were captured after extremely hard fighting, the 1/52nd losing thirty-two men killed and six officers and 202 men wounded. The second brigade of the Light Division were placed in the village of Arbonne.

On 9 December the passage of the River Nive was forced, but this led to a strong counter-attack on Arcangues on the following morning. The pickets were driven in but the threatened assault on the churchyard did not materialise. The fighting continued over the next two days but never became more than a heavy skirmish. On the 13th Soult altered his attack on Wellington's right on the opposite side of the river but this was defeated by Lord Hill, bringing the battle to an end. During this fighting the 1/52nd lost four men killed and six officers and fifteen men wounded, with another four men recorded as missing.

On 9 December the 2/52nd embarked at Ramsgate as part of General Sir Thomas Graham's force that landed in Holland.

1814

General Graham's army moved forward in co-operation with the Prussian forces under Prussian General Bulow against Antwerp. Despite a bombardment little was achieved before General Bulow was ordered to march away. The only further operation undertaken in this campaign was the glorious failure of Bergen op Zoom. The 2/52nd, however, did not suffer any casualties.

Wellington's army rested through the worst of the winter until the Light Division moved to La Bastide-Clairence in February. The 1/52nd in the left brigade of the Light Division was in reserve near Saint-Boès. As the other attacks on these heights had stalled, they were launched against the French right wing. Advancing across marshy ground in line, the regiment halted in front of the French line and fired a series of destructive volleys that tore the heart out of the French defence, and with support now arriving from the other divisions, the battle was won.

On 10 April the Battle of Toulouse occurred, but the Light Division were hardly involved. Peace was announced and the army marched slowly towards Bordeaux, no doubt hoping to be soon back in Britain. The 1/52nd were embarked in HMS *Dublin* and they disembarked in Plymouth on 28 July, where the training establishment of the 2/52nd joined them from Hythe Barracks and all of the fit men exchanged into the first battalion, the 1/52nd receiving 357 men from the 2nd Battalion. On 27 December the regiment marched to sail for America, embarking at Portsmouth on 4 January 1815.

1815

The 1/52nd arrived at the Cove of Cork on 20 January, making two unsuccessful attempts to sail for America, being beaten back on both occasions by severe storms. Fortuitously this meant that when Napoleon's escape from Elba became known, their orders were changed to Belgium.

On their arrival in Belgium, the two battalions met at Grammont and all of the fit men of the second battalion were transferred to the first battalion. Those deemed unfit were transferred to the second battalion before it marched for England. By this order 233 men transferred into the first battalion but some 318 men transferred to the second battalion as unfit for service, including no fewer than twenty-six sergeants.

The actions of the 1/52nd at Waterloo are well renowned. Remaining much of the day in reserve, they were heavily involved in the defeat of one of the three attacks of the Imperial Guard and the subsequent advance that finally crushed French resistance.

The 2/52nd was disbanded at Canterbury on 31 March 1816.

2. VOLUNTEER J W FIRON AT BELLE ILE, FERROL AND CADIZ JOURNAL[12]

Although this journal, written by a learned soldier, refers to a period prior to the *Peninsular War,* the period of service he covers is one that rarely receives a mention. J W Firon does not appear in the muster lists of the 52nd in 1800 and was clearly not an officer, given that he carried a musket and bayonet. This means that he was most likely serving with the regiment as a Volunteer, in the hope of gaining a commission by bravery. There is no record that he ever joined the regiment officially. The regiment's service at Belle Ile, Ferrol and Cadiz in 1800, however, certainly deserve to be included.

Some remarks and observations on the 1st Battalion of the 52nd Regiment leaving Netley Camp[13] to embark for foreign service. Taken on board merely for amusement.

24 June 1800
On this day the right wing marched from camp to South Quay; when they embarked in hoys & for Cowes road, where lay the *Thetis, Experiment* and *Iphigenia* frigates,[14] for the embarking of the regiment, the former being headquarters and commodore's ship. On the day following the remaining part of the battalion came safe onboard. We remained a week at anchor waiting for orders. Cowes is a very pleasant

12 Museum of the Oxfordshire Soldier reference SOFO 2021.

13 There was a military camp at Netley from 1794.

14 HMS *Thetis* of 38 guns, HMS *Experiment* of 44 guns and HMS *Iphigenia* of 32 guns.

place, not more than a mile over, there are about 4,000 Dutch soldiers in our pay.[15]

1 July
A signal given for sailing, accordingly the three frigates got under weigh and after sailing a few knots, the wind changed, we were forced to put back. On the day after, we again attempted to pass the Needles, but the wind being still in the wrong point, and it being a dangerous place to pass with a contrary wind, we anchored in Yarmouth till noon next day, when the Commodore finding no probability of getting by the Needles, we returned with the wind to Spithead. In passing Cowes we found our 2nd Battalion, the 13th and 79th Regiments had embarked that day, we suppose for the same destination as ourselves. We passed them very close but not so as to speak with them. When we embarked we had left them in camp, being the only regiment there.

10 at night – We are now nearly clear of the Isle of Wight, it is a remarkably fine night. The moon shines with brilliancy and soon but the sea and sky to be seen. It forms a grand prospect for those unacquainted with the sea. Sitting on the poop for two hours, the fineness of the evening affords me some pleasing and some unpleasant reflections in a retrospective of past occurrences.

4 July
The wind is now westerly, so that we make very little way. Are now in the centre of the English Channel and have a view of the Channel fleet.

½ past 10 pm. For a few hours we saw some ship ahead. Not knowing what to make of her, our ship being the Commodore fired a signal for the other two to tack and keep close. It is now so misty that we cannot see from stem to stern and have just escaped an accident, the *Experiment* having come so close that we had like to have been foul of each other before it was discovered, but by mutual exertions we got clear. Our lights are now hoisted and drums are beating on the poop.

5 July
I have hitherto continued very well, but numbers of our men are very sick; and although I pitied them I think I never laughed so heartily in my life as when they were staggering on the deck. The frigates have this day kept very close. The wind is now west and therefore quite

15 The Dutch Brigade consisted of about 4,000 troops that had escaped to Britain after the Anglo–Russian army was driven out of Holland in 1799. They formed four line battalions, a rifle battalion and four batteries of artillery in the Isle of Wight. They were disbanded at the Peace of Amiens in 1802.

against us. We were in the morning in sight of Portland, but have now lost it.

6 July
We have a strong wind and although in the same point, we sail 7 knots an hour, but being forced to tack about so often, we do not gain more than 3. I have laid in a good stock of tea, coffee, sugar, butter, soap &c, but if we do not make better way, which we cannot while the wind is in this point, I fear I shall be forced to come on the ship's allowance before we reach our destination; but we do not know what that is to be, but it is supposed Gib[raltar]. We are to fall in with the Grand Fleet in order to learn where we are bound to. We are now in view of Torbay, the sailors, marines and soldiers are remarkably clean, it being Sunday. Yesterday for some hours we had a view of the French coast, but did not see any appearance of an enemy. The French have few vessels out but corvettes and these are not able to cope with us. We have passed several of our ships of war in the Channel, to which we gave signals. We are now bearing SW by W. A few hours back we saw a strange vessel on our starboard, we gave a signal to the *Iphigenia* to chase her, which she did. Got within gunshot and hailed her, which she not answering fired at her. This caused her to tack about, and when boarded was found to be Swedish, they let her pass. We witnessed it all and at first supposed her to be French.

7 July
Noon, wind the same. We are not likely to clear the Channel yet. Our sailing these 7 days might have been accomplished in 24 hours. We have just tacked and are steering to anchor in Torbay.

6 pm. Anchored in Cawsand Bay 4 miles west of Plymouth; where lie two 3 deckers and 4 frigates. Cawsand [is] a small town and apparently the inhabitants are mostly fishermen. It is on a level with the sea and backed by 3 mountains, on one is a church, the steeple of which now serves for a telegraph. On the left-hand hill which is very high there is a lighthouse, seen of course at a great distance. Here I expected to have gone on shore, but sailing away very suddenly, was disappointed. While we lay here and at the Isle of Wight, boats came constantly to us with bread, butter and vegetables. The impositions of the inhabitants at every place we arrived at for every article, are almost incredible.

8 July
We are now steering in search of the Grand Fleet. We are informed they are off Brest and since that at Quiberon. One of our frigates has

just passed us with a French lugger captured this morning and also a merchantmen which the lugger had captured the evening before.

9 July
Sailing against the wind; remarkably rough sea and we are much tossed about. An English ship has just passed which we hailed, but she could give no account of the Grand fleet. We are now steering WSW only 3 knots an hour.

10 July
I arose at 4 this morning, delightful weather, a perfect calm. We saw a cask afloat, took it up but found it contained only water. A brisk gale has just risen. We have boarded this day 3 vessels, they proved neutral. We board all we meet.

4pm. We have now a fine view of the Grand Fleet at a great distance. From the top gallant yard, I counted 16. Wind now abates. We expect to join them at 3 in the morning. I and 3 others tied by the sailors to the mast, as it is customary to serve all that go aloft not belonging to the ship and seldom they let you go without paying a bottle. Yet although the sailors were close, I made my escape down by a single rope, but I have torn the skin from the palms of my hands. We can very plainly see Ushant lighthouse on the French coast.

11 July
We are now in the midst of the Grand Fleet, some leagues west of Brest. I rose purposely to see them and a very magnificent appearance they make. Our captain is just gone onboard Earl St Vincent's ship.[16] We shall soon know our destination. The fleet consists of 25 sail of the line besides frigates.

10 am. Bound for Quiberon Bay and are directing our course thither. We understand our army has made a landing in some place in that bay, but were repulsed several times before landing.

12 July
We are not more than 30 leagues from Quiberon, with [a] favourable wind we shall reach there tomorrow. We have now crowded sail and are chasing a French lugger, the wind so still we gain very little. She was bearing for a vessel which we suppose is one of our merchantmen, but seeing us, she declined it. She has now got her boats out and is rowing to avoid us. We have just sent a boat with an officer of marines

16 Admiral John Jervis, Earl St Vincent, commanded the Channel Fleet from 1799–1801.

to board a ship on our larboard [side] which proved to be Prussian. An English frigate is bearing towards the lugger with whatever wind is in her favour. We have the merchantman safe. The frigate has taken the lugger and is just pass[ed] us.

13 July Sunday
We have now a smart wind and expect to get in Quiberon Bay by noon. Observed 3 vessels ahead of us. Cast anchor in front of Belle Ile (lately fortified prodigiously – they hoisted the red flag and got under arms, intending to land the next morning).

14 July
Weighed anchor and sailed for an island a few leagues from Belle Ile. I am now landed on French ground, having come by the first boat to pitch a marquee for the colonel. This place is beyond all description, our line of tents is close to the village, but such *holes* – our pigstyes [sic] in England are preferable to some of their huts, for the inhabitants are naturally slothful. They are of very dark complexion and indeed we should be brown enough if we continued here any length of time, from the excessive heat. I could not have believed that at so short a distance from England (as we suppose that with a fair wind it is but 3 days sail) there could be so much difference. We cannot purchase a single article here, there is not so much as a shop or public house in the place. It is said that the inhabitants are transported here from France, as ours may be to Botany Bay. The women do all the slavery, such as threshing corn and beating hemp. The latter is very common at this season. Groups of them sit half naked at this employment. The whole of their dress is not worth a dollar, except the cap which might serve nearly to make a man a shirt; for the part which goes under the chin in England, reaches down to their hips. Their clothing is generally coarse blue or brown cloth, with sleeves that would serve to cover their whole body.

I have not seen a tree since I came to this island. There are many acres of wheat fit for cutting and some score bullocks quite small. Their horses are likewise small. You may hire a horse a whole day for a shilling. The place is chiefly rock and sand. The sand reflecting the sun casts a great heat; when undressing to bathe, we cannot bear our feet upon it. The usual hour of mounting guard is 10 in the morning for the other regiments, but our guard relieves every morning at six; after which time there is no parade till sunset. The whole regiment bathes every morning immediately after mounting guard, by beat of drum, they all strip together, go into the water and dress together, with as much regularity as the manoeuvres on parade. The men are ordered to be out in the sun as little as possible during the heat of the day and not at all without a hat. This place is called the Isle of Houat and is enclosed as it were by two others and the continent; the Isle of Hordie [Hoedic] lies to the south of us about 3 miles. Belle Ile about 7 miles to the SW and the continent about 9.

The French have kept an incessant fire for several days from Belle Ile. It is supposed there are about 15,000 army in that island and scarcely a place for landing. There is one remarkable battery in it which mounts 140 pieces of cannon. It is not supposed we shall attack it, for we are no more than 3,300 men; namely the 21st,[17] 23rd,[18] 63rd[19] and 52nd Regiments. General Maitland[20] who is now going to England says he can take it with 20,000 men, with the loss of 3,000 and that it will cost government no more than 30,000 guineas. It is supposed we are only placed here to attract the attention of the French. We are in perfect safety, having 14 frigates lying round the island. Our Grand Fleet has the Brest fleet blockaded. We are very well considering we are upon such a miserable place. Our provisions come from the shipping, we frequently get fish from the inhabitants but not at a reasonable price, yet cheaper than in England. We have also procured from the ships, tea, sugar, tobacco, butter & cheese, which we pay for ourselves.

A few days ago the *Iphigenia* frigate sent her boat with two midshipmen and several sailors to the Isle of Hordie for fresh water and we have not heard anything of them since. They must have either been lost or taken, or gone ashore on some part of France. Lost is not probable as no remains of the boat or crew have been seen. We have taken several prisoners since our arrival, who came under pretence to sell fish but were absolutely spies. We have sent them on board our ships lying off the island. I went yesterday to the lines of the 63rd to visit an old acquaintance and meeting with a party who had been on board with some prisoners, we enjoyed ourselves in passing the grog and wine about briskly, till we all got merry; and coming to our own camp, being full of fun, one of them took hold of a firelock and ran against me several times, till losing all patience I threatened to draw my bayonet, however he stabbed me in 3 different places, but not of any consequence. We have had plenty of mirth about it several times since.

---

17 The 21st Royal Scots Fusiliers.

18 The 23rd Royal Welsh Fusiliers.

19 The 63rd (West Suffolk) Regiment.

20 General Thomas Maitland.

20 July
The French have begun their harvest here, which they would have done long before, but for fear of us, however now they are not in the least annoyed at us. Whatever milk or fish we have from them we buy at a reasonable, or rather an exorbitant price if they require it. They make very little progress in their reaping, for they carry the corn to the barns on their shoulders. They have no such thing as a cart, waggon, or wheelbarrow. The women reap more than the men. We are indifferently off for water, although we have not wanted yet.

The French are firing continually from Belle Ile and we can distinguish them plainly by our glasses. The night we landed, some sailors 8 in number, went in the guard boat to a small battery on the coast, spiked the guns and came clear off, taking two 6 pounders, but not without having several shots fired at them. It was a very rash attempt but the sailors were intoxicated and past all fear.

23 July
Two frigates arrived with provisions and landed enough for 10 days. It is the general opinion we shall embark soon for England or Ireland. When these frigates passed Belle Ile, they had several shots fired at them from the batteries, one of which passed between the fore and main mast, but did no harm. It is surprising how near some of our cruisers go to their shore, to entice their vessels out. The following circumstance may appear almost incredible, but I am convinced of its reality; having been in company with a midshipman who was an actor in the business; but when the valour of British sailors is considered, the improbability will be lessened. A boat with 2 officers and 18 sailors attacked a French vessel containing four 24 pounders & boarded her and after a severe conflict took her prisoner.

26 July
This day, one of our 74's coming too near the rocks was in a dangerous situation and stuck fast. She fired several signal guns, on which boats from the other ships in the bay came to her assistance and the tide fortunately rising, they got her off safe.

The French here have got in their harvest. The manner they have of threshing, or parting the grain from the straw is singular. They place the sheaves on the rocky part of the island, a person stands in the centre, holding by a rope two or three horses who run round to trample the grain.

I must correct what I said in a former part, that they have no carts; they have a kind of cart which they take to pieces occasionally.

I have not entered any remarks in this journal for these few days past and have at all times written very unconnectedly. I have been several times on the point of stopping it altogether, for of late nothing particular has occurred.

We have had two cutters from Guernsey and Jersey which supplied us with liquors, tea, sugar &c which articles have been of great relief to us, as the stock we brought with us was nearly exhausted.

6 August
Noon. We have a fine prospect of about 60 sail of shipping off Belle Ile, which we presume are coming to join us.

17 August
8 am – 68 sail, including ships of the line, have cast anchor just off the Isle of Houat. We are to embark onboard the ships we came in and join them.

18 August
10 am – The whole of the troops (the sick excepted) embarked and joined the squadron. We expect to sail daily, but for what destination we know not, it is supposed Tenerife. Our fleet now consists with our ships, which lay here before, the transports &c of about 90 sail. We have 8 sail of the line besides frigates and about 15,000 troops. 3,000 of the Guards have parted with the fleet in a misty night of the 14th instant. We hope to fall in with them when we put to sea.

21 August
Sailed, but nothing particular happened till . . .

25 August
3 am – Arrived before Ferrol on the Spanish coast. The fleet cast anchor and put out their flat-bottomed boats to disembark us. We lay opposite a battery mounting seven 24's. The *Impeteux*[21] of 96 guns and several frigates and cutters ran close ashore to cover our landing, should the battery oppose us.

4 pm – The boats filled with soldiers rowed towards land. The battery commencing a slight fire at us, we returned in the rear of the ships of war, which soon demolished the battery. The Spaniards quickly deserted it and fled in every direction over the hills which are amazingly high; so that the troops landed without any further opposition.

21 HMS *Impetueux* was an ex-French 74.

As the Guards had not joined us, the Second Battalion of the 52nd were appointed to commence the attack. We took several prisoners; those most intelligible we selected for our guides, as the town to be stormed was about 5 miles off.

9 pm – We arrived on the summit of a hill, the town quite before us. Spain is all alarmed, fires are upon the hills, as signals (I suppose) that the enemy is landed. Here we lay upon our arms till break of day.

26 August

At 4 am – Marched towards the town[22] under a smart fire from the enemy, who were well sheltered behind the rock which entirely covers the ground, but as we were also invisible to them, their shots passed over our heads and did little execution. We soon came on a level with them and commenced a heavy fire from right to left. They ran in the greatest confusion and we pursued them. Our men fell fast but the enemy much faster. We drove them into the town and came under fire of their batteries and gunboats, protected however by a wall. Our First Battalion only was engaged at the beginning, the Second then joined. General Manners[23] and Lord Cavan[24] finding it impossible to take the place without first taking their batteries (which we could not effect, as their gunboats would play so powerfully upon us) caused us to retreat to the ground we occupied in the morning in order to re-embark in the evening.[25]

We are now embarked, perhaps to attack Ferrol in some other direction. It appears a neat and handsome place. I think I never saw so fine a prospect as it presents. It is built in a broad valley and well-fortified by nature as well as art. There is but one side from which it can well be attacked by land, for two large forts or batteries and a branch of the sea come round the south side, where their gunboats are, these can work well upon the land, besides 2 ships of war and 5 frigates lying in the harbour. Yet the town would inevitably have been ours, but it was impossible for our ships to come up. The passage is

---

22 Firon's note – At this time the two picquets of 100 men encountered each other. The author being in the British picquet was slightly wounded in the arm by the sword of a Spanish officer, who he presently saw dead at his feet.

23 Major General Robert Manners.

24 Major General Richard Lambart, 7th Earl of Cavan.

25 Firon's note – At this period the author while on the way to fetch water from a spring exposed to the enemy's fire, having volunteered to do so, was thrown by the wind of a passing cannon ball into a chalk pit. Falling on his face, most of his teeth were broken out and his eyesight considerably injured. The tide had been rising and the gunboats of course so much the more on a level with the ground the army occupied.

narrow between large rocks, so as to admit only one ship at a time, with tremendous chains from rock to rock both under and over the water to defend the passage. I believe had it not been for the chains, our heavy ships would have forced a passage in spite of their batteries, which if they could have done and engaged the vessels and gunboats, the town might have been easily taken by the soldiers.

27 August
We have now weighed anchor, and I suppose we are going to a station near the town. It is rumoured that the sailors are this evening to attempt cutting the chains. It will be a warm undertaking for them in the boats, but I never saw so desperate a set of fellows as they are in general. Last night after the army got onboard, I remained ashore with a party of sailors and we set fire to all the places we well could. A very large lighthouse to the SW of the town we set fire to about 9 o'clock at night, which had a grand appearance. We then set fire to a signal or telegraph house on the hill, which spread for hundreds of yards round and burned for a considerable time. The regiments on shore and not engaged in the action were plundering all the time and driving scores of cows, calves, pigs and sheep down to the beach where they were killed and sent on board. They were killing and roasting all the day; the poor dumb creatures were knocked down and butchered in a most shameful manner.

Opinion

1
The fleet which joined us at Houat was commanded by [Admiral] Sir John Borlase Warren and Lieutenant General Sir James Pulteney commanded the troops. Generals Manners, Lord Cavan, Coote,[26] Morshead[27] and Maitland had respective commands in case of dividing the troops into brigades for landing.

When this joining fleet came in sight of Houat the French inhabitants of the island assembled in great numbers and were rejoiced to find them English, they had by some means got an idea that they were Russians and their chief cry was 'No Russians, Good English, Good English'. This was probably from policy, though it is well known that the English as an enemy, are the most humane power under the canopy of heaven.

26 Major General Sir Eyre Coote.
27 Major General William Morshead.

2
When we got into the Bay of Biscay we were 5 days subject to its motion. I had frequently heard of Biscay being a troublesome place and I found it verified. I am informed that its effect is more remarkable in calm weather than in a moderate storm or strong wind, as its extraordinary motion is occasioned by a meeting of several tides.

3
During the encampment at Houat, I was sent for some time on board again to take charge of our baggage, in the course of which time I ventured upon the most hazardous enterprise that occurred to me during the whole expedition.

Every night after sunset, a boat with an officer and 8 men, each armed with a cutlass and brace of pistols, besides in the boat a carronade, at least an 18 pounder, goes from every ship of war along the coast, to watch the manoeuvres of the enemy. This we call the Watch boat, upon this exploit I begged leave of the captain of the ship to let me go. He seemed very much against it, but at length he gave his consent. So like a second Don Quixote I set sail at 8 pm. When we had rowed about 2 hours, the sea began to roll, the wind was boisterous and came to quite a hurricane, in so much that we were obliged to make land, which was the continent. The night was dark enough to conceal us from the enemy had we met with any. At length getting to shore, we landed in front of a small battery of 3 guns. Our first object was to spike the guns. This done we intended to seize the sentinels, but in the midst of our career we were overheard, and numbers too many for us, came down with great rapidity, so that we had scarce time to get to our boat and bear off, when they in like manner got out boats and followed, but providence so directed that through the darkness and the sea running very high, they either lost or left us, so that we for that time escaped the enraged enemy. Had they overtaken us, I am sure that our boat would have given battle while cutlass and pistols supported us, and in the end we determined to go to the bottom rather than surrender. Having escaped one danger, we fell into another. We were all night rowing and steering we knew not whither in a miserable condition and expecting every moment to make a watery grave; but at length the sable habit of night gave way to the beaming of sol from behind the distant hills, ushering in with joy a beautiful and resplendent morning; when to our surprise we found ourselves 30 miles from any of our shipping, consequently in danger of being taken suddenly by some of the French cruisers. We ought to have been back again by order at 8 o'clock, but could not by any means arrive before 3 in the afternoon, which we did to the great joy of the ship's crew who all imagined that we were either taken or lost. This was the greatest danger and fatigue I have sustained since leaving old England.

4

I likewise omitted to mention in its proper place that the day prior to our landing at Ferrol, the soldiers on board each vessel were called on deck and addressed by their officers, to encourage them in the attempt in which they were to engage. Colonel Henry Conran[28] spoke to his men in the following manner:

'soldiers – On account of the Guards not coming up, our regiment is appointed to make the landing first, and on reading the General Orders I think it a particular favour which confers the greatest honour upon us, that the general should choose and approve the 52nd for so glorious an enterprise. And brother soldiers, I trust that we shall conduct ourselves as soldiers and true patriots to our king and country. We shall be well paid for our courage and valour, with Spanish dollars. We shall have a comfortable Christmas at home in Old England . . . .' (then concluding with a smile) 'Brother soldiers, many of you, by this glorious undertaking, will be enabled to roll in your carriages.'

When he had done we would have given him three cheers, but the captain of the ship stopped it, for fear of alarming the fleet.[29]

From our first landing, the behaviour of our regiment was such as to meet the general's approbation, which the following orders issued by General Sir James Pulteney will in a great measure show.

Renown,[30] 26 August 1800
General Orders
Although Lieutenant General Sir James Pulteney under all the circumstances of the case judged it expedient [not] to make any attack upon the town of Ferrol, he has much pleasure in signifying his complete satisfaction in the general conduct of the troops under his command. It fell to the lot of the Rifle corps and the 1st Battalion of the 52nd Regiment to have the greatest opportunity of distinguishing themselves, but he is persuaded that under similar circumstances the same gallantry and zeal would have been shown by all the troops under his command &c.

The orders ran to a considerable length, but contained nothing further of consequence, except that one regiment seemed to have incurred the general's disapprobation and I will not by any means

28 Lieutenant Colonel Henry Conran, 52nd Foot.
29 It might have indicated a mutiny.
30 HMS *Renown* was a 74-gun ship.

mention its name, as it only arose from a misunderstanding of a few in the regiment.

I shall now continue my journal.

28 August 1800

We are out of sight of the place we landed at and it is conjectured that we are steering for Lisbon. We now think it was not intended to take Ferrol if attended with any difficulty but merely to alarm the Spaniards and make them draw away their forces from the Portuguese army while we might make a descent on some other place. We are acting chiefly I believe on speculation.

Considering that our regiment was engaged from 4 in the morning till 3 in the afternoon, our loss was very small, the whole was only 9 killed and 40 wounded. Among the dead was a Captain Torrens[31] of our light company whom we interred in the sea this day.

Yesterday in getting away, we ran foul of the *Experiment* and carried away our main yard and injured the *Experiment* greatly.

I forgot to relate the following circumstance which I myself witnessed. Two sailors carrying a box of ammunition suddenly lost it from their shoulders by a 24 pound shot from the Spaniards without any further damage. The foremost finding the box drop began to quarrel with his comrade for letting it fall, but finding it was carried away by a cannon shot, he declared he would look for the ball and have it fired back again. Such is the undaunted spirit of British seamen; bravery and disregard of death are the characteristics of these sons of Neptune and rulers of the waves.

29 August

We are just arrived in Vigo Bay and anchored. There is no preparation for attack. We have been in view of Spanish land since break of day and are in expectation of making a descent quietly. The soldiers are in general much chagrined at not waiting to work matters more effectually where we left, as they wished to be handling the Spanish dollars.

4 pm – We understand it is not intended to land here; 33 boats of sailors from the different ships of war are to enter the bay this evening to discover what it contains. Vigo is a neat town in Galicia, with a good harbour, remarkable for a sea fight in 1702, of the English and Dutch against a squadron of French men of war with 13 Spanish galleons and their cargo.[32] The English took 4 galleons and 5 men of war, the

31 Captain Samuel Torrens, 52nd Foot.

32 Note written by AS [?] – A million in silver specie.

Dutch took 5 galleons and 1 man of war. 14 men of war and 4 galleons were destroyed.[33] Moreover while this was transacting, the Duke of Ormond[e][34] with some land forces drove the Spaniards from their castle which defended the harbour. Vigo is situated 8 miles SW of Redondella and 260 NW of Madrid.

30 August

The boats are returned and have brought with them a French corvette mounting 22 guns. She made a gallant resistance and our boats were repulsed twice before they properly boarded her. Many merchantmen were in the bay. They have sent a flag of truce, but its object is secret to us. We are going forward and displeased at being so long idle. We are all at a loss to conceive what we are about.

Anchor weighed and come about 6 leagues north, where we are to water. Some of our regiment have been to Oporto for fresh provisions and have brought a large quantity of melons, grapes, &c. The Spanish coast is very rich and fertile. This evening has been a tremendous gale. Several of our ships are blown ashore and although we had 3 large anchors out, we were dragged. We are about 8 leagues from the fleet and are fearful that one or more of our ships are blown up, as we perceived about midnight a terrible blaze and soon after heard a great explosion. When we join the fleet tomorrow we shall learn further particulars.

31 August

We have joined the fleet and find that the explosion was of our own *Stag* frigate,[35] which had been driven ashore and it being impossible to get her off, the crew blew her up, lest she should fall into the hands of the Spaniards. A Guernsey cutter was also driven ashore and with all hands taken by the Spaniards.

Her crew came onboard this day with a flag of truce, when the Spaniards took the cutter, they found onboard £800. The captain said his loss amounted to £1,200 more. The merchants of Vigo humanely collected the latter sum and presented it to him, together with the £800 they had taken and all his crew on board again with the flag of truce.

From what I could learn and indeed I see nothing to hinder it, we could have blown the town to pieces, but it is reported they have paid us

33 The Battle of Vigo Bay was fought on 23 October 1702. All of the French fleet of fifteen of the line, two frigates and a fireship were all destroyed or captured. Of the Spanish treasure fleet five were captured and eight sunk.

34 General James Butler, 2nd Duke of Ormonde.

35 HMS *Stag* was a 32-gun frigate.

£50,000 for a ransom.[36] The fleet has received orders to prepare for sea. We weighed anchor, but the wind being contrary we again anchored. A number of Spaniards have been all day cutting and carrying away the remains of the frigate.

1 September
6 am – A signal hoisted for the fleet to weigh anchor. We understand we are bound for Portugal and that the ships of war have received orders to quit the fleet of troop ships, the Spanish fleet being near at hand. We are to make the best of our way to Lisbon.

10 September
Bearing SSW fine favourable weather. The fleet all in sight and we keep well together.

11 September
It is now the general opinion that the whole of us will not put into Lisbon. We have a slight breeze and are sailing SSW.

12 September
We have observed two strange vessels for some time to the leeward. The *Dolphin* frigate[37] is directed to chase them. We have a very clear prospect of the Portugal coast. The country is fertile but their cattle are said not to be so good as ours. We have this day been in chase of a vessel for 2 hours, crowded all sail but at last found her to be English.

14 September
We are now opposite Lisbon but bearing towards Gibraltar, so that we do not put in as we expected and remain quite ignorant of what place we are bound for. The vessels the *Dolphin* chased on the 12th proved to be English transports.

We are now in sight of Cape St Vincent with a fine view of the land. On one point stands a large convent now turned into a fortification upon a large scale; it is somewhat in ruins. Farther south is a battery on the point of the cape which appears to occupy a large space of ground. We are bearing away from the land so that we lose sight of the objects.

16 September
A signal is given for each captain to come onboard the commodore. The captain of the *Thetis* is to sail for Faro, for fresh provisions.

36 This was a false rumour.
37 HMS *Dolphin* was actually a 10-gun brig.

We understand that provisions are so very scarce up the Mediterranean, at Minorca and the adjacent places, as to cause our troops to remove and that they are now in and off Gibraltar waiting for us to join them. In that case we shall be about 26,000 strong. We have now a fine evening. The moon and stars have a doubly brilliant and affecting appearance from the water; and the serenity of the weather, which is remarkable, adds greatly to the gratification of a contemplative mind.

17 September
We are now bearing under a fair wind for Faro. At 4 pm saw a strange sail ahead. At 5 pm opposite the land, 12 or 13 leagues distant.

18 September Thursday
Came to anchor at Faro, all our officers are gone ashore to dine at the English consul's. They were not allowed to land for some time, through fear that we had been up the Mediterranean and had brought sickness, they are now returned. The inhabitants would not give more than 18 shillings for a guinea.

20 September
Passed Ape's Hill.[38] At 5 pm ran into Gibraltar, saw the convoy getting under weigh. Received several shots from the Spaniards in passing Gibraltar point. A signal from Lord Keith[39] then in Gibraltar, kept us under weigh. Sailed forward to Tetuan Bay[40] on the Barbary coast where many of the fleet are watering. The Gibraltar fleet under Lord Keith is arrived in the Gut and is very formidable. We are kept prepared for action as the Spanish gunboats are annoying the passage of the shipping very much and they do not hesitate to attack one of our 74's, when calm they have so much advantage.

I was surprised to see a town and bay of the Spaniards full of shipping, so nigh Gibraltar; and firing batteries at us as we passed, when a fleet of ours is so near. The balls passed us fore and aft and the sailors say they were very well directed. The captain ordered a musquet to be fired at them occasionally from the poop, by way of derision, but even this I must say roused the British spirit in all hands aboard, as I firmly believe we never fear meeting two to one and sometimes more.

---

38 Ape's Hill is now Europa Point on the tip of the Rock of Gibraltar.

39 Admiral George Elphinstone, 1st Lord Keith was Commander in Chief in the Mediterranean.

40 Tetuan Bay lays off Tetouan in Morocco.

However, I am fully persuaded that the strength of their fortifications is capable of resisting the most tremendous force that can be sent against them. This town of Algeziras [Algeciras] and Gibraltar seems to hold each other in defiance. They are on opposite sides of the same bay, so that the inhabitants of the one can see the inhabitants of the other walking on the shore.

23 September
We are still in Tetuan Bay about 9 or 10 leagues from Gibraltar. Nothing material has happened. Last night the *Cyclops*[41] ran foul of us and both suffered some small injury, but were disengaged in about an hour.

25 September
Received orders to sail again for Gibraltar, the whole of the ships having watered.

At Gibraltar. We remained till 2 October, which gave us an opportunity of getting many articles we wanted.

2 October
Received signal to weigh anchor and join the convoy which lay about 6 leagues off.

3 October
The whole fleet passed Gibraltar for Cadiz and on the . . .

5 October
Came to anchor about 4 leagues off Cadiz. Every preparation was made for landing. Every man received 3 days provisions and one day's grog. A flag of truce from the town, which delayed our landing.

6 October
Noon. The First Brigade was all embarked in the flat-bottomed boats[42] and we expected orders every minute to row to land. Another flag of truce came from the Spaniards and soon afterwards the men in the boats were ordered to repair on board their respective ships; this sudden alteration gave rise to several rumours. The prevailing opinion was that they had agreed to pay a very large sum as a ransom for Cadiz and its vicinity. Another opinion was that our admiral and general thought it imprudent to land, on account of a dreadful fever which

41 HMS *Cyclops* was a 28-gun frigate.

42 The total invading force was 24,000 in three divisions, 100 men standing in each boat.

raged there and carried off numbers daily.[43] I believe that but few in the fleet know the real cause of our not landing, but time will elucidate this great secret. I have heard from good authority that the admiral and general differed in opinion about landing; that it was Sir Ralph Abercromby's wish to land immediately after casting anchor, as the sea was then calm, but afterwards it became so rough and the surf ran so high, that it was dangerous for the flat-bottomed boats to attempt a landing.

7 October
Again weighed anchor, and when at sea we found ourselves bound to Gibraltar again. I omitted to observe that before we left Cadiz, a vessel with despatches and letter was sent to England and by the neglect of a person on board upon whom I depended, I was disappointed in sending a letter which I had written to London.

We had scarcely a breath of wind for 3 days and when it rose it proved quite against us. We did not make the Gut of Gib till the 11th and on the 12th anchored in Tetuan Bay. Finding the weather stormy, the fleet received orders to weigh anchor again. The main part of the fleet put into Gibraltar. Our frigate, the *Thetis*, with many others had orders to keep out at sea. For a whole week we were beating about under a perfect storm, not a sailor or soldier lay dry in his hammock for several nights. We lost our jib boom, fore stay sail, anchor &c, the rocking of the vessels was so great that we could not

43 From the Annual Register – Letter from Governor General Thomas de Morla:
5 October 1800
To the English Admiral
The affliction which carries off in this city and its environs thousands of victims and which threatens not to suspend its ravages till it has cut off all who have hitherto escaped, being calculated to inspire compassion, it is with surprise that I see the squadron under the command of your Excellency come to augment the consternation of the inhabitants. I have too exalted an opinion of the humanity of the English people and of yours in particular, to think that you would wish to render our condition more deplorable. However, if in consequence of the orders your Excellency has received, you are inclined to draw down upon yourself the execration of all nations, to cover yourself with disgrace in the eyes of the whole universe, by oppressing the unfortunate and attacking those who are supposed to be incapable of defence. I declare to you that the garrison under my orders, accustomed to behold death with a serene countenance and to brave dangers much greater than all the perils of war, know how to make resistance which I shall not terminate but with their entire destruction. I hope that the answer of Your Excellency will inform me whether I am to speak the language of consolation to the unfortunate inhabitants, or whether I am to rouse them to indignation and revenge. May God preserve Your Excellency, Thomas de Morla

get any water upon deck from the hold, but were obliged to drink rum instead.

13 October
Another storm. A signal hoisted for us to weigh anchor and bear off once more for fear of being dashed to pieces upon the rocks, this being a very dangerous place. In the course of the night the fleet was so scattered that we could not see more than 2 ships besides our own in the morning.

16 October
Still the wind not abated, and we found our main sheet in tatters. With a great deal of trouble another was hoisted and providentially the people on board received no hurt.

19 October
The wind abated and we came to anchor in a bay called San Lucar,[44] whereby this time a number of our ships were anchored. One of the captains informed us that all the shipping was safe from any damage, which he said, very seldom happens in such a large fleet, especially in this part of the world.

Here we got necessary articles for our sick, as we had upwards of 70 soldiers laid up, besides sailors in our ship. In the evening we made towards land, when Admiral Lord Keith arrived and took the command from Sir John Borlase Warren, who went to Malta.

23 October
We left Cape San Lucar and touched on the town of Tangiers, it lies near the shore in a valley. The inhabitants are very numerous and being Mahometans [Mohammedans] I observed with interest during our previous stay there, their morning and evening devotions upon the beach, washing their hands and crying aloud with their hands raised toward heaven.

In the evening we arrived at Gibraltar. At the same time one of our sailors fell overboard, but providentially was saved by the boatswain.

The Spaniards took a cutter belonging to us, with their gunboats, she having no gun to protect her.

26 October
Orders came to leave our ships, accordingly we landed on the Rock.

---

44 Near the Spanish city of Sanlúcar de Barrameda.

27 October
The companies were divided and sent onboard the following transports, *Lady Jane*, *The Nelly*, and the *Baily of London*. But the 63rd Regiment on landing relieved the 44th that had lain on the Rock. The reason of our leaving the *Experiment* &c was that they were going on to Malta in their way to Egypt. We sailed for Lisbon.

6 November
Arrived at Lisbon and lay [at] quarantine for 5 days.

11 November
Landed in a noble square, where is the building appropriated to the meeting of merchants, which in London we call the Royal Exchange. From this place (the Placa da Comercia [Praça do Comércio]) the regiment marched through the town to the barracks of Campo de Ourique.

Lisbon being the capital is inhabited by the nobility and is very populous; its length is estimated at 5 miles and all along the riverside are many well-built storehouses. The Royal Exchange is a fine piece of workmanship and the best statue I ever saw, represents John the Great, the grandfather of the present Queen of Portugal, on horseback.[45] Father up the town are many well built houses and noble churches. About a mile from the town is the Aqueduct of Alcantara,[46] which supplies Lisbon with water from a distance of above 100 [36] miles. It is the most wonderful building I ever saw, having upwards of [blank, fourteen] arches[47] belonging to it of a considerable height. Numbers of the inhabitants gain their livelihood by selling water from this place and the many different fountains in the streets.

The cattle for riding[48] are chiefly mules, the waggons, if so I may call them, are but clumsy vehicles and are drawn by bullocks. The chief firing here is charcoal and fir wood, as there is but a small quantity of coal in the country. The milk is mostly that of goats, cow's milk is very dear, as much as 6d per quart.[49] Fruit is cheap, a hat full of oranges or grapes may be had for a few half pence. On our first landing we were surrounded by English residents enquiring for news from England.

45 The statue of King Jose I on horseback caused many soldiers to call the square 'Black Horse Square'.

46 The Aguas Livres Aqueduct was built in 1746.

47 The arches carrying the Alcantara valley number fourteen, the total number of arches are 109.

48 Horses and mules etc are frequently referred to as cattle at this time.

49 About £1.50 in today's terms.

12 December
Two of our officers disagreed, owing I believe to intoxication, fought a duel and were both wounded.

17 December
Marched from Campo de Ourique to Belem quay, to embark for England on board the following transports, *The Lady Jane, The Nelly, Prince George* and the *Flora.*

This being the Queen of Portugal's birthday all the guns from the different batteries were firing and two yachts on the Tagus were fitted up and decorated with the Colours of all nations, for a pleasure excursion of the Royal family and had a beautiful appearance as we sailed away.

26 December
Our 20 transports and the convoy attempted to put to sea, but the wind being contrary, we were obliged to return into the river. All along the shore are villages and batteries adjacent to each other, so that the defence is very complete. Near the town is the Castle of St Christ[opher] situated in the water, by which it is quite surrounded. This is well fortified.

29 December
We sailed again and proceeded pleasantly for 3 days when there arose a violent storm which continued 4 days, during which we lost our fleet.

9 January 1801
Came up with a fleet of about 40 sail bound for India, but never again overtook our own. In this last hardship that we sustained, we suffered greatly in coming through the Bay of Biscay and at Scilly we were near being dashed to pieces against the rocks so well known by the name of the rocks of Scilly. In so much that the captains of some of the transports gave up all hope of relief and began to supplicate the All Supreme in whom all power rests, both by sea and land, for mercy in their desperate situation and the benign power of the Almighty brought us once more to hail our native land.

11 January
We arrived at Spithead, dropped anchor and lay at the mother-bank for 5 days, when new weighed and sailed up the harbour and lay quarantine until orders came to sail for the Downs on 21 January.

Arrived the next night about 10 o'clock. From thence sailed immediately for Ramsgate where we arrived . . .

25 January
And part of the regiment landed the same day; but a great misfortune happened to the ship I was in by running foul of the pierhead. She struck so violently as to be very near sinking and was obliged to put to sea again for 2 days, till another pilot brought us into the harbour. Then one of our men at landing fell overboard and was crushed between the pier and the ship and we never found the least remains of him.

28 January
Marched to Canterbury, there remained till 2 November and thence to Deal barracks.

Summary	
At Isle of Houat	38 days
Vigo Bay	3 days
Tetuan Bay	5 days
Gibraltar	7 days
Cadiz	2 days
Gibraltar	4 days
Tagus River	17 days
Lisbon Barracks	37 days

3. LIEUTENANT COLONEL SIR JOHN COLBORNE LETTER DESCRIBING ATTACK ON THE UPPER TESON REDOUBT, 1812[50]

Dublin, 26 April 1859
My dear Captain Moorsom,
You will find I think, the following a correct version of the capture of the Upper Teson redoubt, as the plan of attack and details were arranged by me, and carried into effect under my immediate orders and inspection. Sir J[ohn] Jones in his *Journal of Sieges*, gave a very erroneous and unfair account of this affair so creditable to the Light Division in describing which he might have [allowed?] himself of an opportunity of demonstrating, that success in assaults can only be expected from high discipline and order and not from bayonets and forlorn hopes, without a fire on the defences. The failure in the assault of Fort Christoval at the First Siege of Badajoz was probably caused by an irregular rush of fine soldiers, without sufficient protection.

Memorandum 8 January 1812
The Light Division marched from El Bodon or through it, early on the 8th and reached the ground in front of the Upper Teson about noon. The detachments intended for the assault of the redoubt were *not* volunteers. They were companies commanded by the senior captains of each battalion; two from the 43rd, four from the 52nd Regiment, two from the 95th, and one each of the Portuguese battalions. Four companies were selected for the advanced guards, to occupy the

[50] The Soldiers of Oxfordshire Museum – Reference SOFO 2141A.

crest of the glacis and open fire, while the party with the ladders in charge of Captain Thompson of the engineers[51] in the *rear* of these companies could be brought up and be assisted in placing the ladders for the assault. In the rear of this whole, the companies destined for the actual escalade followed. In this order we started and advanced, after a caution had been given by me in respect to *silence* and each captain had been instructed *previously* where he was to post his company, and how he was to proceed on arriving near the redoubt. An officer of the 95th and two sergeants had been stationed before dark on the brow of the hill, to mask the angle of the redoubt, covering the steeple of a church in Ciudad Rodrigo. When we reached this point marked by the officer of the 95th, I dismounted and again called out the four captains of the advanced guard and ordered the front company to occupy the front face and the 2nd the right &c. Captain Mulcaster of the engineers[52] suggested that it would be better to *wait* for the light ladders which were coming up, I however thought that no time should be lost, and proceeded with the *very heavy* ladders which had been made during the day. When about fifty yards from the redoubt, I gave the word double quick. This movement and the rattling of canteens alarmed the garrison, but the defenders had only time to fire one round from their guns before each company had taken its post on the crest of the glacis and opened fire. All this was effected without the least confusion and not a man was seen in the redoubt after the fire had commenced. The party with the ladders soon arrived and placed them in the ditch against the palisades, so that they were ready when Captain Mein of the 52nd, came up with the escalading companies. They got into the ditch by descending on the ladders and then placing them against its fraises.[53] The only fire from which the assailants suffered was from shells and grenades thrown over from the rampart. During these proceedings Gurwood[54] of the 52nd, came from the gorge and mentioned that a company could get in by the gorge with ladders, I desired him to take any he could find. Thompson [Thomson] of the engineers had no opportunity of being of use, the whole arrangements were executed by the exertions of the captains of companies and the order preserved by them. We entered the redoubt by the ladders safely, no resistance or opposition was made. The company at the gorge had forced open the gate, or it had been opened by some of the defenders endeavouring to escape. Captain Mein, I believe, was wounded from

51 1st Lieutenant Alexander Thomson, Royal Engineers.
52 2nd Captain Edward Mulcaster, Royal Engineers.
53 Sharpened stakes protruding from the ramparts.
54 Lieutenant John Gurwood, 52nd Foot.

a shot from one of our own companies as he was mounting on the rampart. Most of the defenders had fled to the guard house. Not one man was killed or wounded after we entered the redoubt. The force under my command was collected outside and marched down to the rivulet at the bottom of the glacis of the place and covered the working parties opening the first parallel till moonlight. Had the redoubt not been taken, five days would have been required to attack it regularly. The governor had been in the redoubt half an hour before we attacked it. The investment in fact, had been completed some days before the 8th by the guerrilla cavalry. The Light Division returned to El Bodon about 12 on the 9th, relieved by another division. In my report to General Craufurd I recommended the four senior captains and two subalterns who I believe were promoted. This is a long and heavy account, but the affair was a very remarkable, successful operation. Seaton

4. LIEUTENANT COLONEL JOHN HUNT *PENINSULAR WAR* DIARY[55]

John Philip Hunt became an Ensign in the 52nd Foot in March 1799, he became a Lieutenant in November 1799, then captain in the 96th Foot in December 1802, transferring back into the 52nd Foot in February 1803 and was then promoted major in September 1808 and brevet lieutenant colonel in April 1812, before becoming a confirmed lieutenant colonel in the 60th Foot in November 1813. During part of 1808, he was an aide de camp to Sir John Moore and then rejoined his regiment in the retreat to Vigo, and served at Sabugal, *Fuentes de Oñoro,* Badajoz, Salamanca, San Millan, the Pyrenees, and San Sebastian. He was seriously wounded at San Sebastian and that ended his war.

This diary begins abruptly in April 1812. There are markings in the two volumes we have, which seem to indicate that it originally consisted of three volumes, but unfortunately the current whereabouts of the first volume is unknown.

7 April 1812. Camp before Badajoz.

8 April. Ditto.

9 April. Ditto

10 April. Ditto.

11 April. Marched to Campo Major [Maior] 4 leagues.

12 April. Marched, bivouack near Arronches 4 leagues.

13 April. Marched to Portalegre 4 leagues.

14 April. Marched to Nisa 5 leagues.

15 April. Marched to villages between Vila Velha [de Ródão] & Retaxo &c 4 leagues.

16 April. Marched to Castelo Branco 3 leagues.

17 April. Halt.

---

55 Reference Museum of the Oxfordshire Soldier – SOFO 2195 & 2195B

18 April. Marched to Loizo [Lousa], Escalha Enema [de Cima] & Debaxo [Escalos de Baixo] &c 4 leagues.

19 April. Halt.

20 April. Marched to Sao Miguel de Acha 3 leagues.

21 April. Marched to Penamacor 4 leagues.

22 April. Marched to Sabugal & villages adjacent 4½ leagues.

23 April. Marched to Aldeia Velha, Alfaiates &c 3½ leagues.

24 April. Fuentedeguinaldo (Spain) 3 leagues.

25 April. Halt. J'etois a diner avec le chef aujourd'hui. [I had dinner with the chief today]

26 April. Marched to El Bodon 1¾ leagues.

27 April–1 May Halt. This movement was made in consequence of Marmont entering Portugal & ravaging the whole country in the direction of [blank – Abrantes?] & as far as Castelo Branco, where I am sorry to say, he found a considerable supply of provisions. Luckily the bridge over the Tagus at Vila Velha [de Ródão] was removed in time, therefore no time was lost in reconstructing it when we arrived at Nisa. The enemy retired before us and I understand that as soon as Marmont, who had proceeded towards Celerico where we had a magazine, heard [that] the Light Division had crossed, he faced about & retired with the utmost celerity. The whole of their track was marked with devastation and even in Spain (particularly at El Bodon) they behaved in an unprecedented cruel manner to the inhabitants. It appears Marmont attempted nothing against Ciudad Rodrigo, the governor of which behaved most admirably.

Went on the 28 [April] to Ciudad Rodrigo. This town is by no means so strong as Badajoz, indeed it has no pretentions to the name of a regular fortification, being merely surrounded with a wall (which is old) [and] badly flanked. The ditch is by no means deep & in the middle is constructed a *fausse braye*[56] which certainly covers the foot of the wall. Upon the whole it appears to me not capable of resisting a siege and indeed in many places exposed to escalade. The Spaniards are occupied in repairing the breaches and in constructing the following outworks at the extremity of the ground to the [blank – north?] (where we approached lately) is a redoubt [with] 3 guns *en barbette*,[57] tolerably well-constructed with a ditch palisaded. About 50 yards to its rear is a small work which protects the rear of the former, it has 1 gun *en barbette* and to the rear of this and on the site of the flattened redoubt is a Fort

56 A fausse braye is a lower wall built in front of the fortress curtain wall, to protect the base of the wall from artillery fire.

57 Artillery en barbette means that they were raised by a platform to fire over a parapet, rather than through an embrasure.

Wellington, of some strength. It commands the ravine which runs near the town on this side, on the opposite side of which is a smaller fort (Craufurd). To the northward is a redoubt called (Castanos) about 200 yards from the place, of some strength.

2–14 May. Halt.

15 May. The regiment inspected this day by General Alten.

16–23 May. Halt.

24 May. J'etois a diner avec le chef aujourd'hui. [I had dinner with the chief today.]

25–26 May. Halt [at] El Bodon.

27 May. The division was reviewed by the chief this day. He expressed his approbation of the corps, but was not satisfied with the performance of the Brigadier & Staff.

28 May–10 June. Continued at El Bodon until the . . .

11 June. Marched to a bivouac about a league beyond the Agueda upon the Salamanca road.

12 June. Halt.

13 June. Marched to a bivouac about a league beyond the Yeltes River 3 leagues.

14 June. Bivouac 4 leagues.

15 June. Bivouac near [Blank].

16 June. Came in sight of the enemy's cavalry within a league of Salamanca, which were soon driven in with some little loss on both sides.

17 June. Marched towards Salamanca, found it evacuated by the French, with the exception of about 800 left in the fort[58] which they had constructed on top of a convent to command the passage of the bridge. Forded the Tormes in consequence, about a league above the town. The ford rather deep, note: a better [one] about a mile lower. Bivouacked in a wood on the bank of the river, 3 miles from Salamanca; went into the town, which has suffered considerably, most of the convents being destroyed. The inhabitants pretended to feel a good deal of satisfaction at our advance, in which however, I suspect they were not very sincere.

18 June. Marched towards Toro, in which direction the French had gone, halted about 3 miles beyond Salamanca. The country is everywhere well cultivated, covered with the finest crops of grain, almost sufficiently ripe to cut.

58 Note by Hunt – There were also two smaller forts connected by a covered way, both with the larger, all of which are extremely strong and well-constructed. Three supporting forts were constructed by the French, San Vincente, San Cayetano and La Merced.

19 June. Aldeaseca [de la Frontera] 1 league, bivouac near Aldeaseca [de la Frontera].

20 June. In consequence of Marmont advancing with all the forces he could collect, we moved this day to a position on the Toro & Valladolid side of Salamanca where Lord Wellington drew up his army in expectation of being attacked there. Went to the front as Field Officer of the day and occupied an advanced post near the enemy.

21 June. Position near Salamanca. The enemy made no movement of consequence but contented themselves with a distant partial cannonade which did us very little injury and manoeuvring upon the right which brought on a little skirmishing.

22 June. Position near Salamanca. The enemy this day attempted to establish themselves upon some high ground immediately in front of our right which commanded a view of this position, from which however they were soon driven from by some regiments of the 7th Division but not without some loss on our side.

23 June. Position. This morning at daybreak we discovered the enemy had broke up and gone off. Lord Wellington suspected from the direction they took, that their intention was to cross the Tormes higher up, in which opinion he was confirmed by reports in the evening being brought in that the French were preparing to cross it above [Alba de] Tormes. We (the Army) received orders in consequence to get under arms and the whole except a division or two moved to the right and the Light Division were ordered to march to the high ground on the banks of the Tormes, the 2nd Brigade about a mile & half in front of the First upon the road leading along the banks of the river to Salamanca, the enemy being in force a few miles in front and their videttes placed close to the Tormes about a mile in front of the village of Aldealengua.

24 June. Near Aldealengua. This morning a heavy firing was heard at daybreak on the opposite side of the river and when light, we discovered a strong corps of the enemy driving in a brigade of our cavalry. The cavalry (German Brigade) retreated gradually before them and seemed, although they were without much infantry or artillery to keep them in check, and although the enemy got very near them with their gunnery fortunately lost but few. About 10 am Lord Wellington sent the 1st & 7th Divisions across the Tormes and reinforced the cavalry with another brigade, which the French seeing began to retire, but a few hours afterwards observing Lord Wellington and withdrawing the infantry to the other side, they advanced a second time, which compelled Lord Wellington to move them back again, about 4 pm the enemy retired towards Alva [Alba] de Tormes. This night, between 10 & 11 o'clock, the light companies of the 6th Division stormed one of

the small forts in the town, which the enemy still held notwithstanding we had kept up at intervals a very considerable fire upon them, and were after a most obstinate contest, repulsed with very considerable loss. General Bowes killed[59] with 15 officers & 140 rank & file killed & wounded.[60] Several reasons are given for the failure, but I believe it was much too strong to be carried by escalade without having been regularly breached &c &c.

25 June. Post near Aldealengua. Nothing of importance took place this day. It is said the enemy are waiting for reinforcements which occasions their remaining in our neighbourhood, which is certainly probable. At present they are in not a sufficient strength to attack us in position and I understand that unless Marmont receives his expected succours soon, he will be forced to retire from want of provisions.

26 June. Post near Aldealengua. Got under arms at 11 last night, in consequence of a false alarm, which was particularly annoying as we were obliged to fall in before daybreak (ie 3 o'clock) every morning.

27 June. The forts in the town which had certainly made an admirable defence, this day surrendered in consequence principally of the convent in the large fort having been set on fire by red hot shot from one battery and the garrison were alarmed for the safety of their magazine. They were allowed to take with them their personal baggage, the officers their portmanteaus & the men their knapsacks. I understand they were a fine body of men and were about 800 strong in the commencement of our attack, of which number they lost upwards of 100,[61] our loss I fear numbers nearer 400.[62]

Sunday, 28 June. Bivouac near Aldealengua. This morning at daybreak we discovered the enemy had retired after destroying the villages they had occupied. About 11 am received an order to march immediately to Castellanos [de Moriscos] 1 league.

29 June. Marched to a bivouac in a wood near Parada de Abullos [Parada de Rubiales] 3 leagues.

30 June. Marched to the village of Castrillo [de la Guareña] on the banks of the small river of Guarena in the neighbourhood of which we bivouacked, 2 leagues. The enemy are still retreating in the direction of Valladolid, at least the main body is upon that road, but they have I hear a column of 9,000 men upon the Toro and another of 2 divisions

59 Major General Barnard Bowes was killed on 24 June 1812.

60 Oman quotes six officers and 120 men killed and wounded in this premature assault.

61 The French lost three officers and forty men killed, eleven officers and 140 men wounded. About 600 men were made prisoners.

62 Allied losses were five officers and ninety-four men killed and twenty-nine officers and 302 men wounded.

upon the Madrid roads, but their columns can so easily concentrate on either front, that it is with me a matter of doubt which road it is their intention alternately to take. Their vedettes are rather more than a league in our front.

1 July. Marched to Nava del Rey, a town of some consideration 4 leagues. Were received by the inhabitants with a great deal of joy principally owing to our having saved them from a large contribution which the French had levied, but not collected. They I understand retired from it only on our approach.

2 July. To Rueda. About 9 am our advanced cavalry came up with the enemy who had continued in their neighbourhood, I presume from not expecting us to advance so far, much later than usual with them. It is said they were in the greatest possible confusion, most of them drunk, having found immense quantities of wine in this place and I have no doubt had we attacked them, we should have made great havoc, but our chieftain for reasons (which I have no doubt were unanswerable, but which remain *a secret)* allowed them to pass quietly the *Douro* at Tordesillas, about five miles distant. 3 leagues.

3 July. Bivouac Rueda. Went on duty as Field Officer of the day. At daybreak marched towards Tordesillas. Formed upon the heights on this side of it, made a great show of our force for the purpose of alarming them and preventing them from detaching any people to *Pollio* [Pollos] which place the 3rd Division took possession of, crossing some regiments, together with a brigade of cavalry to the right bank of the Douro at a ford near that village, in doing which I believe they lost but few. Returned in the evening to the bivouac.

4 July. Bivouac near Rueda. A day of rest!!! Rode to Medina del Campo, about 6 miles distant, to take leave of General Sir T[homas] Graham, who is compelled by ill health to return to England, to the deep & heartfelt regret of the whole army. Medina del Campo is a very large town but the houses are extremely old, built in a very bad style and altogether in a most ruinous condition.

5 July. Sunday Rueda, halt.

6 July. Rueda, halt. The whole country for some leagues round Salamanca produces immense quantities of corn, cultivation being carried to the highest perfection, from Nava del Rey to the Duero, the country has quite a different appearance, the soil being almost everywhere sandy is not so well suited for corn as for the vine, which covers the whole of the land and (as far as the eye reaches) it is one continued vineyard. That made here is a light sort of white wine, by no means unpleasant & not unlike Vin de Graves. Rode this day to

La Secca [La Seca] a very extensive village about 5 miles to the south east (towards the Duero). The harvest is now ripe and the people were all busied in gathering it in and winnowing & sifting the corn, which is all prepared in the open air, the farmers never putting it in stacks or bins unthreshed.

7 July. Rueda, halt.

8–15 July. Continued halted at this place without any particular movement on either side being made, until this day, when it was discovered at daybreak that the enemy had moved from the posts they occupied upon the right bank of the Duero to *their right.* In fact, Lord Wellington had been aware for some days past that they intended moving towards that part and had accordingly moved off several divisions to *our* left in order that they might be quite prepared if the enemy should dare to cross the river lower down, which however I understand is not likely, though their intentions are unknown. I mean of course to the public, our chief I take for granted is well acquainted with their object.

About 6 pm the chief shifted his quarters, which had been since our advance at this place, to La Sana [del Rey] on account of its central situation. The 1st Brigade of our division and General Pack's Brigade of Portuguese at present attached to it, moved also in the evening to Foncastin about a league off. J'etois a diner avec le chef aujourd'hui. [I had dinner with the chief today.]

16 July. This evening about ½ past seven were unexpectedly ordered under arms and soon afterwards ordered to march to the rear. Marched all night and arrived about daylight at Castrejon [de Trabancos], near which we bivouacked together with our First and Pack's Brigades and 4th Division. 4 leagues.

17 July. Halted near Castrejon [de Trabancos].

18 July. About daybreak a report arrived that the enemy were advancing; got under arms and soon afterwards we observed the enemy in force moving down towards our left, in order to turn the position which our First Brigade occupied in front of the village of Castrejon [de Trabancos]. About this time Lord Wellington arrived and it appeared from the questions he put respecting our disposition &c that he had not expected this movement on the part of the enemy. The ground to our left favouring the advance of the enemy, we drew our 1st Brigade off from the village and retired in contiguous columns followed by the enemy, who pressed us hard and occasionally fired on us with their artillery but with little effect, which we considered as extremely fortunate. We were completely within the range of their guns. We continued moving on until we reached a position in front

of the village of Canizal and just behind the small river of Guarena [Ermita], where we drew up in order of battle. The enemy attempted the centre with one division of infantry and some cavalry but were repulsed with some loss by the 4th Division. In this affair the 27th & 40th Regiments distinguished themselves. The enemy also lost a general of brigade (cavalry) named Carrier who was taken it is said by Major Krauchenberg[63] of the hussars.

The march this day was extremely fatiguing and several men unfortunately fell into the hands of the enemy, having fallen out of the ranks through fatigue. Went on advanced picquet this evening as Field Officer of the Day.

To the latter part of the day, with the enemy upon our flanks close to us, the head of their column being almost in a line with ours, evidently with an intention of reaching the pass in our front before us. Notwithstanding we were so near and an action seemed inevitable, we got to the position without coming to blows and without losing scarce a man, excepting those who fell out through fatigue.

19 July. We expected the enemy would have attacked us this morning at daybreak, but they remained quiet until the afternoon, when (about 5 o'clock) they formed and after making a show of advancing, they commenced moving with their whole force to their left to turn the right of our position, occupying the high ground in their front, being separated from them by a deep ravine. Soon after we arrived the enemy commenced a cannonade, which we answered with our horse artillery, but the ground on which they stood commanding us and their guns being of heavier metal, we fell back and formed under cover.

20 July. This morning, soon after daybreak we observed the enemy in motion and soon discovered they were all in full march towards our right, still proceeding to turn the right of our new position. They appeared to move with great rapidity and in better order than usual; soon after their intention was ascertained by our great chieftain. He moved the army also to our right and as we moved on the *cord*, while the enemy were compelled to march upon the arc, we consequently reached some ground which had been marked by our commander for a position in their front, before the heads of their column appeared. Our division & the 3rd were ordered to proceed by a direct road which ran through a wood in the rear of this new position, towards the village of [Blank] where we halted for a few hours and as the enemy still proceeded to their left on a road which went directly towards Salamanca, we were in the course of the afternoon put in motion again

63 Brevet Major Georg Krauchenberg, 1st Hussars King's German Legion.

and marched in a parallel direction with them. We reached the village of [blank] about 7 in the evening where we halted with great part of the army during the night.

About 2 next morning 21 July we commenced once more our march and proceeded by a circuitous road (in order to clear the road we had halted upon for other columns) towards our old position in front of Salamanca, which we reached about 8 in the forenoon. And were in the act of crossing it, being ordered to within a short distance of Salamanca, when we were suddenly stopped by a new order to go to the village of Moriscos in front of the right of the position. We halted until 6 in the evening when we were ordered under arms and directed to cross the Tormes at the ford of St Martha [Santa Marta de Tormes] in consequence of the enemy having moved their whole force across at Huerta. We reached our bivouac on the left bank of the river with [in] a very short distance of Salamanca about ten and halted for the night. About 9 this night (whilst we were on the march) came on one of the heaviest storms of thunder, lightning & rain I ever remembered; the thunder burst directly over our heads and stunned several persons in our division, but providentially without injuring anyone materially, although the bolt must have fallen close to us. The report was so loud that it frightened the horses, mine rushed forward and was very near through me, but the most singular event attending it took place in Major General Le Marchant's Brigade of cavalry, viz 3rd Dragoon Guards, 5th Dragoons [Guards] & 4th Dragoons, which had just taken their ground for the night, most of the men being fatigued had lain down in a line in front of their horses, which were tied together by troops, the horses alarmed by the tremendous explosion rushed forward over the men and wounded badly near fifty of them. Several of the horses afterwards separated, having broken their halters and the next morning about 40 were missing, supposed to have galloped off towards the enemy.

22 July. About 6 this morning, several shots were heard in our front as from skirmishers and we afterwards understood that Lord Wellington had moved towards the enemy for the purpose of reconnoitring them, in the course of an hour the firing became more brisk and we found afterwards that the enemy had attempted to get possession of a wood some distance to our (their) front but were driven back by the 7th Division. The fact was that they were anxious to discover the situation of our army and had pushed on to the wood for that purpose, but finding it disputed they desisted. About nine we were ordered to advance and we moved to the wood just mentioned. We now discovered that our whole army had assembled within a short distance of us, to our right,

with the exception of the 3rd Division & a brigade of cavalry. The army were in several massive columns formed under cover of some extreme high ground which concealed them from the enemy and they were so placed as to be ready to proceed at once to any part the chief might think necessary. From this disposition, we all saw that something of consequence was on the eve of taking place. The enemy being about two miles to our front in a wood and as we understood was preparing to move towards our right in order by threatening our communication with the rear (Ciudad Rodrigo) induce Lord Wellington to uncover Salamanca, which any further retrograde movement on our part must invariably occasion. It was not long however before we learnt (what indeed was pretty apparent from the manner in which our army was disposed) that, as soon as the enemy debouched from the woods (which partly concealed him) sufficiently to be laid hold of, Lord Wellington was determined to attack him. At this moment we saw the 3rd Division, which had just crossed the Tormes (having remained on the right bank of that river during the night) in full march by our rear along the road leading from Salamanca towards Ciudad Rodrigo, to preserve, *as we then thought*, the communication from being cut off. The situation of our army remained thus for some time. On the left of the whole was the wood I have before noticed, behind which in reserve was placed a brigade of cavalry, some horse artillery & the Light Division, farther to the right and towards the front was placed the army in several massive columns all covered & concealed by this high table hill (one of the Arapiles) on which was placed a battalion with some guns; the 3rd Division & Don Carlos' Spaniards had halted about 2 miles in the rear, but considerably farther to the right upon the Ciudad Rodrigo road & most of the cavalry were still further to the right but rather to the front of the 3rd Division.

The enemy were separated from us by a valley and placed behind several hills (two remarkable hills called the Arapiles) some of rather a considerable height, which run in a line along our front, the left of which (advanced a little towards our line) and was (almost a perfect round hill).

We remained thus for some time (3 or 4 hours), at length about 3 o'clock the enemy began to form their columns & they debouched from the wood towards their left. Several of our columns immediately issued towards our right in double quick time, forming in two lines, the right stretching almost as far as the round hill upon the left of the enemy. As soon as this movement commenced, Marmont garnished these hills (of his) with artillery and began a very heavy cannonade upon our columns which continued without ceasing, though without the effect which was to be expected from artillery so favourably placed upon our uncovered troops. This fire was answered by some guns placed about the centre of our line.

Upon the first movement of our columns we observed the 3rd Division and cavalry rapidly moving to the left of the enemy & in a very short time they arrived at the round hill and completely outflanked them. It is said that Marmont had not the smallest idea that Lord Wellington intended to attack until he saw the 3rd Division moving to their front, he then endeavoured to rectify his error, but it was too late, for their troops formed in great confusion & disorder. He endeavoured to dispute possession of the important hill upon his left, the key to his position, but it was soon carried in the most masterly style by the 3rd Division, which having thus completely turned the enemy advanced [sic] without a check along their line, to their right, doubling back one division after the other and our cavalry upon *its* right taking advantage of the enemy's broken state, charged repeatedly through them, which produced such a panic in this part that it is said they through [sic] away their arms by hundreds and ran in towards our men, surrendering themselves and near 3,500 were taken.

Although nothing could have resisted the 3rd Division; yet the enemy committed several mistakes which I presume arose out of the confusion they were in on finding themselves outflanked, the division placed upon the hill instead of taking up a strong defensive position which they might have done, having artillery I hear, upon the light companies of the 3rd Division, which advancing in the front, approaching, moved forwards, consequently turned in a circular form as they were; necessarily got into disorder and soon fell back. Immediately it was discovered that the division had turned them, the whole line advanced and ascended with rapidity & in most admirable style the hills in their front which they gained, almost immediately the enemy giving way at all points and the whole were thus carried and kept possession of, with the exception of the most considerable hill, almost to the right of the whole, which it fell to the lot of the 4th Division to attack. Upon our troops gaining the summit in the first instance, they found in their front a regiment of 4 battalions almost at the foot of the opposite side of the hill, behind which upon a height farther to the rear was drawn up 2 divisions of the enemy. Upon seeing these troops so near them they immediately commenced firing without waiting to be formed, which being observed by the officer commanding the enemy, he rapidly & in excellent order, formed into columns and advanced against our people who continued firing upon them until they got close to them, when they gave way and the enemy who had not yet fired a shot, regained possession of the hill, but they kept it a short time only, for the 6th Division coming to their support, the 4th Division formed again and so deprived the enemy of their short-lived advantage. Thus was the whole front of the enemy defeated without a check excepting in this instance and in another which General Pack's Brigade of Portuguese attacked a hill (the larger Arapile) defended by a stronger body of the enemy and although they carried it, yet being unsupported they were driven back during being taken in flank, but another corps moving to their support, the enemy were driven back completely. Whilst these events were transacting the Light Division were put in motion and we marched to the support of the 2nd Division, but before we arrived near them, everything being recovered, we wheeled to our left and advanced against a corps of the enemy which had remained in reserve upon their right and in our front. On approaching the high ground occupied by the enemy we deployed into 2 lines (the 43rd the first & 52nd the rear line) and covered by the 95th formed in our front in extended order, with part of the 95th & 1st Cacadores in column upon our flanks, we advanced to the attack supported by the 1st Division which followed close in our rear.

23 July. Got under arms at daybreak and moved towards the Tormes, but the enemy having all retreated by Alba de Tormes to our right, we brought our left shoulders forward and crossed the river by a ford near Huerta, followed by the 1st Division & preceded by the Heavy German Brigade of cavalry. After halting a little time, we (1st & Light) formed in two columns parallel to each other & moved on in pursuit of the enemy who were about 2 leagues in our front. About 9 am the cavalry in advance came up with their rear guard which they found formed in squares with artillery upon the road leading up a considerable ascent, for the purpose of covering the retreat of a number of stragglers &c. Our cavalry formed 3 squadrons in line, at some distance from each other and which the flank squadrons hemmed in the scattered enemy, driving them upon the centre of the enemy's square and I believe took the whole, consisting of 1,500 men prisoners. This was one of the most gallant actions ever performed by cavalry.

About ten came in sight of the enemy in full retreat across the heights a league in our front, but in consequence of our men being extremely fatigued, we were obliged to halt near the village of [blank] where the troops bivouacked 4 leagues.

24 July. Marched at daylight in pursuit of the enemy through Penaranda [de Bracamonte] to Flores de Avila, here we bivouacked, 3½ leagues.

25 July. Bivouac near Flores de Avila, halt.

26 July. Bivouac near Aldeaseca 3 leagues.

27 July. Marched at daybreak as usual at 3 o'clock to Montijo [Montejo de Arévalo], 3 leagues.

28th Marched this morning at 3 o'clock. Passed through Arrevola [Arévalo], a large town but like most of the Spanish towns, in a state of decay & ruin, not so much owing to the war as to the state of the country, though it must be at the same time, granted that if this war has not produced this fallen state it has assisted the decay & certainly prevented any improvement. Arrevola [Arévalo] is placed between 2 rivers (at least a small river [Arévalino] unites with the River Adaja just below the town). It appears strongly situated and had formerly a castle of some strength, but which is now in a state of ruin. Reached Olmedo about 9 & went into quarters, 3 leagues. This was also headquarters today, Lord Wellington having halted yesterday at Arrevola [Arévalo].

29 July. Marched at 3 am for [Arrabal de] Portillo, but when we arrived within ½ a league of it, were halted and ordered to Pediajo de Portillo [La Pedraja de Portillo] about 3 miles to the left of the former, in quarters, 4 leagues. Headquarters at Madajos [Mojados] on the River Cega *1 league in our rear.*

30 July. Marched before daybreak (3 o'clock) for Bocillo [Boecillo] near the Duero [Douro] which we reached about six. Halted for a short time until the chief had reconnoitred, in about a hour we received the order to advance. We forded the Duero near Bocillo [Boecillo], at least a little higher up, without the smallest opposition from the enemy, he having retired towards Tudela the night before, indeed the left banks so effectually command the opposite one, that an enemy could never maintain himself there. We found they had evacuated Valladolid in great disorder, leaving about 800 sick & men who were so badly wounded as not to be in a state to be removed. Went that afternoon to Valladolid which is a very extensive but so ancient a town as to appear in a most dangerous condition. The houses in general appearing to totter from their foundations.

31 July. Bivouac near the ford of Herrera [de Duero] on the Duero. Halt.

1 August. Marched at 3 this morning to Tudela de Duero a middling sized town on the banks of the river where it makes almost a right angle. At the point of the angle is a bridge of stone across the river but at this time it was rendered useless by one of the arches being blown up by the enemy about a month before, 1½ leagues.

2 August, Sunday. Tudela de Duero. In consequence of the dragoon sent with the dispatches losing his way, did not receive the order to march until the evening of this day instead of yesterday & as we ought

to have marched at 3 in the morning, we proceeded at 7 this afternoon to ford the Duero just below the bridge. The ford was not very good even at this season, but in winter I should conceive it impracticable. We reached the place of our destination Aldea Major [Aldeamayor de San Martin] about ten at night, where the 2nd Brigade went into quarters, the 1st bivouacking near the *town*. Headquarters at Cuellar 5 leagues in our rear. 1½ leagues.

3–5 August. Aldea Major [Aldeamayor de San Martin]. Halt

6 August. Marched this morning at 3 am by Le Bovale [Portillo?] & Cogeces de Rio Seco [Cogeces de Íscar] to El Pino and encamped on the River Cega near the Ponte del Pinon. 3½ leagues.

7 August. Continued our march this morning at ½ past 3 am by Remondo and from there by the right bank of the River Piron through Fresneda [de Cuellar] and Mudrian towards Tramerso [?] and encamped on the right bank of the River Piron near Puente del Roble [?]. The headquarters were this day in Segovia or Viomily [?] 3 leagues.

8 August. Marched at ½ past 3 this morning, passed by Carbonero [el Mayor] and Tabanera [la Luenga] and arrived at our bivouac on the banks of the River Eresma near Yanguas [de Eresma] about eleven, having been delayed considerably by the bad marching of the 1st Division which preceded us, 3 leagues.

9 August Sunday. Marched at 4 am by [Los] Huertos, the ford of Ortouna [Hontanares de Eresma?] and passing through the villages of Valverde [del Majano] & Madrona, encamped with the 14th Light Dragoons, 1st Hussars [KGL] & 1st, 4th & 5th [Dragoons] on the Riofrio near the Palacio del Riofrio. The palace is a very fine building, built upon rather high ground & commands a view of some extent, though the country is not of the most picturesque description. We were bivouacked in the park belonging to it, at least if I may be allowed to call it so, for it was mainly a sort of forest walled in, though it certainly had great capability of improvement, a fine stream running through the middle, which might have with little labour been a fine stream of water. This was formerly used as a hunting seat by the late royal family. About 5 miles to the northward of this is situated Segovia, where I rode soon after I had refreshed myself and washed off the dust with which we are always covered every march. This is a town of considerable extent & great antiquity, but now in a state of rapid decay, presenting a melancholy picture of the state of the country. It has a very fine cathedral, the architecture of which is extremely pleasing, in it are several handsome chapels and I think I never saw in one church, so many windows of painted glass, the colours of which are remarkably brilliant, there are also some good pictures which are not often met

with in Spain. One of the monks told me that King Joseph about 7 days before, had been there and on his departure had carried all the plate, candles, books &c to be carried away. Segovia has also a castle of singular appearance and of great antiquity, but from its position being commanded on all sides, is a place of no strength and has been kept in repair I believe, only on account of its being useful as a state prison. The French had thrown into the ditch, which is of great depth, a great quantity of gunpowder and also some guns and gun carriages. There were also some guns and mortars (spiked) left on the platform in front of the castle. Memo, this is [the] Tower of Segovia which *Le Sage* has celebrated as the prison of his hero *Gil Blas*.

Headquarters this day at San Ildefonso, a royal palace about two leagues towards the Sierra de Guadarama, 3 leagues.

10 August. The whole of the troops marched this morning soon after daylight towards the Guadarama Pass. After proceeding about 2 leagues, halted in a bivouac near the village of Otero de Herreros 2 leagues.

11 August. Crossed the mountains which divide Segovia from Old Castille by the pass (called from the mountains) the Guadarama Pass, the road over it being the principal one leading to Madrid, is most excellent and it is a fine monument of human industry. We halted in the park belonging to the Escurial [Escorial] which is very extensive and might be made with a little care, remarkably fine, 4 leagues.

The Escurial [Escorial] is situated at the feet of the Guadarama Sierra about ½ [a] league to the westward of the pass. This extraordinary palace is by no means so extensive or magnificent as I had conceived from the description given of it by the many authors who have written concerning it. It is however certainly a very singular edifice built in the form of a gridiron in consequence of its founder the bigoted Philip 2nd having made a vow to erect it upon the day of Saint Laurence who we are told was grilled upon such an instrument. The church in the centre of the palace, is most beautiful, it has a simplicity about it extremely pleasing though at the same time it does not diminish the magnificent grandeur for which it is so celebrated. The ceiling is very finely painted but the part most worthy of observation is the mausoleum or burial place for the kings & queens of Spain who have died since Charles 5th, whose body is also there. The Royal Tomb is of a circular form, the floor and sides of the most beautiful marble as well as the steps on which you descend, start from the body of the church. The bodies are deposited in marble boxes of a very handsome form, which are placed above one another in niches, twelve on each side the entrance door, the kings on the one, the queens on the other side of it.

12 August. Halted. Bivouac near the Escurial [Escorial].

13 August. Marched at 4 am for Las Rosas [Las Rozas] 3 leagues. On the night of the 11th, a smart firing of cannon was heard in the direction of Madrid and we since found that a serious affair had then taken place in a village about half a league to the right of the one we are now in. It appears that the French came so unexpectedly upon the Portuguese cavalry that they gave way in the utmost disorder & confusion and the consequence was that 3 guns & howitzers belonging to Captain Macdonald's Troop of Horse Artillery[64] attached to the advanced cavalry, were taken[65] besides about 40 horses and in addition to a number of men of the German Heavy Cavalry which relying upon the Portuguese had unbridled their horses and were refreshing themselves when these cowardly rascals fled in such haste that they literally had not time to get their horses out of the stable before the enemy were among them. The particulars of this very bad affair is not exactly ascertained but enough is known to prove it [to be] one of the most disgraceful occurrences that has happened for a long time past.

14 August. Marched at ½ past 3 am for Villaverde, a village within four miles of Madrid, 3 leagues. Went this day to Madrid, which viewed from the environs & adjoining country appears of the size of a village in comparison to London and it certainly is by no means so large as one would expect to find the capital of so considerable a country as Spain. Upon entering it from the Toledo road, one crosses the small River Manzanares by a very handsome bridge about 300 yards from the city and contains a very considerable number of excellent if not magnificent houses. The style of building too, is extremely light & pleasing in general, but I must allow that the shops are bad, very confined & very dirty. There are several excellent coffee houses at which I have no doubt on other occasions very fair entertainment is to be found, but our presence completely upset everything and I believe in the course of a very few days, the cellars were almost universally drank dry, which augurs rather unfavourably as to the abundance of its supplies.

It presented on our entrance one of the most gratifying sights possible, almost every house had silk hangings or rich tapestry hanging on the outside of the windows, which gave a remarkable gay appearance. The inhabitants too, seemed delighted at the change of fortune and expressed their joy in the most animating manner. Indeed, just when we entered it, they had fresh reason to rejoice, for the enemy

64 Captain Robert Macdonald commanded 'E' Troop Royal Horse Artillery.

65 Three cannon were captured by the French cavalry but when they were eventually forced to retire they left the cannon behind.

who had been left in the Retiro, a fortified palace situated upon a spot which commanded most of the town & in which they had 200 pieces of cannon, had a very short time before ordered to surrender. We found that on the preceding night, the 7th Division had carried some barracks just outside the works, in such gallant style, that when the governor saw on the following day (the 14th) everything prepared for escalade (the 3rd & 7th Divisions being formed ready), he immediately hung out a flag of truce and sent proposals to give up the place.

It was also said, we had succeeded in cutting off his water from the place and besides, having a considerable quantity of gunpowder in the interior of the work, he was fearful of our red-hot shot setting it on fire and blowing them all up together. About 4 I had the pleasure of seeing the garrison march out about 1,900 strong, well clothed & well-appointed troops, mostly French. They marched out with the honours of war, ie the officers retained their swords & portmanteaus, the men their knapsacks, laying down their arms on the glacis.

The Royal Palace of Madrid is one of the most splendid in Europe; not so much from its extent, or from the appearance of its exterior (which is certainly handsome, but being unfinished is not very imposing), but from the costliness of its decorations. The suite of apartments (called the State) are singularly beautiful, indeed it is said that Bonaparte, when he saw them, observed that they were the finest in Europe. For my own part, they far exceeded any idea I had ever formed of even Eastern magnificence. The ceilings are admirably painted by the first antique masters of most of the different schools and the collection of pictures is also most valuable. The walls are covered with the finest tapestry, the gilding is extremely rich without being tawdry, in short, the *tout ensemble,* surpasses description and absolutely disarmed the *critique* of the most fastidious spectator, for although I was in there frequently, I never heard a single individual discover a solitary fault.

The Museum of Arts & Science is also well worth attention, the collection of different marbles in particular being very beautiful. It is not however, so large or is there in it so much *variety* as in Montague House,[66] but it is much better arranged.

The Prado is a public walk & ride on the eastern side of the town, not unlike (and confining it to the walk & ride) St James Park and it is also embellished with several fountains, those of Neptune, Apollo &c &c

66 The second Montague House (the original being destroyed by fire in 1686) was described as the grandest private residence in London by some margin. It was sold to the trustees of the British Museum in 1759, who demolished the property in the 1840s to build the present edifice.

are very fine, but the eye looks in vain for the fine canal & meadow which ornaments our own.

Most of the principal people frequent it of an evening and particularly on Sundays; formerly it was considered disgraceful for anyone but the *Roturier*[67] to walk but '*Tempora mutantur, nos et mutamur in illis*',[68] few even of the nobility have now either horses or carriage.

19 August. In consequence of the water being unwholesome at Villaverde we moved this day to Getafe about 2 miles farther from Madrid.

24 August Getafe. This evening Lord Wellington gave a grand ball & supper to the chief nobility of Madrid, at which a certain number of officers were invited. It is scarce necessary to observe that it was most splendid. The State apartments of the Royal Palace were thrown open on the occasion, all brilliantly illuminated. The dresses were all rich & splendid, both ladies & gentlemen being in their full court dresses. In short, I believe (indeed was told) that nothing in England was ever seen finer. There were several bands of music stationed in the galleries, besides bands in the ballroom, which played alternately and the waltz, cotillon & 'country dance' were danced. There were about 200 ladies present, who were not only richly but in general tastefully attired, yet the want of beauty was singularly striking. There were undoubtedly among them some very pretty women, but I saw none that I could call really beautiful. The supper was admirably conducted and served with a sort of grandeur in the Banqueting Hall, a very fine large & well-proportioned room in which were placed three long tables containing about 400 covers. They afterwards placed at the bottom of the two side tables, two square smaller ones, but there were still some who did not obtain seats. For my own part, I preferred being a spectator, the *coup d'oeil*[69] being most magnificent & pleasing. After supper the dancing recommenced and continued until broad day.

I feel that I have given a very imperfect & inadequate description of this magnificent assembly, which I shall ever remember with pleasure & gratification. I certainly have been better pleased at a much more humble ball, but that was from my partners. This however delighted from the scene itself, a ball and banquet given in the most splendid Royal Palace in Europe.

1 September. This morning the chieftain with his Staff, heads of departments &c left Madrid for the north, where the remains of Marmont's army had been collecting and were becoming troublesome,

67 The Common People.

68 Latin: 'Times are changed, we also are changed with them.'

69 A glance that takes in a comprehensive view.

in spite of the Spanish army of Galicia, which in fact are worth very little. Lord Wellington left in Madrid the hussars & 14th Light Dragoons, 3rd & Light Divisions of infantry and the Spaniards under Don Carlos. He has with him therefore Anson's, Ponsonby's & the German brigades of cavalry, the 1st, 5th, 6th & 7th Divisions of infantry. I must also state that the 4th Division are stationed at the Escurial [Escorial] at the foot of the Guadarama pass.

10 September. We continue in Getafe. Nothing of importance has taken place since, but rumour states that Soult has raised the siege of Cadiz & has marched for Valencia to join Joseph & Suchet at that place. This is now the sickly season in these southern climes and we have a great number of officers ill. About ½ past 3 (pm) poor Coates died.[70] He had been taken ill soon after he joined the regiment on the 18th ultimo from England & had only lately come up from the rear, but his constitution was destroyed & the fever returning, carried him off in a short time.

Went this afternoon to the Bull Fete at Madrid. The theatre or place in which the bull fights are exhibited is a large building in the form of a circle. The inward circle in which the bulls are fought about [blank – 60?] paces in diameter, is surrounded by a wooden wall for the purpose of separating the animals from the spectators, about 5 feet high, outside of which there is a passage which goes quite round, about four feet wide, the outer wall of which is about 6 feet high. Behind which commences the seats for the common spectators (a sort of parterre) these benches about 14 in number are placed one above another and are continued the whole extent of the circle. Above the back part of these is a row of boxes (balconies) for the higher classes. As this area is not covered over, these boxes are let, in proportion to their being more or less exposed to the sun, the Royal Box being in the centre of the shade. I should have observed this circle is entered in three places, where the gates are, by which the bulls &c enter. About 4 o'clock [the] Fete commenced. The *parterre* was crowded with men, women & children & most of the boxes were full in every part & on every face was depicted gaiety and an air of impatience for the expected pleasure. After clearing the inwards circle of the crowd, the guards placed themselves at extended order in the passage above mentioned. The picadors and toreadors then entered. The picadors were two men, very finely dressed, mounted on (but sorry) horses, armed with a pike about the length of a halberd. The toreadors were dressed in fancy dresses of different coloured

[70] Lieutenant Baker Coates, 52nd, Foot is recorded as having died on 9 September, but this appears to show it was on 10 September.

silks, they made certainly a very handsome appearance, they were 8 in number, one of whom was called by distinction the matador, this being the chief actor, often making their reverences to the governor & the spectators. One of these *gates* was thrown open and a bull rushed furiously into the circle, after looking around with the most enraged aspect, he rushed forward at the first toreador he fixed upon. The man instantly threw down a cloak which he carried on his left arm (his only defence) and leaped over the wall into the passage, the bull for a moment stopped at the cloak, but almost instantly pursued him to the wall, which stopped his progress. Sometimes indeed (and I saw one bull at this fete do it) the bulls leap into the passage where the guards are placed whose only means of avoiding his fury is either to leap into the circle or escape by one of these *intersecting barriers.* The animal then turned about and pursued another, who escaped the same way; sometimes indeed the bull stops at the cloak which is thrown at him. It always however invariably diverts or checks his progress; the animal then eyed one of the horsemen and rushed at him, the picadors remained boldly waiting his attack which he received upon his pike that was firmly couched. The pike entered the animal's shoulder and turned him off. He then, more furious than ever, rushed at the other picador who received him in the same manner, but either the shock was more furious or the horse was too weak, for it (the horse) was turned by its violence completely round and the bull immediately gored the poor animal in the belly and tossed him repeatedly, the wound was so large that the internals instantly protruded, notwithstanding which he was not suffered to retire, it being a point of honour for the man to remain as long as their horses can keep their legs. The toreadors then extricated the horseman by throwing their cloaks at the bull, who turned about and attacked them in return. He made afterwards several other similar attacks upon the horseman, some of which alarmed us a great deal for the safety of the Picador, for several horses were thrown over and it was by mere good fortune that the enraged beast attacked the horses instead of the man who laid under him and who indeed was not able to stir, scarcely without assistance, the horseman's thighs and legs stuffed with wool so that the horns of the bull may not penetrate the *leather pantaloons.* The destruction of horses sometimes is very great, this day *nine were killed,* three of which were *killed by one bull.* When the bull has attacked the horsemen three times each, the men on foot provide themselves with darts about 2 feet in length resembling arrows, the points of which are barbed and with these they rush at the bull and stick them into his neck and shoulders. This is attended with a good deal of risk, it being necessary that the man should *face* the animal and not stick from behind. Occasionally but not often these darts have a number of crackers affixed to them, which on being stuck into the bull, are by the shock set on fire and go off with loud explosions, these torment the bull to madness and he rushes furiously about the circle, turning up the ground & foaming with rage. After having continued this for some time, during which more or less address[71] in striking the darts are exhibited by the several combatants, which is proportionately applauded by the spectators, the matador enters armed with a *sword* and his cloak over his left arm. This is considered the most interesting part of the whole and every eye is directed to him, with the greatest anxiety and certainly his part of the performance requires great courage, address and activity. Upon the bull fixing him, then stands upon his guard firmly and when the beast rushes at him, he plunges the sword into the spinal marrow of the neck, which almost immediately kills him. Sometimes indeed the vital part is not exactly hit and the skill of the matador is more or less appreciated by his success in this particular.

The above description with little variation, applies to every fight. It is astonishing how fond the Spaniards are of these feasts and even when the poor horses are nearly faint with loss of blood, their entrails hanging almost on the ground, the most delicate female looks on without any feeling of compassion and would indeed oppose the animal being permitted to retire, such is the force of custom! For my own part, I am not desirous of attending another for although the appearance of the spectators and the dresses of the combatants, all of whom are remarkable well-made fine men, are extremely interesting and the noble appearance of the bull when he first rushes into the arena and excites an agreeable anxiety & solicitude, yet one soon gets weary of the uniform sameness of the spectacle and when the disgust one feels at the mangled state of the defenceless horses is taken into the account, I am by no means surprised at the dislike evinced for the amusement by the officers in general.

6 October. In consequence of Soult having raised the siege of Cadiz and proceeded in the direction of Madrid, General Hill moved with his army towards Aranjuez & Toledo, near which and on the banks of the Tagus it continues cantoned. The intentions of Soult are not ascertained, but it is certain that he is moving towards us. I think it is merely to draw Lord Wellington from the north, which it will not effect.

Getafe 10 October. The 2nd Brigade has remained stationary until this period. Yesterday we received accounts from the army before Burgos, the castle at which place, Lord Wellington had been besieging

---

71 Aplomb.

since the 17th ultimo when he first broke ground before it. This fortress it appears was of greater strength than was at first conceived, it is placed in a commanding situation and had been strengthened by some important outworks which the French had constructed for being upon the main road to Bayonne, from which most of their supplies come into Spain. It had been always regarded by them [as] of the utmost importance to secure their communications.

The outwork called Fort San Filippe [Miguel] was carried by storm by the light companies of the 42nd & 79th [& 24th] Regiments, supported & assisted by detachments from the several regiments of the 1st Division upon the [blank – 19 September]. On the [blank – 22 September] a breach was made in [blank – the first wall] by springing a mine and it was immediately escaladed by detachments under Major Lawrie[72] of the 79th, which failed owing principally to their leader being killed, the troops suffered considerably. Another mine was sprung on the [blank – 29 September] ultimo and a breach was made, which was entered by a sergeant & 4 men, but owing either to a mistake or misconduct, the main body of the storming party missed their way and these men were driven out again. A third breach was however effected on the 5th [October] instant at midnight, by the same means and the work instantly stormed by the 24th Regiment, in a most gallant style. It was at least carried with a loss of about 10 killed & 40 wounded. It being understood that the castle itself must soon fall, it is said that Lord Wellington will immediately come to Madrid leaving sufficient force under Sir Edward Paget to watch the remnant of Marmont's army.

21 October Getafe. This morning a route arrived for the brigade to march immediately. At 8 am got under arms& proceeded through Villaverde to a ford (the 2nd below the bridge) across the Manzanin [Manzanares], which is so swelled by the rain as to become a formidable river. We proceeded to Ribas [Rivas de Jarama] but finding on our arrival it would scarce hold a regiment, the 52nd was ordered a league further to San Fernando [de Henares], a royal manufactory near the *Jarama* River 3 leagues.

23 October. Marched this morning at 8 am to Vicalvaro, a village situated within a league of Madrid. 1 league.

25 October. Marched this morning to Alcala [de Henares], a large town near the small River Henares. Alcala [de Henares] was formerly celebrated for its university, but at this time there are neither professors

[72] Major Andrew Lawrie, 79th Foot, was killed on 22 September.

or students, it is still however in a better condition than most of the Spanish towns I have seen. 3 leagues.

26 October. Alcala [de Henares]. Halt.

27 October. An order arrived late last night for us to march this morning to Arganda [del Rey]. We accordingly marched at 7 am crossing the river Henares by the bridge over it about a mile from the town and proceeding through the very strong pass immediately on the opposite side, we arrived at our destination about 2 pm. At 9 pm an order suddenly arrived for us to march immediately back to Alcala [de Henares], which we reached before daybreak the next morning. 8 leagues.

We have lately made several extraordinary movements owing to the mistakes or ignorance of the present chiefs. Yesterday's movement for instance was perfectly ridiculous, but Lord Wellington is we understand returned from Burgos and we trust everything will go on right again. After having spent uselessly and fatally several weeks before Burgos and losing some thousands of valuable lives, he had been obliged to raise the siege. From what cause he could have made so fatal a miscalculation respecting its capability of defence is unknown and therefore my commenting upon it must be improper.

28 October. Alcala [de Henares]. Yesterday several thousand Spanish troops marched to this town from the banks of the Tagus and also from Guadalajara. The men in general are stout and some of the regiments seem well clothed, but their officers appear mean in their persons and are in short the worst part of their army, the consequence is that very little can be expected from them. They are badly fed and their whole interior economy entirely neglected.

Everyone is still ignorant of the cause of all these movements which are so contradictory, that it is perfectly impossible to form any opinion upon them. But it is surmised that Soult & Suchet are directing their march, in unison, to this point and it is possible that Lord Wellington has ordered this retrograde movement in hopes of inducing them to cross to this side of the Tagus, Soult I fear is too cunning a fox to be so easily caught.

29 October. Halted at Alcala [de Henares]. The last conjecture I find, is what most conjectures generally are when founded upon rumour & common reports, ridiculously absurd; as orders arrived this morning for the troops at Alcala [de Henares], Spaniards as well as English, to march without delay to a league beyond Madrid, where we arrived after dark & where we found assembled the whole of General Hill's forces together with the 3rd & 4th Divisions. In passing Madrid, we observed the Retiro on fire, which blew up with loud explosions and we then learned that in consequence of 25,000 men having reinforced

the French army in the north, Lord Wellington was compelled to retire before them, to withdraw his troops from this part and what was most distressing, to sacrifice Madrid, so hard was he pressed!!! Bivouacked near the village, 5 leagues.

30 October. Marched this morning back to Madrid to cover the retreat of the 4th Division & Kempt's[73] Brigade which however *on that account* was not necessary as they were not followed & we were halted in the avenue which runs round the town opposite to the palace. At about 10 am General Cole[74] desired me to take four companies to a store of bread, corn & flour in the city which the inhabitants had broken into and were plundering. On my arrival I soon dispersed the mob without being obliged to having recourse to violence. The store contained several hundred thousand rations which were distributed to the troops and after they had taken every man as much as they could carry, there remained still a considerable quantity which I gave to the famished poor of Madrid, first admitting the old & helpless and after a great many of that description had satisfied themselves, I let in the rest of the mob and such a rush I never witnessed; after which I withdrew my men and for the last time left Madrid. It was with real heartfelt sorrow that I saw this fine city left to the rapine & revenge of the enemy, who I was convinced would make the inhabitants repent the enthusiastic reception they had given to us. The whole town appeared in mourning, the streets deserted and on every face was depicted anxiety & dismay. Soon after I joined we moved again to the ground we bivouacked on the preceding night, 2 leagues.

1 November. Marched at 7 am. Passed by Rozas and reached our bivouac near the River Guadiana about 3 pm, 3 leagues.

2 November. Continued our march at 7 am, arrived near the village of Guadarrama about 3 pm when we bivouacked, 3 leagues.

3 November. Marched at 7 am, ascended the Guadarrama pass and proceeded by Espinosa [El Espinar] to near the village of Villacastin where we bivouacked, 5 leagues.

4 November. Marched at the usual hour, after proceeding about two leagues a report was sent to General Cole, who had the direction of the rear guard composed of the 4th & Light Divisions (the latter always forming in the rear of the whole) that the enemy were following close, the 2nd Brigade (ours) was ordered to halt behind a bridge to bring off the stragglers, stores &c, of which in a retreat there always were great

[73] Major General James Kempt.

[74] Major General Galbraith Lowry Cole.

numbers. About 4 pm we continued our march and arrived at our bivouac near the village of Villaneuva de Gomez (or Blascosancho).

5 November. Marched at 7 & bivouacked near the village of Fontiseiros [Fontiveros], 4 leagues.

6 November. Marched at 7 & bivouacked with the 2nd, 3rd, 4th Divisions & Hamilton's Portuguese in position behind Flores de Avila, 3 leagues.

7 November. Marched as usual, passed by Penaranda [de Bracamonte] & bivouacked within a league of Alba de Tormes, 4 leagues.

8 November. Marched about 9 am, crossing the bridge over the Tormes at Alba de Tormes and bivouacked in a wood near Calbarassa de Ariba [Calvarassa de Abajo], 3 leagues.

9 November. Halted in bivouac.

10 November. Marched at 7 into Salamanca, our division went into the Irish Convent, dined with Sir Edward Paget[75] who received me & behaved with the most cordial friendship.

11 November. Halt Salamanca. Got under arms at daybreak, about which time several shots were heard in the direction of Aldealengua. We were consequently ordered to march to the old position near Castellan[os] de Moriscos, where we found the 5th & 6th Divisions encamped, the 1st Division being in Villares [de la Reina]. Remained until 4 pm when we moved back to the town.

12 November. Halt, Salamanca.

13 November. Halt, Salamanca. Dined with Lord Wellington who was in the greatest possible spirits.

14 November. About 10 am a sudden order was sent to us to march immediately, a report having arrived of the French crossing the Tormes about 2 leagues above Alba de Tormes. We moved to a wood near the Arapiles where we bivouacked. The army being in the woods in front of us.

15 November. At 9 we were ordered to march, proceeded with the whole of the army in retreat towards Ciudad Rodrigo, bivouacked after dark in a wood near [blank]. The enemy's cavalry followed us close & made many prisoners, besides taking a great quantity of baggage & stores.

16 November. Marched at 7 am. The whole army, Spaniards as well as English in full retreat in 3 columns. The 2nd, 3rd & 4th Divisions under General Hill forming the left column (as we retreated); the centre composed of the 1st, 5th, 6th, 7th & Light Divisions under Sir Edward Paget; the right column being the whole of the Spaniards.

75 Lieutenant General Sir Edward Paget.

The Light Division formed the rear guard, bivouacked near Cocos [Robliza de Cojos], 3 leagues.

17 November. Marched about 7. Soon afterwards the enemy's cavalry appeared in sight, in close pursuit, formed in contiguous columns to bring off the stragglers, in which order we retired for some distance. About 11 the enemy came suddenly upon us with great force, we formed again in close columns to be prepared against their cavalry and were at one time ordered to form the square. Their cavalry however made no attempt upon us, but their infantry advanced in force with a considerable number of skirmishers in their front, we accordingly wheeled into columns & continued our retreat, covered by our skirmishers, which were furnished by each battalion. As their skirmishers were very numerous I sent out P[atrick] Campbell[76] with his company. We then descended some very steep heights, at the foot of which was a perfect plain which extended to the River Huebra about 3 hundred yards from these heights. Our men continued their march in excellent order though followed close by their infantry and under a fire of artillery which opened upon us from the heights we had left, notwithstanding which, we reached the river with little loss. Our men crossed it by two fords up to their middle, we then formed in columns contiguous to each other. Shortly afterwards I was ordered to take five companies & follow Lord Wellington, who was proceeding reconnoitring along the banks of the river which run along the front of our position. The enemy were discovered endeavouring to cross it on our left in order to turn us. Lord Wellington rode up to me and ordered me to drive them back and by no means to let them up, telling me he would send the remaining five companies of the regiment to my aid. I immediately deployed into line and advanced in that order. As soon as we got within 60 yards of them, I ordered the men to cover themselves and give them a volley, which they did most effectually, notwithstanding their arms were extremely wet, it having rained violently the whole day. The enemy soon fell back, retiring up the hill on the opposite bank of the river which ran between us, and as this hill was extremely steep and well covered with wood, it gave them great advantage over us. Notwithstanding which, they liked so little our fire that they fell back entirely in the course of about an hour. In this affair we unfortunately had 1 Captain (poor Dawson[77]) & 2 men killed, two captains & 38 men wounded. We remained quiet all night and slept upon our arms; nothing further occurring.

[76] Captain Patrick Campbell, 52nd Foot.

[77] Captain Henry Dawson, 52nd Foot, was killed at San Muñoz.

18 November. This morning we were ordered to march at 5 but the divisions who were to precede us delayed our march until past 7. We then proceeded without being followed by the enemy, at which we were not a little pleased, as we were compelled by the repeated stoppages to halt most disadvantageously and completely exposed to their fire, had they continued their pursuit. After the most severe march I have ever experienced, the latter part of the way for *miles* being up to the knees in water, we reached after dark, our bivouac on the face of some hills immediately behind St Esperito [Sancti-Spíritus].

19 November. Marched again this morning at 7 for Ciudad Rodrigo, in the suburbs of which we went into quarters.

Thus terminated the retreat from Salamanca in which we experienced greater hardship than ever I remembered in my life. In the first place the rascally commissaries had made no arrangement for supplying the division and we received no bread whatever during the whole retreat. The weather too was most severe, extremely cold and constantly wet, and to sum up the whole we had the rear guard, which compelled us frequently to help to cover the stragglers &c of the divisions in our front and we consequently arrived late, always in our bivouacs, when our men were so plagued with want of food, with having been exposed for so many hours to the inclement weather, their clothes never having been dried since we left Salamanca, that they had neither the will or ability to make for us.

22 November. We remained in the suburbs until this day when we were ordered to San Felices el Chico [Saelices el Chico]; on our arrival near the village, we found it occupied by some dragoons and were compelled to bivouac in a neighbouring wood, which was most annoying as it was perfectly unexpected.

25 November. We continued in the bivouac until this day suffering most severely from the cold, it having been a hard frost all the time, but luckily fine day weather. So severe indeed was the weather that two men died from the cold, absolutely frostbitten. At 10 am we were ordered to march back to Ciudad Rodrigo where we went into quarters.

26 November. Suburbs of Ciudad Rodrigo, halt.

30 November. Marched this day to Nave d'Aver [Nave de Haver] (Portugal), the most wretched, ruined village in the peninsula.

20 December. Continued until this day at Nave d'Aver [Nave de Haver], when the 52nd marched to [Fuente]Guinaldo (Spain). The inhabitants having applied for a British regiment and Lord Wellington who has gone to Cadiz to arrange for the ensuing campaign, sent orders for our battalion to be sent there.

[Fuente]Guinaldo. The battalion remained in these cantonments the whole winter and certainly we were altogether as well off for *quarters* as any part of the army. The situation was however extremely bleak and being removed as it were from the rest of the army we depended wholly upon *ourselves for society*. With respect to rations we were in general very well supplied. *Notwithstanding I never spent a winter so unpleasantly* in the whole course of my life and rather than pass another such a time, I would give up all my future hopes of military advantages.

The dearth of amusement, sameness of society, want of occupation (*that* caused by the regiment excepted) no books, no capability of changing the scene, horses out of condition. In short without enumerating more miseries we were driven absolutely to sit too long at table as the only relief (I speak of myself) against the cheerless, wearisome existence it was our fate to linger out. Absent from all that was dear to me in the world, seeing *scarce one* in whom I took an interest or who felt interested about me, it was with the utmost difficulty I could prevent myself falling into a perfect calluosity of feeling approaching to Mrs ___.

1813 [Fuente]Guinaldo. Commencement of the Campaign of 1813
20 May. This morning an order (which we were prepared for) arrived for the regiment to march to Carpio [de Azaba], there to be encamped & where the brigade was to be assembled, but as I was not considered sufficiently recovered from my attack of ague I was directed by the surgeon to remain at [Fuente]Guinaldo.

21 May. Proceeded to Ciudad Rodrigo & by good luck procured the same billet in the suburbs I occupied at the termination of the late retreat, 3 leagues.

22 May. Proceeded to overtake the regiment which had the preceding day crossed the Agueda by a ford above Molinos de Flores. Reached the intended bivouac some time before the regiment and conceiving myself quite well, joined, but I had scarce dismounted when the ague attacked me, from which I had been free for more than ten days. Camp between San Espirito [Sancti-Spíritus] & Martin de Rio [Martín de Yeltes]. Superseded by Colonel Gibbs[78] this day having had the command 1 year & near two months, 4 leagues.

23 May. Got on this day to San Munoz, 2½ leagues.

24 May. Halt, San Munoz. This day had a very severe fit of ague [all] day.

25 May. Continued our progress to [blank – Robliza de Cojos?]

[78] Lieutenant Colonel Edward Gibbs, 52nd Foot.

26 May. This day was again attacked by the ague. When the fit terminated I exerted myself to get on to Castrejon, 1½ leagues.

27 May. Reached Salamanca, which the troops (cavalry) had entered the day before & near which the Light Division had arrived in the evening. It would seem that the French commandant had conceived we were not so near, for he waited so long that our cavalry came up with him. The few cavalry he had went off leaving the infantry, who formed squares and resisted every attempt our cavalry made to charge them. I understand they received with firmness several discharges from our horse artillery which was brought up quite close. At last they got away, losing about 300 men killed, wounded & prisoners. Their force was [blank] cavalry, 3,000 infantry. If Monsieur had stopped a little longer, the Light Division would have arrived & not one would have escaped, 3½ leagues.

28 May. Salamanca. Owing to the infernal ague was ordered to remain here. Another fit this day. These repeated attacks weaken me considerably.

29 May. Salamanca.

I was regularly attacked by the ague every second day until the 12 June, when it gave way to the bark (under providence) which I took in large doses (½ an ounce a dose) about two hours before the time the fit was expected, and continuing free from any symptom I persuaded the Inspector Mr Robb[79] to permit me to start for the army, though I had ten days leave unexpired, but as I was aware I should be obliged to travel short stages, I was anxious to set out, that I might *stop the mouth of malice*, accordingly I left Salamanca on the 20th in the evening.

20 June. To San Christobal de la Cuesta. This village is situated on the left extremity of the celebrated position in front of Salamanca which Lord Wellington took up about this time last year. 1½ leagues.

21 June. To Fuentes del Sauco [Fuentesauco], 4½ leagues.

22 June. To Villabuena [del Puente]. A small village to the right of the Toro road, 3 leagues.

23 June. To Toro. In consequence of the morning being extremely wet & stormy, was prevented setting out till noon (when taking advantage of a cessation of the storm) left my little dry quarter and reached this place about 3 pm. Toro is situated on the right bank of the Duero, which runs at the foot of the hill on which the town is placed. This river is here broad, deep & fast, but has a tolerable good bridge over it, commanded completely by the town. The centre arches of this bridge have been repeatedly broken down by both parties according

[79] Deputy Inspector of Hospitals John Robb.

as each found such a proceeding expedient. It was lately destroyed by the French before their retreat, but was speedily repaired by the British. The town being on a considerable elevation commands a most extensive view of a country extremely picturesque. The Duero is seen for miles winding its course through a plain, at this time, rich in luxuriant crops of all sorts of grain until it reaches the town, below which, its banks are covered by groves of very fine elm, alder &c. Toro having changed its masters so often and being almost always a military post, has in consequence, suffered severely. It appears very thinly inhabited and the few people remaining in it exhibit the most striking marks of poverty, from being fleeced so frequently by the French, 3 leagues.

Unfortunately it would appear that the last page is missing from this journal, as the next journal begins five days later.

Palencia 28 June. Left Ampudia about 5 this morning and proceeded to this place (city) which I reached about 9. I had scarce got into my quarter with my baggage when I was attacked by a fit of the ague, the most violent of any I have yet had. I begin now to despair of getting quit of it, as the heat is now getting intense. Thus, I am once more compelled to halt, 4 leagues.

29 June. This is a very ancient city, about the size of some of our respectable county towns, it is situated on the banks of the Pisuerga in a valley of some extent, of a circular form, the circumference bounded by hills & might like our Bath be compared to a punch bowl. The French have left their *mark* here as well as everywhere else.

30 June. Another severe fit.

1 July Palencia.

2 July. Finding my enemy did not make his expected attack this morning, at least confined himself to a feint, I determined upon proceeding on my journey; for I found the heat so great in this city owing to it being deprived by its situation of a circulation of air, that I felt my health getting progressively worse and I was also anxious to reach Reynosa [Reinosa], a fine town only a few leagues from the Esla and an hospital station. I therefore started at 4 & got to Amusco about 7 where I procured an excellent billet, which the good old woman who showed me my apartment, took care to tell me had been occupied by Wellington himself when the army advanced. I call this poor woman (she was the housekeeper) *good,* because she is almost without exception the only one who has ever received me in their houses with a real welcome, 3 leagues.

3 July to Santillana [de Campos] 4 leagues. I observed today that the leagues were each marked by having a village situated at their termination, passed a canal with a *lock* almost the only one I have seen in this barbarian country, but I never remember to have seen a barge on the two or three I've seen, or any proof of navigation & strongly suspect this to be not completed.

4 July. Fearing an attack of the enemy this morning at 7, I was detained until 2 pm, when finding myself a sound man, I took a very slight dinner and proceeded to Herrera [de Pisuerga], whither I had sent previously my orderly sergeant to procure a billet and draw 3 days rations and where I arrived before ½ past 6, 4½ leagues. The country through which I have hitherto passed, since I left Salamanca has had one general feature without exception, flat, open, without wood or almost tree and cultivated (where there is any cultivation), with corn or the vine. Of course, there cannot be, to the traveller, a more disagreeable country to journey in for even in its best attire its sameness gets tiresome, but when bare or fallow, it is most cheerless and wearisome.

5 July. To Aguilar de Campo[o], 4 leagues. The face of the country is completely changed, having become extremely mountainous. The climate has also changed with it, fine fresh breezes instead of the stilting heat of the plains, the good effects of which I already exercise & am getting stronger every day.

Aguilar de Campo[o] is a very old town, surrounded by a wall with towers & protected by a castle built on a mountain at the foot of which the town is situated, but all is now in ruins! The Pisuerga, over which there is a stone bridge, runs close to the town and there are several groves of fine poplars leading to the several gates, which render the exterior very agreeable. The interior is however most melancholy, most of the houses uninhabited & the streets deserted.

In the very ancient church, near the altar, is a fine monument erected to the memory of Don Fernando Marriquez, Duke of Aguilar & Conde de Casteneda & his wife, who died in the year 1560. Their statues as large as life & extremely well cut in marble, are placed kneeling towards the altar. The costume (drapery) is admirably finished & they still appear in the highest preservation.

6 July to Reynosa [Reinosa], 6 leagues. I intended to have halted half-way as directed in my Route but finding every house in the village (Fombellida) uninhabitable, continued to this place. Reynosa [Reinosa] is very agreeably situated in the midst of some very high mountains, the sides of which are covered to the summit by groves of trees. One or two of the highest excepted, which have now a considerable quantity of snow on them. The principal source of the Ebro is about three

miles above the town, but the river, which runs close to it, is here very respectable, it abounds with trout of the finest species. There is also a remarkable spring close to the town, which issues from rather a steep bank and forms a large bason of the finest water, from which it runs in a considerable stream towards the Ebro. I was told that this town was situated higher than any other in Spain & the air was certainly very cool at this season of the year and in winter the cold I understand is intense. The houses are adapted to the climate, indeed several are built in a singular manner to the houses in the neighbourhood of Gottenburg [Gothenburg] in Sweden.

7 July, Reynosa [Reinosa], halt.

8 July. Proceeded to Cilluazello [Cilleruelo de Bezana], 4 leagues. The road leads through a narrow valley among the mountains. For the greater part of the way, the country showed the highest cultivation of the richest soil and I think I never saw [sic]. The different crops of wheat, barley hemp, peas &c more luxuriant. Within three miles of the village the valley widens considerably and forms a very extensive heath.

9 July. To Villacaya [Villarcayo], 4 leagues. The road today was romantic beyond description, it laid over and among some exceeding high mountains & through forests of beech, oak &c. Passed by several small villages situated in the valleys & hollows, the ground around which was highly cultivated. The houses in these villages are in general good and it appears to be in a flourishing condition.

10 July. To Momedeana [Momediano], 3½ leagues. This little village is situated in a glen surrounded by mountains & large forests. I had at first some difficulty in procuring a billet, the Corregidor took me to a most miserable hovel, but perceiving a much better house near, I insisted upon having it in spite of the jolly old priest, its owner, who I contrived in the end, by rather violent behaviour, to bring to his senses. He had by way of a housekeeper, a very good looking young woman who told me she was his *niece.* This is the universal custom, every cure takes care to provide himself with a handsome niece. Passed through Medina [Medina de Pomar] ½ league from Villacaya [Villarcayo], an ancient town but in decay.

11 July, to Sessa [Teza de Losa], 3½ leagues. Being informed that San Martin de Loisa [Losa], the place marked in my Route was infected by a malignant fever, I quartered myself in this little village situated on the side of a mountain near the main road.

12 July. To Fresneda, 3 leagues. Finding Osma, the village appointed for my resting place this night occupied by a party of the Staff Corps, [I] continued on to this little place very pleasantly situated on the side of a mountain near a very narrow but highly fertile & well cultivated

valley. This day was rather warmer than usual & I had a slight attack of the enemy, which is alarming now I am about to leave the mountains & their salubrious air.

13 July. To Nanclares [de la Oca], 3½ leagues.

14 July. To Vitoria, 2 leagues. The road from Fresnada to Nanclares [de la Oca] was extremely rugged and very difficult (though not impracticable) for artillery; at the same time it was picturesque beyond description, passing over mountains covered with the finest walnut, oak &c, it continued so until Nanclares [de la Oca].

At this latter village the mountain road falls into the 'Carmino Reale' from Bayonne to Burgos. And there also commenced the action of the 21 June, which terminated so gloriously for the British arms. The French commanded by Marshal Jourdan, the king present in person, were posted across a valley about three miles broad, the sides of which were for some distance very rugged & steep mountains; on *their* left in particular which continued almost all the way to Vitoria. On their right, the mountain terminated much sooner, but the ground was hilly for some distance, in their front was the River Burgos [Zadorra], rapid but *fordable.* It seems they rested here in the utmost confidence and had no idea of being attacked.

As soon as Lord Wellington saw their disposition, he perceived that their right could be easily turned & he determined on the attack. Ordering Sir Thomas Graham to move upon that point, General Hill commanding on the right. The French disputed the action on the (our) *right* & centre for some time until they discovered General Graham's corps, when they retreated in the utmost haste, leaving their artillery to the victors, who took 188 pieces of cannon of different calibres,[80] our loss was severe, particularly in officers and I have to lament one of my oldest friends & most esteemed companions, poor Ridewood.[81] Indeed, as I have never heard of his being wounded, when I was suddenly told by one of his men that he had died two days before, having lingered so long, I received so serious a shock that it brought on a fit of the ague. I regret most bitterly his death, he was as gallant a soldier & as good an officer as any in this army. His loss will be felt by many, for he was highly respected & the regiment he commanded will not soon have such an officer at their head. Farewell poor Ridewood!

---

80 It is normally stated that 151 cannon were captured.

81 Lieutenant Colonel Henry Ridewood, commanding the 45th Foot, was an ex 52nd man. He was severely wounded at Vitoria and died on 11 July 1813.

I also lost another very old friend, poor Adams of the 5th[82] whom I regret most sincerely. Poor Currie of ours also was killed.[83] His loss must be felt & regretted by everyone that knew him; by his regiment the 52nd in particular. In which he was an honour & an ornament.

15 July Vitoria, halt. This is a city of considerable magnitude & in a more flourishing condition than any I have seen in Spain. The French having remained in it since 1808 undisturbed until now. Of course, the inhabitants are not the best patriots, but in fact are entirely in their interest. In consequence of my health not being quite so good, I continued here until the19th, when feeling rather better I determined to proceed to my regiment.

19 July. To Salvaterre [Salvatierra],[84] 4 leagues. The fields on both sides of the road were entirely laid waste the whole way by the contending armies (road good).

20 July. To Lacunza [Lakuntza], 6 leagues. The road laid along a narrow but highly fertile valley, bounded on each side by mountains covered with wood. A considerable river (the Arga [Arakil]) winds along it & the villages are innumerable. Road not good.

21 July. To a small village about ½ a mile to the right of the main road [Irurtzun?], leading from Pamplona to San Sebastian and Bayonne and about ½ league after the cross-road from Lacunza [Lakuntza] enters it. It was situated most delightfully at the foot of a well wooded mountain and commanded a view of Pamplona distant about 2½ leagues (road bad) 4½ leagues.

22 July. To Huarte, 5 leagues. After proceeding from the little village about 2 leagues, we turned off to a commissariat station for rations about a league from the road, we then continued round Pamplona to this village. Pamplona appears a very considerable city and strongly fortified. It is blockaded by the Spanish army under O'Donnell[85] and as the French garrison are short of provisions, it is expected soon to fall. I understand they consist of about 3,000 men, they make frequent sallies to procure forage and it is difficult to ascertain if they succeed or not, so various are the different accounts. For my own part I fear it will hold out *yet* some time, particularly as it seems rather loosely watched.

23 July. Being obliged to take Madeira last night, I was afraid of the weather this morning, it raining most violently and consequently was compelled to halt. I had travelled hither from Vitoria with Captain

82 Captain John Adams, 5th Foot, was killed at Vitoria.

83 Captain James Currie, 52nd Foot, was killed at Vitoria.

84 Now Agurain.

85 General Henrique O'Donnell, an Irishman in the Spanish army.

Dalhunty, Paymaster 45th Regiment,[86] who had been to the latter place to see poor Ridewood (with whom he always lived) but was too late as he died two days before Dalhunty arrived. There were also 4 other officers in company, who as their division was only 3 leagues off, left me to join it.

24 July, To Orquin [Orkin] near Lanz [Lantz], 4½ leagues. The road today was extremely bad and had I not known that artillery had gone by it I should have called it quite impracticable. Finding Lanz [Lantz] where I intended to halt, full of troops. I turned off to my left to this small village delightfully situated in a vale surrounded by the wildest & most picturesque mountains. Within two miles is a larger village called Arraiz [Arraitz].

25 July, to San Estevan [Santesteban], 4 leagues. Soon after leaving Orquin [Orkin], the road passing by Arraiz [Arraitz] on the left, began to ascend the mountain, over the summit of which it went. On reaching the top the view was most wild, a series of mountains and vallies [sic] for a very considerable extent, in fact I cannot conceive a wilder country in the habitable part of the world! The descent was, as the ascent, by a winding road at the foot of which is the village of Donna Maria [Donamaria], about 2½ miles distant from which is the village of San Estevan [Santesteban]. The road on the whole practicable but most difficult for artillery, ie *for light guns*.

26 July. Learning yesterday that the Light Division were on the frontiers at Beira [Bera] & at Lessaca [Lesaka] (which was headquarters) I proceeded for the latter place about 5 am. At the distance of about a league I met Lord Wellington & Staff and I found that in consequence of a forward movement of the enemy under the command of Soult, he was going to remove farther to the rear. On approaching Lessaca [Lesaka] I met the division on full march, joined my regiment and after having fallen back 3 leagues, encamped on the summit of a very high mountain about two leagues in front of San Estevan [Santesteban].

27 July. This evening about 7, received an order to march to Zubieta & encamp. Owing to the difficulty of the road & darkness of the night, did not reach it until 5 the next morning, although I had in the morning rode the greater quantity of the same road in an hour & ¼. I was on horseback from 11 am until 5 the following morning excepting about an hour and in my weak state of health was consequently not a little fatigued.

28 July. Zubieta.

---

86 Paymaster Marcus Dalhunty, 45th Foot.

29 July This evening we received at 8 o'clock an order to march to [blank – Lekunberri], 4 leagues. Owing to the difficulty of marching at night in such mountainous & difficult roads, we were the whole night marching a league, and did not reach our ground until 1 pm this day, the 30th.

30 July. On the 26th instant it appears the enemy attacked General Hill at the pass of Maia [Maya] and being very superior in force, succeeded in possessing himself of it (particularly). Our loss was considerable, but the enemy's much greater.

Soult also forced the pass of Roncesvalles, which compelled Lord Wellington to collect his troops near Pamplona and I hear he has made repeated desperate attacks on our position, losing immense numbers of men without gaining an inch. The particulars have not yet reached me, but I understand that finding himself foiled there so completely, he has withdrawn, either to wait for reinforcements; to attempt to force his way by some other road; or to return beyond the frontiers. Our situation was critical, between Sir Thomas Graham at Irun and the chief and we were destined to move to either point as might be found most necessary. We are now encamped on the *main* road from Pamplona to San Sebastian and are about 6 leagues from the position & are under orders to be prepared to march at the shortest notice.

31 July, Camp near [Blank]. At 2 pm received an order to march immediately and to proceed to the position the division occupied before it fell back. On reaching Lissa [Leitza] we found it getting dark and as ever gained so little by marching in the dark, we halted near it & encamped, 2 leagues.

1 August. Marched this morning at 4 am and after the most fatiguing march I ever experienced, arrived about 7 pm at the ground where we encamped on the 26th, 5½ leagues.

2nd. Marched at ½ past 4 am and proceeding through [blank – Igantzi?] & Lesacca [Lesaka], arrived about 11 at the position immediately behind the village of Beira [Bera], the last Spanish village before which are posted a very strong corps of the enemy, on extremely strong ground. To our left on the other (the left) bank of the Bidassoa river is encamped Longa's corps of guerrilla infantry, about 3,000. The 1st Brigade having been ordered to attack the right of the enemy's position, we were directed to move about 2 pm to support them.

It may be necessary to state here that the enemy had suffered such loss in their attempts to force Lord Wellington at Ostiz that he was obliged to retire with precipitancy. The chief closely pursued him with the 4th, 7th & 6th Divisions on the roads towards the Porto de Maia [Puerto de Maya] and took & destroyed great numbers of them on this day, the 2nd. The enemy had halted on some very high ground on the above roads, from which Lord Wellington determined to drive him and he sent orders for us to attack his right flank in order to make him quit the strong ground he occupied. This appears to have had the effect desired, for he soon made a retrograde movement and the following morning was completely off. It is said that this excursion of Soult's cost him 20,000 men, our loss must also have been great, but the particulars have not yet reached me. In short, it is so difficult to keep up any communication in this mountainous region, that we are quite ignorant of the operations of our next neighbour!! After a spirited affair of the 3rd Battalion 95th, who drove the enemy from a precipice 'as it might be called', in the most gallant manner, the night having approached we returned to our camp.

3 August. This morning we marched to the ground we formed on last night, but as Soult had retired, we were soon after ordered back to camp. At noon we received an order to cook & be in readiness to execute any order we might receive. We then understood Lord Wellington had determined to attack the position of the enemy in our front, but we remained quiet all night. It was said that he had intercepted a letter from Count Gazan,[87] which stated that their ground here was so strong, they were under no apprehensions of our succeeding against them and as we had seen them reinforced by several fresh battalions (we presumed from the retreating army, the former troops not having advanced with Soult) it was hoped no attack on the front of the position would be attempted.

Our situation is a singular one, as we are close to the enemy, our centries [sic] within pistol shot of each other and yet perfectly quiet. I have said the Bidassoa runs to the westward at right angles at the foot of their right. This river flowing past Lesacca [Lesaka] (the headquarters ½ a league distant) separates us from another ridge of hills or rather mountains on which is the camp of the guerrillas under Longa. Excepting a few shots occasionally from them and the firing at San Sebastian, there is here no appearance of hostility. How long this extraordinary life of ease will last is unknown, but it certainly cannot last long.

8–12 August, Camp at Beira [Bera]. Yesterday [8th] sent a letter no. 7 to my wife enclosing a bill on Coutts[88] for £60. Nothing extraordinary has occurred, each party reposing and refitting following the late operations. A calm preceding a storm.

87 General Honore Theodore Gazan.

88 Coutts & Co. bank was established in 1692.

13–18 August, Camp at Beira [Bera]. Perfect tranquility has prevailed during the above days & no indication of hostility on either side. The French are employed in constructing works on the several roads leading to their different positions which however determines nothing as to their future views & we are in utter ignorance with respect to any further operations. Yesterday I rode to the summit of a very high mountain near the pass of Echellar [Etxallar], which commanded a most extensive view of France and great part of the enemy's position. They are encamped with great regularity on the roads at the entrance of the several passes and appear in considerable force. Our camps on the opposite side of the mountains, that separate the two armies are equally respectable and (without taking into consideration the character of the contending troops) leaves no cause for apprehension on our part.

The town of Bayonne, of which I had a good view, is of no great extent, with a harbour of little consideration, I did not observe a single ship in it. The country bordering on the frontier is apparently unproductive, exhibiting few marks of fertility or cultivation. The difference between the frontiers of the two kingdoms presents a striking contrast! In comparison France seems a perfect plain, with the wild picturesque scenes of mountain above mountain on the Spanish side.

26 August, Camp near Beira [Bera]. Nothing has occurred or alteration been made in our respective positions from the 19th up to this day. I lament to say however that desertion to the enemy has become alarmingly frequent, for which it is difficult to account.

27 & 28 August. On the 28th an order was sent in the pages of a letter to General Alten to select from his division 100 British & 50 Portuguese with 1 field officer, 2 captains, 6 subalterns, 'for the purpose of giving an example of distinguished valour & conduct in an enterprising moment'. Accordingly volunteers were called for and after due considerations I claimed the command of this gallant band, being the senior field officer not commanding, which with some difficulty I claimed, it having been promised to Major Napier[89] but I asserted my seniority & succeeded. It was understood that service for which we were required, was to storm San Sebastian and it was heard that the 5th Division who had been engaged in the siege of that place had become completely dispirited.

The party as above paraded at 5 pm and proceeded to Lessaca [Lesaka] where we were put under canvas for the night.

29 August. Marched to Oiartzun [Oyarzun] where we encamped, 3½ leagues.

89 Major William Napier, 43rd Foot.

30 August. Marched in company with a similar party of the 4th Division & 400 of the 1st Division destined for the same service to near San Sebastian & encamped. Waited on Sir Thomas Graham who invited me to dinner.

31 August. About 12 last night received an order to assemble at a point fixed upon by 2 am from whence the three detachments were to proceed to the trenches. Soon afterwards moved there accordingly into a convent where we remained until about seven, at that time I was sent for to Sir Thomas Graham's to receive my instructions, whither I repaired with Colonel Cooke 1st Foot Guards[90] & Major Rose 20th Regiment,[91] the commanders of the other two divisions. We were directed to wait upon Sir James Leith[92] who told *me* that he intended he should take my men (150) with 200 German light infantry to the advance part of our trenches for the purpose of keeping down the fire of the enemy upon our people as they advanced to the assault. The remainder of the 1st & 4th Divisions were to remain in reserve. Soon after this I posted my men according to these directions and about 11 everything was prepared for the assault. The troops appointed for this purpose rushed out and gained the breaches but made no further progress, the few individuals who crossed over were soon driven back and observed that our men conceived they could do no more. At this moment, the men showed themselves to the enemy (who were all regularly & extremely well posted) opened a most tremendous fire from their several works with all kinds of firearms and the destruction was shocking. The party under my command kept up also a good fire upon the enemy, but the latter were too well covered & too advantageously posted to be much injured by it and we were *also too few* for such a service.

The 1st Brigade of the 5th Division having got this far it was soon necessary to order the more troops to their assistance and I am sorry to say a good deal of confusion began to prevail. Sir James Leith ordered me to move my men forward to show the way, which although I then considered as not very fair, at a time when the failure of the others was anything but encouraging and as my men were so scattered along the works, yet as soon as I supplied them with a little ammunition I ordered them to move on. With about 20 men I gained the breach & reached the top, where, as I was examining it, I was struck on the breast with a spent ball which however only sickened me for a moment. Finding myself only bruised, I endeavoured to prevail on the men below to

90 Lieutenant Colonel Richard Cooke, 1st Foot Guards.

91 Major Alexander Rose, 20th Foot.

92 Lieutenant General Sir James Leith.

follow me, but finding the precipice too deep on the other side and the troops not much inclined to follow, excepting my few brave companions of the 52nd, who were but a handful, I proposed to go to another breach which seemed more practicable and notwithstanding the constant fire of the enemy, which every moment killed numbers, I succeeded in gaining.

On reaching the summit, I found myself only with about *ten* of my men, the rest including Captain R[obert] Campbell,[93] Lieutenant Harvest,[94] O'Connell 43rd[95] &c were either killed or disabled. I however endeavoured to lead on the men of the other regiments underneath who were principally Portuguese & observing a part where I could descend into the town, I exerted myself to rouse the soldiers. At length while in the act of taking hold of the colour of a Portuguese regiment with one hand and stepping over the crest of the breach, I received a ball under my left knee which knocked me completely over and put an end to all further exertion on my part. Two of my men undertook to lead me off and with the blessings of providence I was conveyed safe from farther injury to the convent where we had assembled in the morning. Soon after this I heard the troops had forced the town but the loss was immense on our part. I certainly think I was treated with little consideration, if I had been ordered with my 150 men of the Light Division to form the advance of the assailing column I think much loss would have been prevented, as I have no doubt that our men selected from the most desperate of the whole division, would have done anything, if sent in a body, but dispersed as they were, seeing the other troops fail, seeing them refuse to advance, their ammunition nearly expired, what could possibly be expected. In short, I think we were unfairly treated, but I saw so much bad arrangement that this behaviour ceases to surprise me. I have now to state the loss of my little band:

It consisted of at first:

52nd Regiment – 1 Field Officer, 1 Captain, 1 Subaltern, 3 Sergeants, 35 Privates
43rd Regiment – 1 Subaltern, 3 Sergeants, 30 Privates
95th (1st, 2nd & 3rd Battalions) – 1 Captain, 6 Sergeants, 35 Privates
17th Portuguese Regiment – 1 Subaltern, 1 Sergeant, 20 Privates
1st & 3rd Cacadores – 1 Subaltern, 2 Sergeants, 30 Privates

93 Captain Robert Campbell, 52nd Foot.
94 Lieutenant Augustus Harvest, 52nd Foot.
95 Lieutenant John O'Connell, 43rd Foot.

Total 1 Field Officer, 2 Captains, 7 Subalterns, 15 Sergeants, 150 Privates

Mr Fitzgerald Volunteer with 52nd Regiment wounded
In addition to the above
Names of the Officers
Brevet Lieutenant Colonel [John] Hunt 52nd Regiment Wounded Severely
Captain Robert Campbell 52nd Regiment Wounded Severely
Lieutenant [Augustus] Harvest 52nd Regiment Killed
Lieutenant [John] O'Connell 43rd Regiment Wounded Mortally
Captain [Alexander] Andrews 3rd Battalion 95th Rifles No injury recorded
1st Lieutenant Eaton 2nd Battalion 95th Rifles Wounded Slightly
[2nd] Lieutenant [William] Hamilton 1st Battalion 95th Rifles Wounded Severely
[2nd] Lieutenant [James] Percival 1st Battalion 95th Rifles Wounded Severely

The names of the 2 Portuguese ensigns are unknown to me[96] and I do not know at this date what the casualties among the men amount to.[97]

Near San Sebastian. Continued here until the 16 September, when a Medical Board having recommended me two months leave of absence, I procured through the interest of Sir Thomas Graham a passage onboard the *Creole* frigate,[98] Captain Forbes,[99] which was returning to England with Admiral Martin,[100] who had been sent out by the government to Lord Wellington to ascertain the nature of the naval force he required to cooperate with the army. [Robert] Campbell who was wounded & had remained with me constantly, accompanied me on board and it was impossible for any people even in our situations to be treated with greater kindness & attention than that we received from Admiral Martin, Captain Forbes and every person on board, which I shall ever remember with gratitude.

96 Their names are not recorded in Moises Gaudencio & Robert Burnham's *In the Words of Wellington's Fighting Cocks.*

97 Moorsom's *History of the 52nd Regiment 1755–1816,* pp.202–3, names every soldier of the 52nd who were in the attack. Of three sergeants and thirty-five corporals and privates, two sergeants were wounded, three corporals were wounded and two privates were killed and eleven wounded.

98 HMS *Creole* of 36 guns.

99 This would appear to be an error as the captain of HMS *Creole* was Captain Robert Mackenzie, Royal Navy.

100 Admiral Sir Thomas Byam Martin.

After a very pleasant quick run of 4 or 5 days we anchored in Plymouth harbour, where I landed the following morning and shortly afterwards set off for London, which I reached in the course of a few days having travelled up by easy stages on account of my wound.

Finis

Spes et Fortuna, Valete
Sat me Lusistis;
Ludite nunc alios.

[Hope and Fortune, farewell
You have made sport of me enough
Make sport of others Now][101]

101 The final lines of La Sage's novel *Gil Blas*.

5. BREVET MAJOR WILLIAM ROWAN REMINISCENCES[102]

Strictly Private

William Rowan became an ensign in 52nd Foot in November 1803, a lieutenant in June 1804, captain in October 1808 and a brevet major in March 1814. He served at Sicily, Sweden, Walcheren, Vigo, Sabugal, Vitoria, the Pyrenees, Bidassoa, Nivelle, Nive, Orthez and Toulouse. He fought throughout these campaigns without being wounded, but was wounded at the Battle of Waterloo. He later served in Canada, becoming Lieutenant Governor of Upper Canada, and later returned as Commander in Chief, North America in 1849. He effectively retired from the Army in 1855 but was promoted field marshal in 1877 and he died at Bath in 1879.

1803–04

In June 1803, having just completed my fourteenth year, I joined the Antrim Regiment of Militia as an Ensign, my oldest brother being one of the majors of that corps.[103] Shortly after I proceeded with the regiment to do duty in the Dublin garrison, where we arrived immediately after the suppression of Emmett's Revolt.[104]

In the month of November following [1803] I was very unexpectedly Gazetted to an ensigncy in the 52nd Regiment of Light Infantry, on the recommendation of the colonel, Major General Sir John Moore KB and joined it before the end of the month at Shorncliffe camp in Kent,

---

102 Museum of the Oxfordshire Soldier, reference SOFO 2085.

103 Major John Rowan of the Antrim Militia.

104 A rising led by Robert Emmett aimed to capture a number of key locations in Dublin including Dublin Castle, but it failed dismally. Emmett was captured and hanged.

where I had the good fortune to find my brother Charles a captain,[105] my brother Robert a lieutenant[106] and my Uncle Charles captain and Paymaster of the same corps.[107]

The 52nd Regiment about this period had attained such celebrity from its superior discipline and efficiency as a light infantry corps, under the command and instruction of Lieutenant Colonel Mackenzie,[108] afterwards Lieutenant General Sir Kenneth Douglas Bart,[109] Sir John Moore was permitted by the Commander in Chief, Field Marshal the Duke of York, to nominate the successors to all vacant commissions &c in the regiment, consequently when a second battalion was added to the regiment in 1804 I was & every step promotion was given to the officers serving in the corps, by which I obtained a lieutenancy.

1805–06

We were stationed at Hythe and Shorncliffe on the coast of Kent, within sight of the French army assembled near Boulogne until the middle of 1806, when the 1st Battalion with several other regiments proceeded to Sicily, where Sir John Moore succeeded to the command of the troops assembled in that island.

1807

In 1807 Sir John Moore left Sicily, taking with him a considerable portion of the force for the purpose of making a demonstration at Lisbon, but circumstances having occurred to render such a step inexpedient, he returned with the troops under his command to England. The 52nd landed at Portsmouth and marched to Canterbury.

1808

The battalion to whom I belonged accompanied the expedition under the command of Sir John Moore and [Admiral] Sir James Saumarez which was ordered to the Baltic to cooperate with the King of Sweden, but this being found impracticable, after remaining several

105 His elder brother Charles (fifth son of eight and two daughters) had been commissioned an ensign in 1797 and became a captain in 1803.

106 Robert Rowan was appointed as a captain in August 1804 but resigned his commission in August 1807.

107 Charles Rowan was appointed as paymaster in November 1798, the paymaster equating as the lowest captain in a battalion. He transferred to the 13th Royal Veteran Battalion in August 1814. He retired when on full pay with the Royal Veteran Battalion in May 1816 and died in 1819.

108 Brevet Colonel Kenneth Randoll Mackenzie.

109 Mackenzie changed his name to Douglas in 1831 and died in 1833, therefore Rowan's memoir was written between these two dates.

weeks in the harbour of Gothenburg, the expedition returned to England and from thence proceeded to reinforce the army serving in Portugal, which we joined the second day after the Battle of Vimiero [Vimeiro].[110] The 1st Battalion 52nd with the reserve of the army under Major General Paget,[111] occupied the heights of Belem during the embarkation at that point of the French army under Marshal [General] Junot,[112] after the Convention of Cintra. The Reserve then crossed the Tagus and marched to Estremoz on the frontier to compel the evacuation of Elvas by the French garrison.[113] We rejoined the main body of the army under Sir John Moore at Salamanca and moved with it upon the position occupied by the French at Sahagun and Valladolid. Previously to the commencement of the retreat of the British troops from Sahagun, I was promoted to a company and removed to the 2nd Battalion 52nd Regiment, which with the 1st Battalion 43rd and part of the 95th Rifle Regiment formed a Light Brigade under the command of Colonel Robert Craufurd[114] until the embarkation of the army after the death of our lamented chief Sir John Moore at Corunna.

1809

Upon the return of the army to Great Britain, the two battalions of the 52nd were reorganized at Deal in Kent, and in the spring of 1809 the 1st Battalion proceeded to the peninsula and the 2nd Battalion to which I belonged, formed a part of the superb but defeated expedition which was ordered to the Scheldt under Lord Chatham and Sir Richard Strachan. I had the good fortune to be an amateur in the batteries during the bombardment of the town of Flushing and while our squadron of line of battleships passed the town, pouring in their broadsides. It was a splendid sight, but the fire of the ships did little injury to the defences of the place, which I had an opportunity of examining on entering the town with the Royal Regiment on the 15 August, my brother James[115] being a captain of that corps, which was selected to take formal possession of the place.

110 Fought on 21 August 1808.

111 Major General Sir Edward Paget.

112 General Jean Andoche Junot.

113 The Elvas garrison was to give up the fortress under the terms of the Convention of Cintra.

114 Brevet Colonel Robert Craufurd commanded a brigade in the Corunna campaign composed of 1/43rd, 1/52nd & 2/95th, but it was not officially described as the Light Brigade.

115 Captain James Rowan 1st Foot, he transferred to the 22nd Portuguese Line Battalion in July 1810

1810

During a part of this year I served with my battalion in London on the occasion of the riots caused by the arrest and committal to the Tower of Sir Francis Burdett, by order of the House of Commons.[116]

1811

On the 22 January I was married to Martha Spong[117] at Town Malling[118] church,[119] Kent. Returning to breakfast at the house of a friend I found a letter awaiting me, ordering me to proceed *forthwith* to join my regiment which was then on its march, for immediate embarkation with several other regiments to reinforce the army in Portugal!!!

Under the peculiar circumstances thus, so active operations were expected to commence as soon as their force should join Lord Wellington, I could not with any degree of propriety apply for leave of absence to remain behind my regiment. Accordingly at the expiration of a week I reached Spithead just as the fleet was getting under weigh & embarked in the *Argo* frigate.[120]

We joined the Light Division of the army in Portugal during the pursuit of [the] French army under Massena[121] from their position at Santarem and on the 3rd April we had a sharp action on crossing the River Coa near Sabugal; of which action Lord Wellington said in his official despatch 'although the operations of this day were by unavoidable circumstances, not performed in the manner which I intended they would be, I consider the action that was fought by the Light Division, by Colonel Beckwith's Brigade[122] principally, with the whole of the 2nd Corps to be one of the most glorious that British troops were ever engaged in'. Shortly after this action I obtained leave of absence to return to England to join the depot of the regiment and

---

116 Sir Francis Burdett was a radical MP and a major thorn in the government's side and when he published a copy of his parliamentary speech in the *Weekly Register* criticising the government, he was charged with libelling parliament. His arrest was attempted at his house but prevented by a mob, however learning that his friend Sir Thomas Cochrane was planning to resist his arrest with organised violence, he allowed himself to be arrested and he was conveyed to the Tower of London.

117 Of Aylesford in Kent.

118 Now known as West Malling.

119 The Parish church of West Malling is St Mary's.

120 HMS *Argo* was a 44-gun frigate.

121 Marshal Andre Masséna.

122 Beckwith's Brigade consisted of 1/95th, 1/43rd & 3rd Caçadores.

was so fortunate as to be offered a passage from Lisbon in Her [His] Majesty's ship *Abercrombie* of 80 guns.[123]

1812

I was employed on the Recruiting Service at Manchester for 12 months and subsequently commanded the 2nd Battalion of the 52nd Regiment after its return to England in this year.

1813

In January I embarked at Portsmouth in command of a strong detachment to join the 1st Battalion 52nd Regiment on the peninsula, landed at Lisbon and joined the Light Division at Fuenteguinaldo in Spain, a short time previously to the opening of the important campaign in the month of May. On the 26th of that month we drove the enemy from Salamanca. In June we moved against the French position in front of Burgos and compelled them to retire, when they blew up the castle and abandoned the town. We then crossed the River Ebro and on the 18th (my birthday) we had a stirring affair, when our brigade unexpectedly and to our material surprise, near the village of San Millan cut in between the two brigades of a French division on route to Vitoria by a road that crossed the one on which we were marching our regiment; [we] immediately wheeled into line and dashed at one of the brigades as it attempted to form on some high ground to our right. It did not however, want to receive us, but after a desultory fire it dispersed in all direction among the hills. We pursued for some time, taking several hundred prisoners and capturing all the baggage. A[n] inferior French officer was hit by a soldier of the 52nd who took his decoration of the Legion of Honour, which has been in my possession ever since. Of this affair at San Millan Lord Wellington said in his despatch 'Major General Charles Alten with the Light Division drove the enemy from San Millan and afterwards cut off the rear brigade of the division of which he took as prisoners, killed and wounded many and the brigade was dispersed in the mountains.'

Three days after, on the 21st of June, we obtained the brilliant and decisive Battle of Vitoria, taking 151 pieces of brass cannon, Marshal Jourdan's baton, 2 eagles,[124] 415 caissons, 100 forage & forge waggons, all the baggage, provisions, cattle, treasure and a considerable number of French prisoners.[125] The official despatch says 'Major

123 HMS *Abercrombie* of 74 guns was an ex-French ship named *Hautpoult* that was captured on 17 April 1809.

124 This is not correct, no eagles were captured at Vitoria.

125 Around 2,800 men were captured.

General Vandeleur's Brigade[126] of the Light Division was, during the advance upon Vitoria, detached to the support of the 7th Division and Lieutenant General the Earl of Dalhousie[127] has reported most favourably of its conduct.'

We continued to pursue the shattered French army until the Light Division captured their *last gun,* one howitzer only escaping into Pamplona. For several weeks we occupied a position in the Pyrenees near the frontier town of Vera, which was occupied by the picquets of our brigade. During the whole of this period the French continued to fortify their position on the heights immediately above the town. At daylight on the morning of the 31 August about 15,000 French passed the River Bidassoa at the fords below the town of Vera and within sight of our bivouac, for the purpose of attacking the left of the Allied army and relieving the garrison of San Sebastian. This attack completely failed, a heavy rain came on in the evening and rendered the fords impassable before the rear of the French could recross the river. Early the following morning, their rear-guard made a rush at the bridge near Vera, which was only defended by picquets of the Rifle Corps. This picquet was soon overpowered, the captain[128] and many of the men killed and not being properly supported, the passage was gained and four of the enemy's brigades escaped, which must have surrendered had the precaution been taken by Major General Skerrett[129] who commanded the brigade. Only a corporal's picquet was actually on the bridge when it was attacked. Lord Wellington's report of this affair says 'The fall of rain during the night had so swollen the Bidassoa that the rear of their (French) column was obliged to cross the bridge of Vera. In order to effect this object, they attacked the posts of Major General Skerrett's Brigade of the Light Division, at about 3 in the morning, both from the Puerto de Vera and from the left of the Bidassoa. Although the nature of the ground rendered it impossible to prevent entirely the passage of the bridge after daylight, it was made under the fire of a great part of Major General Skerrett's Brigade and the enemy's loss in the operation must have been very considerable.'

Previously to the scene just mentioned, the Light Division was deployed in the operations connected with the battles of the Pyrenees,

---

126 Major General John Ormsby Vandeleur commanded the 2nd Brigade of the Light Brigade from September 1811 to June 1813.

127 Lieutenant General George Lord Dalhousie commanded the 7th Division.

128 Captain Daniel Cadoux, 95th Foot, was killed along with sixteen of his men and a further forty-three wounded out of a party of 100 men.

129 Major General John Skerrett commanded the 2nd Brigade of the Light Division from July to October 1813.

but it was engaged with the enemy only on the last day, viz 2 August & had immediately after re-occupied its former position near Vera.

On the 7th of October the Allied army crossed the River Bidassoa. On this occasion the Light Division stormed the extremely strong fortified position overlooking the town of Vera, our brigade captured 3 guns and 400 prisoners. The official despatch stated 'Colonel Colborne[130] of the 52nd Regiment, who commanded Major General Skerrett's Brigade in the absence of the major general, on account of his health, attacked the enemy's right in a camp which they had strongly entrenched. The 52nd Regiment under the command of Major Mein,[131] charged in a most gallant style and carried the entrenchment with the bayonet. The 1st and 3rd Cacadores and the 2nd Battalion 95th Regiment, as well as the 52nd Regiment distinguished themselves in this attack.' Napier says 'with shrill cries the French followed, but just then the 52nd appeared, partly in line, partly in column, on the platform and raising their shout rushed forward. The red uniform and full career of this regiment startled the hitherto adventurous French, they stopped short, wavered and then turning fled to their entrenchment, the 52nd following hard, entered the works with them. The riflemen and Cacadores who had meanwhile rallied, passed it on both flanks, and for a few moments everything was hidden by a dense volume of smoke'. I saw however the British shortly rallied again and the whole mass emerged on the other side, the French, now the powder playing, the others proceeding until the second entrenchment, half-way up the present slope, enabled the retreating troops to make another stand. The exulting and approving cheers of Kempt's Brigade[132] now echoed along the mountain side with renewed vigour the men continued to scale the craggy mountain, fighting their toilsome way to the top of the Puerto. Meanwhile Colborne having carried the second entrenchment above the star fort, was brought to a check by the works on the very crest of the mountain, from whence the French not only plied his troops with musquetry at great advantage, but rolled huge stones down the steep!! On this day the allied army first entered the French territory.

We had an important part to perform in the general action on passing the River Nivelle on the 10th of November. After driving the enemy from the mountain of La Rhune, the 52nd attacked the principal redoubts on the height above the village of Sarre, which was defended by a battalion of the French 88th Regiment. We suffered severely

130 Lieutenant Colonel John Colborne, 52nd Foot.

131 Major William Mein, 52nd Foot.

132 Major General James Kempt commanded 1st Brigade of the Light Division.

from their fire (32 killed, 208 wounded[133]) being unable to get into the redoubt without ladders; but the French mountain was at length compelled to surrender, Colonel Colborne promising that the officers should retain their swords and the commanding officer's orderly man a haversack which was said to contain merely the accounts and other documents belonging to the battalion. Having been ordered with my company to escort the prisoners (800) to the rear, I have ever since continued an impression that the *Eagle* of the battalion was concealed in the above-mentioned haversack and have regretted that I did not adopt some means to ascertain the facts; but I was deterred at the time by the promise made by Colonel Colborne.

In reference to this battle Lord Wellington said in his despatch 'Major General Charles Baron Alten attacked with the Light Division and General Longa's Spanish Division,[134] the enemy's positions on La Petite Rhune; and having carried them, co-operated with the right of the centre in the attack of the heights behind Sarre'.

1814

The Battle of Orthes [Orthez] was fought on 27th of February. On no occasion, I believe, did a single battalion contribute more purposefully to the successful issue of a general action, than the 52nd Regiment did at this battle.

The 4th & 6th Divisions had not succeeded in their attacks on the enemy's position, when Lord Wellington changed his plan of action and ordered the 52nd Regiment which had hitherto been in reserve, to advance in line over a swampy piece of ground, impassable for horses which separated the attacking columns of the 4th & 6th Divisions. This movement was enacted by the 52nd as if the regiment had been at an ordinary field day and it gained the crest of the enemy's position under a heavy fire without check; it was there that the present Duke of Richmond,[135] a captain in the corps was shot through the lungs.[136]

I was promoted to the rank of Brevet Major for this action. Lord Wellington in his official despatch mentions: 'I ordered Marshal Sir William Beresford to turn and attack the enemy's right with the 4th Division under Lieutenant General Sir Lowry Cole, and

133 This can be broken down further into two sergeants and thirty men wounded; six officers, seven sergeants, three buglers and 192 rank & file wounded.

134 General Francisco de Longa.

135 Captain Charles Earl of March, 52nd Foot, became the 5th Duke of Richmond in 1819.

136 The musket ball was never removed.

the 7th Division under Major General Walker[137] and Colonel Vivian's[138] Brigade of cavalry; while Lieutenant General Sir Thomas Picton should move along the great road leading from Peyrehorade to Orthez, and attack the heights on which the enemy's centre and left stood, with the 3rd and 6th Divisions under Lieutenant General Sir Henry Clinton, supported by Sir Stapleton Cotton, with Lord Edward Somerset's Brigade of cavalry. Major General Baron Charles Alten, with the Light Division, kept the communication, and was in reserve between these two attacks.

I therefore so far altered the plan of the action as to order the immediate advance of the 3rd & 6th Divisions and I moved forward Colonel Barnard's Brigade[139] of the Light Division to attack the left of the height on which the enemy's right stood.

This attack, led by the 52nd Regiment under Lieutenant Colonel Colbourne and supported on their right by Major General Brisbane's and Colonel Keane's Brigades of the 3rd Division, and by simultaneous attacks on the left by Major General Anson's Brigade of the 4th Division, and on the right by Lieutenant General Sir Thomas Picton, with the remainder of the 3rd Division and the 6th Division, under Lieutenant General Sir Henry Clinton, dislodged the enemy from the heights and gave us the victory.

I was promoted to the rank of Major for this action. Lord Wellington in his official dispatch mentions 'I ordered Marshal Sir William Beresford to turn and attack the enemy's right with the 4th Division under Lieutenant General Sir G[albraith] L[owry] Cole and the 7th Division under M[ajor] General Walker and Colonel Vivian's Brigade of cavalry; while Lieutenant General Sir Thomas Picton should march along the great road leading from Peyrehorade to Orthes, and attack the heights on which the enemy's centre and left stood, with the 3rd & 6th Divisions under Sir Henry Clinton, supported by Sir S[tapleton] Cotton with Lord E[dward] Somerset's brigade of cavalry. Major General C[harles] Baron Alten, with the Light Division kept the communication, and was in reserve between the two attacks . . . I therefore so altered the plan of the action as to order the immediate advance of the 3rd & 6th Divisions and I moved forward Colonel Barnard's Brigade of the Light Division to attack the left of the height on which the enemy's right stood. This attack led by the 52nd Regiment under Lieutenant Colonel Colborne and supported on their right by Major General Brisbane's and Colonel Keane's Brigades of the 3rd Division and by simultaneous attacks on

137 Major General George Walker.

138 Brevet Colonel Richard Hussey Vivian.

139 Brevet Colonel Andrew Barnard, 95th Foot.

the left by Major General Anson's Brigade of the 4th Division and on the right by Lieutenant General Sir Thomas Picton with the remainder of the 3rd Division and the 6th Division under Lieutenant General Sir Henry Clinton, dislodged the enemy from the heights and gave us the victory.

Colonel W[illiam] Napier who was an amateur in his own view, his regiment the 43rd having been ordered to the rear to receive their clothing states at page 560 volume 6 of his history. 'Wellington seeing that St Boes was inexpugnable had changed his plan of battle. Supporting Ross with Anson's Brigade which had not hitherto been engaged, he backed both with the Seventh Division and Vivian's cavalry now forming one heavy body towards the Dax road. There he ordered the Third and Sixth Divisions to be thrown in mass upon Foy's left flank and at the same time since sent the 52nd Regiment down from the Roman camp with instructions to cross the marsh in front, to mount the French ridge beyond, and to assail the flank and rear of the troops engaged with the 4th Division at St Boes.

Colonel Colborne, so often distinguished in this war, immediately led the 52nd down and across the marsh under fire, the men sinking at every step above the knees, in some places to the middle, but still pressing forwards with that stern resolution and order to be expected from the veterans of the Light Division, soldiers who had never yet met their match in the field. They soon obtain a footing on firm land and ascended the heights, we were at the moment that Taupin was pushing vigorously through St Boes, Foy and D'Armagnac hitherto more than masters of their positions, being at the same time seriously assailed on the other flank by the 3rd & 6th Divisions.

With a mighty shout and a rolling fire the 52nd soldiers dashed forwards between Foy and Taupin, beating down a French battalion in their course and throwing everything before them into disorder. General Bechaud was killed in Taupin's Division, Foy was dangerously wounded, and his troops discouraged by his fall and by this sudden burst from a quarter where no enemy was expected, for the march of the 52nd had been hardly perceived save by the skirmishers, got in confusion and the disorder spreading to Reille's wing, he also was forced to fall back and take a new position to restore his line of battle.

The battle was well fought on both sides, but the crisis was decided by the 52nd and when that regiment was just in movement, only a single Portuguese battalion was in reserve behind the Roman Camp; upon such nice combinations of time and place does the fate of battles turn!!

On the 1st of March the Light Division entered Mont-de-Marsan and captured an immense magazine of provisions &c.

The retreating French army was driven from the position which it had taken up at Tarbes on the 20th of March.

Marshal Soult took up his final position at Toulouse, where he was attacked on Easter Sunday the 10th of April, six days after Bonaparte had expressed his intention to abdicate, but he did not sign the act until the 11 April. However, Lord Wellington was ignorant of these circumstances till he had entered the city of Toulouse on the 12th, on which day the 52nd Regiment occupied quarters in the town.

During the action the Light Division aided and supported the attack made by the division of Spanish troops amounting to about 10,000 men under the command of Don M Freire.[140] The division was twice repulsed and driven back in much disorder, with the loss of 2,000 men killed and wounded. The official despatch says: 'It gave me great satisfaction to see that although the Spaniards suffered considerably in retiring, the troops rallied again as soon as the Light Division, which was immediately on their right moved up'.

The 52nd twice deployed into line to cover their retreat, which immediately checked the French. On one of those occasions, seeing a Spanish captain who had previously been quartered in the same house with me, I enquired why they had not penetrated the tete de pont of the canal immediately in our front, he replied they had made the attempt but found that nothing mortal could get into it, although we could see they had not been near the works.

The French having claimed the victory on this occasion, I would recommend everyone who may be disposed to agree with them, to read the Duke of Wellington's memorandum published by Colonel Gurwood.

After the convention for the suspension of hostilities, we marched to Castel Sarrazin and here received with open arms by the inhabitants who were honestly tired of the war. We remained there till arrangements had been made for the embarkation of the British troops at Bordeaux. On our route to this place a curious scene occurred when the 1st and 3rd Regiments of Portuguese Cacadores, who had for several years formed part of our brigades and fought by our sides were to separate from us on their return to Portugal through Spain. The 52nd Regiment was formed into a hollow square for the Portuguese to march through, followed by the Spanish and Portuguese women with their children, who had attached themselves to the British soldiers and who were to receive provisions from the commissary until they reached their

140 General Manuel Freire de Andrade.

respective homes. At the appearance of the column we presented arms, the band playing the national airs till the whole had passed through the hollowed square. Several of the Portuguese officers embraced our officers weeping like children. The poor women were of course deeply affected at parting from men with whom they had lived for years. It was considered the most humane arrangement that could be made. Nevertheless, several of the women followed the troops to Bordeaux and thence to England.

On the line of march to the port of embarkation, on the 14 June, we were perfectly [delighted?] by orders to form line to receive Lord Wellington for the purpose of taking leave of us. We gave his lordship three hearty cheers, the first and last time we ventured to give expression to our feelings *under arms,* it was well received.

We embarked at Pauillac some distance lower down the Garonne River than Bordeaux on the 27 June, onboards HMS *Ship Dublin,*[141] my brother Edward was one of the Lieutenants.[142] And landed at Plymouth on the 28th whence we marched to Hythe and Chatham in Kent.

141 HMS *Dublin* of 74 guns.

142 Lieutenant Edward Rowan, Royal Navy.

6. MAJOR CHARLES ROWAN LETTER REGARDING WOUNDING OF MAJOR GEORGE NAPIER AT CIUDAD RODRIGO[143]

Charles Rowan, brother of William was appointed as an ensign in the 52nd Foot in 1797, paymaster in 1798, lieutenant in 1799, a captain in the 52nd Foot in June 1803, major in May 1811 and brevet lieutenant colonel in April 1812. He spent much of his time in the Peninsula as a brigade major and later assistant adjutant general to the Light Division. He served at Ferrol, Sicily, the Baltic, Corunna, the Coa, Busaco, *Foz de Arouce*, Sabugal, *Fuentes de Oñoro*, Ciudad Rodrigo, Badajoz and Salamanca. He, like his brother, survived without a wound until Waterloo, where they were both wounded. He retired from the Army in 1822 and became founding Commissioner of the Metropolitan Police in 1829, a position he held for twenty-one years. He died in London in May 1852.

El Bodon, 21st January [1812]

My dear Napier,
Although the news I have to tell will shock you at first, yet after all, it is more a subject for congratulation than condolence. You may rely upon my not deceiving you in any point, and therefore believe that

143 From the *Life and Opinions of General Sir Charles James Napier*. John Murray, London, 1857.

poor George[144] is as well as any man ever was who has sustained the loss of an arm. He has had an opportunity of distinguishing himself in a manner he has long sought for, by leading three hundred fine fellows up the breach at Ciudad Rodrigo; which he did in a style second to none that ever went up a breach. Before reaching the breach itself, they had to scale the walls of the fausse-bray,[145] and he planted the first ladder himself. Nothing could resist such fellows and in a few minutes the place was our own. His wound was by a grape shot, in the elbow joint of the right arm; by which the bone was so much shattered as to render the loss of the arm inevitable, and for which he decided instantly. The operation was performed by Dr Guthrie,[146] and yesterday morning I saw him as well and as unconcerned about it as if he had an arm to spare. I am going again to Ciudad Rodrigo and until he chooses to write to you with his left arm, I will always let you know how he is. I need not tell you he was a volunteer: a lieutenant-colonelcy will not half recompense his deserts.

Amongst others lost on this occasion is poor Dobbs;[147] and Colonel Colborne,[148] a great friend of George, is badly wounded. General Craufurd not expected to live. I now again repeat, that nothing is likely to happen to George; he appears so well you could not tell anything had happened to him. Of course, for many reasons he will go home as soon as the surgeons think it advisable to move. Believe me with the greatest veneration for everybody that bears your name most sincerely yours. Charles Rowan

144 Major George Napier 52nd Foot commanded the Storming Party at Ciudad Rodrigo and lost an arm.

145 A defensive wall standing in front of the main wall and divided from it by a ditch.

146 Staff Surgeon George Guthrie.

147 Captain Joseph Dobbs, 52nd Foot, was killed at Ciudad Rodrigo.

148 Lieutenant Colonel John Colborne, 52nd Foot, was severely wounded.

7. CAPTAIN JOHN EWART LETTER DESCRIBING THE STORM OF CIUDAD RODRIGO[149]

John Ewart was appointed an ensign in the 52nd Foot in November 1803, becoming a lieutenant in March 1804 and captain in the 3rd Garrison Battalion in May 1806 before transferring back to the 52nd in May 1807, transferring to the Royal York Rangers as a major in October 1812. Ewart served in the Baltic and at Walcheren, Vimeiro, Vigo, Sabugal, *Fuentes de Oñoro*, Badajoz, Salamanca, San Millan. He later served in the West Indies, Guadeloupe and the East Indies. He died in 1854.

El Bodon, 21 January 1812

My dear Uncle,
I am happy to assure you that, thank God, I am perfectly well and safe. The official despatches will have informed you and all my kind friends in Lancashire, that the Light Division has been very actively employed lately and with no small pleasure you will hear (knowing how kindly anxious you will all have lately been about me) that Ciudad Rodrigo was taken by the 3rd and Light Divisions at a few minutes after 7 o'clock on the evening of the 19th instant, and though I regret to hear our loss is considerable, yet we must rejoice that this place (certainly of great consequence to the contending armies) has fallen after a siege of only 11 days, during which time, considering the constant firing upon our trenches from the garrison (an officer of their artillery acknowledged

[149] Originally published in the 43rd & 52nd Light Infantry Chronicle of 1893.

that they had fired 7,000 shells alone at us), on the whole we have been very fortunate.

Nothing could be more favourable than the weather has been during the whole time; not a drop of rain has fallen, the nights have been clear and frosty and the days have always been cheered by the sun. Our sick have been very few, though every fourth night a whole division was obliged to lie in the open air, not having any tents, and at these times we were employed in erecting the batteries eight hours at a time, while the enemy were constantly firing at us. In consequence of a small fort upon a rising ground, from which the French themselves bombarded the place in 1810, being taken by storm[150] by a detachment of 500 men of our division (I was too young a captain to be of that party) on the night of the 8th instant, our approaches to the town were at once very close. The last breaching battery was erected within 200 yards of the walls. The governor was summoned on the 16th instant, but refused to surrender. On the 19th two breaches were found practicable, and the 3rd Division (General Picton's) being on duty in the trenches, was ordered to storm the principal one, in which, I regret to hear many brave fellows were lost by the exploding of a large magazine near the entrance of the breach. Among them was General Mackinnon (of the Guards) at the head of his brigade, the 45th, 74th and 88th Regiments. In the meantime our regiment (the 2nd Battalion close in rear of the 1st), were formed behind a mound in the suburbs, where Lord Wellington was, in column of only three men in front, with the 43rd Regiment in a similar manner on our right, so that the two regiments might lead together, as the smaller breach which we were to storm on the left of the 3rd Division was supposed to be able to admit six men abreast. Part of the 95th Rifle Corps and the Portuguese light infantry attached to our division, were employed in carrying ladders and bags filled with wool to fill up the ditch with. In front of the two regiments were 300 men under Major Napier of the 52nd, all volunteers from the division (but of which these again were the senior officers of each rank) headed by 25 men under a lieutenant (Gurwood[151] of the 52nd also). We were not many minutes in gaining the ramparts, though a good deal of grape shot and musketry was discharged upon us from the enemy, by which several were wounded; among them, I regret to say, we have, as a division, sustained a very severe loss in General Craufurd, who is not expected to recover from his wounds; but as a regiment a much more severe one, though we heartily trust it is only temporary, in Colonel

150 This refers to Fort San Francisco, captured on 8 January 1812.

151 Lieutenant John Gurwood, 52nd Foot.

Colborne, who though he has only commanded us a few months, had gained the hearts of every officer and soldier in the regiment. He remained at our head some time after he was wounded, but we fear it will be some time before he can recover.

Major Napier,[152] as brave an officer as ever lived, has lost his right arm, and in poor Captain Dobbs[153] (one of my oldest friends in the regiment), the regiment has lost as gallant an officer as ever led a company into action. As a brother officer, never was anyone more universally regretted by his comrades. His company led our battalion, mine was the fourth and very happy were we all to hear our bugles sounding through the whole place 'cease firing' in a very few minutes.

Many of the inhabitants were plundered and some houses set on fire; none, however, of the Spaniards were killed, and not many of the garrison, who in every direction were attempting to conceal themselves. About 10 pm I was ordered on guard over 700 prisoners in a large barrack, and indeed they were very quiet and glad to have got off so well. I only regretted much that there were some wounded among them and it was impossible to get surgeons to attend. I continued on duty until yesterday at noon, when my charge had increased to above 900 men with 64 officers, all of whom I gave up to be escorted to Lisbon by a Portuguese regiment and came back to this place after my regiment. The 5th Division passed on the road; they have lately been towards Coimbra to get clothing &c and are now employed in levelling our entrenchments and in repairing the town of Rodrigo, into which I heard a Spanish garrison is to be put, but what we shall do next it is impossible to surmise. The Spaniards ought to be very active and 'Boney' will be properly annoyed, I should think. It was reported that Marmont was coming to oblige us to raise the siege with all haste, but now I suppose, we shall not see him in such a hurry, and as we must expect some wet weather, we hope to be left quiet in cantonments, which will be very acceptable to us. I believe few armies could have had sharper work than we have had within the last ten months, and we suppose we shall not advance into Spain just yet, until we see how Blake gets on in Valencia, upon which *much* must depend. Remember me in the kindest &c &c John Frederick Ewart

---

152 Major George Napier, 52nd Foot.

153 Captain Joseph Dobbs, 52nd Foot, was killed.

8. LIEUTENANT CHARLES BOOTH LETTERS[154]

Charles Booth joined the 52nd as an ensign from the 1st West York Militia in May 1805 aged 18. He was a lieutenant in the 2nd Battalion in June 1805. He then joined the 1st Battalion in July 1806, serving in Sicily, and then served with them in the expedition to Sweden, Corunna, the advance to Talavera, the Coa, Busaco, Pombal, Redinha, *Foz de Arouce* and Sabugal (where he was slightly wounded), *Fuentes de Oñoro* and the siege of Ciudad Rodrigo. He was killed at Badajoz on 6 April 1812.

To his brother Thomas:[155]

Shorncliffe near Hythe, Kent 24 May 1805

Dear brother,
Though I took the pains to walk the streets of London three days, solely on account of the great desire I had to get properly equipped, I was under the necessity of leaving town disappointed and joining the regiment of the line in coloured cloths[156] (which rarely happens). On joining my regiment, I saw that Thatcher's[157] sabre was far from being regimental, therefore McKenna[158] advised me to decline accepting Thatcher's kind offer, I shall write to him shortly. Off Weston[159] I shall

154 These snippets from his correspondence were originally published in the 43rd & 52nd Light Infantry Chronicle of 1932 & 1933. Unfortunately, the whereabouts of the originals is not known.
155 His elder brother, Thomas, died unmarried in 1823.
156 Civilian attire.
157 Lieutenant William Thatcher, 1st West York Militia.
158 Adjutant William MacKinna, 1st West York Militia.
159 It has been impossible to identify him with certainty.

receive 2 regimental jackets, 2 pairs pantaloons, 1 pair of buff breeches, 2 pairs gaiters, if anything more you shall know. What I have now got off Weston added to things possible to render useful from the I.W.Y.[160] viz, white kerseymere breeches, 2 pairs with old buff, 2 pairs leather the same, with regimental waistcoats, greatcoat etc will quite equip me for the 52nd. I have reserved my battalion sword and a few other things which will be useful if ever I join a battalion regiment. I shall want from my sword cutler a good sabre, 2 pairs epaulettes (4 in number), 2 buff sword knots (regulation for field days), bugles for my coat, if anything more you shall know.

Of my hatter, 1 regimental cap, feather and bugle, 1 coloured cap to drill in (my other has served me nearly nine months). There is not a possibility of my informing you of the amount of all necessary expenses in equipment yet, for I have not received the bills of which, as soon as I do you shall know their amounts individually. There is yet another expense which though I cannot say I have contracted it in equipping myself for the 52nd, yet I can affirm is one which was necessary and absolutely so, consequently makes away with a material part of my resources. It is customary in all regiments in the service to pay officers their month's allowances in advance and I had received my dues in this manner when I was gazetted, therefore from that time my pay ceased, when I found I had to pay back into the hands of the Committee of Paymastership £5 14s[161] on account of pay, lieutenant's commission received in advance from our paymaster I.W.Y. and though I received ensign's pay from that time in the 52nd Regiment, yet this will be all for two months to come, go to the payment of commission fee (sometimes about £5) and the contribution of the mess of the 52nd which is always paid on an officer's first entrance into the regiment, viz 6 guineas. From this and the circumstances of my having paid £10 of my last allowance (£20 received April 1st) to Faber[162] for things I bought of him before he left our regiment, you may easily imagine a relief of the above kind would benefit me much.

I may with the greatest truth says that while I have been in the army my expenses have been as few, moderate and just as possible. And even then whilst I received pay of lieutenant in the West Yorks and £80 a year, my allowance from the executors, I found this but just able to cover all expenses whatever. You mentioned in one of your letters that it was possible for me to have my allowance increased, which will

160 1st West York Militia, where he had served previously and where his father and brother still served.

161 About £300 in modern terms.

162 This must be Lieutenant Charles Faber West York Militia.

now be doubly acceptable, as receiving only ensigns pay and not even this for some time to come. It is neither my interest nor desire to be uncomfortable, which I am sure a profuse allowance would make me, but it is my wish to appear as comfortable as any moderate person.

I never should love money, but I am convinced I must always have it in sufficient quantity to defray necessary expenses. I know what I have said on this subject will be unnecessary, for you are always the first to point out the wants and contribute to the comfort of anyone of your brothers and sisters, especially those who labour to deserve your attention.

Having now determined in my former opinion of making the army my profession, I am resolved not to be the last in rank or abilities among those who compose it. I am convinced I delight in it and as has already been shown, can do my duty so as to occasion people to take notice of it. I am now in one of the very best regiments in the British army, therefore it is my duty to make myself equal to a commission in it. To do this I must not lose any opportunity of learning drawing and French, though at the expense of losing my breakfast every morning, which would pay for the learning these two most essential accomplishments, many of the officers (they are all very young not exceed[ing] nineteen years for the most part) learn fencing, music, drawing and French at 2s 6d a lesson each. This would amount to a round sum in a half year, such as would not suit me. To learn both, I must not eat at all, the two latter (I think with an addition to my present allowance) I could afford to learn and still continue breakfast, which at home has not often been more than milk and bread, sometimes indulged with a little butter, this I am more fond of and consequently would do me more good than coffee, tea, chocolate, eggs, or all the rarities possible to be enumerated. It is sometimes necessary to invite in my turn a friend to breakfast moderately. But according with the custom of most economical men of the military profession (especially subalterns) I avoid as much as possible invitations on either side. Our mess here appears very moderate after first paying the six guineas, they have mess articles of their own, messed by a sergeant of the regiment. I believe pay about 2s more or less for their dinner each day, drink very little wine, most of them water drinkers. This will suit me, to avoid suspicion I may partake of the bottle at mess (never in my room) once or twice a week. This is the practise of many who are not strictly water drinkers. Tell me your opinion of my learning drawing and French.

. . . I am sure from his [his brother Henry's] letters[163] (do not say to him that I informed you) that he does not exert himself as much as he might do. For from experience I know that if he attends well only to

[163] His brother Henry joined the 43rd Foot as an ensign on 8 March 1806 by purchase.

Latin and Greek his time will be entirely taken up, whereas he informs me that he is now learning the flute! He might as well have told me that he is tired of school. I have learnt the flute myself a little, sufficient indeed to convince me that whoever learns or even attempts to learn it must give up his time to it alone. Then it plainly appears that Harry has time for amusements, not for application to music. It would have been a quite opposite thing if he had informed me he had left off Latin, Greek, French and Mathematics on account of the great application they required and had determined to turn music master. Whoever advises their children to learn dancing and music or such like trumpery while at school encourages them also to be idle, consequently dunces after they leave it.

How I now rejoice that no one could prevail upon me to learn either to dance, sing or play music in order to interrupt my study of mathematics and French which I find Classics not a little contribute to do, dead languages are of very little use.

An admonition from you to our musical brother Henry would make him drop his flute and take up the compass and scales and instead of tuning English, tune French, for he is deficient in both.

26 June 1805
I have now got the most part of my bills of which follows a correct statement.

If you should think anyone of them exceptionable, as not being an expense necessary for equipping me for the 52nd I beg you will consider it accordingly and deduct it from the sum of the whole. I have not been in any difficulty yet and my next quarters allowance up to July 1st will be more than sufficient to pay my small expenses that I may have been at. I am afraid that £50 will not be sufficient to pay the expenses I have been at in changing regiments. I have paid the bills as far as the £50 will go . . . I shall astonish you when I tell you that I soon expect to be gazetted lieutenant in the 2nd Battalion 52nd, without purchase. You were astonished when I once mentioned that I was 2nd Ensign 2nd Battalion, but how will you believe me when I inform you that I never joined the 2nd Battalion, having been drilled in the 1st for five days, during which time only I belonged to the 2nd Battalion.

Eight Ensigns 1st Battalion (I am 7th) will be gazetted lieutenants in the 2nd in three weeks, at least so General Moore (our colonel) told Major Barclay 52nd[164] with whom I am rather a favourite (so his uncommon attention leads me to suppose). With my pay as lieutenant

164 Lieutenant Colonel Robert Barclay.

and £100 or less, I can live profitably, learn French, Mathematics and get a general knowledge of military barracks and get my breakfast in the bargain, all of which I find General Moore expects his officers to attend to.

I expect to be dismissed drill in a month, which I am not a little proud of. I began with eight other officers and as many privates on 7 May and all except two privates have got forward with me. There are now both officers and privates who have been six months constantly at drill in the brigade. I expect in a few days to fall into the ranks and be drilled (as customary) across the country for three or four hours in the Light Manoeuvres.

[In a list of items he had to purchase is listed:]

Spy glass and compass £3[165]
It is an order from General Moore that everyone shall have them for distinguishing the different signals on the coast. The box compass to point out our road as north, south, east or west &c.

6 August 1805
[Charles was transferred to the 2nd Battalion 52nd which was . . .]

. . . of the greatest consideration, otherwise I would have exerted myself in every possible way with the colonel to have let me remain with the 1st Battalion, which being perfectly disciplined and more strictly looked after by the general, would have afforded me a glorious opportunity of learning my duty in every situation, wherein the principal attention of the officer and soldier is required. A second battalion is never so well looked to as a first because the raw recruits joining by one or two at a time keep the regiment (which is nearly composed of recruits) in constant drill, in the marching, manual and platoon exercises &c and when recruits are sufficiently acquainted with which, they join (if fine men) the 1st Battalion and they reap the fruits of our labour.

[Charles had gained leave in London before the battalion sailed for Sicily, while there he walked to Eton on the 12th to see his brother George who was at school there. Leaving London at 8 am, he arrived at Eton at 1 pm.]

165 Approximately £150 in modern terms.

12 July 1806
I was proceeding to call on Dr Blenkinsop, when I met George with his hands full of books, grave countenance and with solemn and thoughtful gait, just quitting the school; he was a little astonished to see me and I, on my part, was as pleased and as surprised to see him so much altered, so stout and healthy and if I am not very much deceived, grown.

He repeated to me with all the enthusiasm of a martinet, their entire routine of business, then launched out in praise of the country about Eton and Windsor. I mentioned Yorkshire in order to see whether he would start at the name or no, he passed the word very coolly. He said he believed he was to go there with young Lonsdale, but he had an invitation to spend the holidays with some young lord or marquis, which he did not know whether to accept or no. Lords, dukes and titles, in fact were nothing there.

He had been promoted lately from the 4th to the 5th Form and from what I could learn from his account of the school discipline (which is very just and strictly observed) he will get famously forward amongst them.

On the whole he likes Eton extremely well. He dined with me at an inn, where he sat until 3 pm when I returned on the road to London. Eton is the dearest place in the kingdom, they charged me 16s[166] for dinner and George did not eat more than a couple of ounces in the whole. A small fish, veal steak and a fruit pie composed our dinner; taken into account a pint of wine which I called for to prevent our being mobbed, for you must know it is a capital offence to dine moderately when the king is at Windsor. Windsor and Eton are but separated by a bridge, as Westminster from London.

Almost every officer I have seen of both our battalions speak in the highest terms of Henry's character and say that he is by no means deficient in attention to drill, on the contrary rather remarkable for his quick progress in it.

Tell William[167] that if he wants to get into the army at all, the foot is preferable on account of the cavalry being completed in officers; and those regiments that are not so in the Army List are deficient in men and will be for some time to come and promotion is very slow. The most advisable step he can take is to get leave to raise men for a lieutenancy, [in the] cavalry, after having purchased his ensigncy in the foot and the regiment he fixes on must be a good one, for probably some lieutenant

166 Approximately £45 in modern terms.

167 William Booth joined the 95th Foot as a 2nd lieutenant on 25 September 1806 and exchanged into the 15th Light Dragoons in 1809.

in the cavalry (who has squandered away his property) may exchange with him for the difference and this is very often occurring.

But I will assure you the cavalry officers in general are esteemed by the foot as a set of insignificant ignorant fellows and whenever a regiment of cavalry come to be brigaded with a foot regiment, the cavalry scarce are noticed.

[Charles sailed in the *Collingwood* transport from Plymouth for Sicily, but was driven back to Ramsgate no fewer than eight times.]

October 1806
On the way out, on a fine bright morning, the anniversary of the glorious Battle of Trafalgar, on the very spot where that greatest of all naval battles was fought the year before, in which the immortal Nelson fell did we meet that same British fleet under the command of that excellent, skilful, gallant and good man Lord Collingwood.[168] Immediately the signal was made by our commander, Sir Thomas Duckworth,[169] for the ships of the convoy to pass under the admiral's stern, the soldiers dressed and paraded on the deck, with bands playing 'Rule Britannia' and colours flying; and as we passed our colours drooped and presenting arms we gave them three hearty cheers, the fine sailor like old admiral taking off his hat and bowing to us, his own brave crew and the rest of his fleet returning our cheers with loud huzzas. My ship in which was our band was curiously enough called the *Collingwood* after him and had a fine large figure of the admiral at her head in full uniform and we led the van in this well suited compliment as Collingwood himself had led the van in the battle. I never felt more elated or saw a finer sight.

[Henry had the possibility of transferring to the 68th Foot[170] as a lieutenant, but declined. Charles wrote with his opinion.]

Sicily [November?] 1806
An unlucky fellow you were, in all account, in not being able to get the lieutenancy. I grant you the regiment is in a poor pickle at present and by no means in the world a proper one for making yourself master of your

168 Vice Admiral Cuthbert Collingwood.

169 Vice Admiral John Cuthbert.

170 The regimental number is omitted in the published account, however a note states that the regiment referred to did eventually become light infantry later. The only regiment to become light infantry later (1809) that was actually stationed in Britain in 1806, as no foreign deployment is mentioned, was the 68th Foot.

profession in at present, but there is a continual revolution in all things. When a regiment acquires the utmost possible pitch of perfection in discipline, it cannot retain that, there never was an instance of it. I have seen an instance to the contrary; the 52nd and 43rd will in turn wear the appearance of the 68th. It is extremely probable that the 68th are desirous to emulate the 43rd and following with the utmost diligence their steps will get to a tolerable state of discipline much easier and sooner than the 43rd or 52nd did. What I argue upon is principally this; the 68th will soon get into notice from their attention to discipline and here is laid open the widest field for promotion, viz full establishment of officers for 1st battalion, a second battalion and as the great use of light troops becomes more and more necessary every day, what body of men is more likely to be converted into a light battalion than the regiment in question, who have been improving upon their system of drill for light troops as practised at present by the 43rd and 52nd. This mode of drill is thought so much of here, that all the regiments in Sicily are taught to go through their field manoeuvres in double quick and imitate this regiment in every particular. Yes, you will laugh at it, fancy a set of the strongest, unwieldy fellows in the army, of which the heavy battalion, as it is called, is composed, forming line from column and changing front to the right or left. It is like an earthquake, the ground shakes again with the heaving of their feet.

The Marquis of Proto, supposed the richest man in Melazzo, was brought before a General Court Martial for stealing and attempting to carry off a knife from the mess room of one of the regiments at Melazzo. He was found guilty and a sentinel who caught him in the act and whom he had accused and brought to Court Martial for seizing and maltreating him, was honourably acquitted. There have been frequent instances of Marquisses pocketing forks, knives and anything they could lay hold of when invited to any public dinner at Messina. This is fact and you can rely on me not joking.

Melazzo September 1807
To his brother Thomas
As to myself, I do not know yet exactly whether it is in my power or not [to purchase a company] for my fortune I apprehend wants a little more improvement from the state it is now in to enable me to take a thousand pounds from it. If this was possible and my money now lodged in London, I should be a lucky fellow indeed, if I could get a company by purchase whilst I am on this service, supposing we were to keep our station here for five years to come. Four of our five officers here have had their money lodged for purchase two years back and

have not the least chance of a company now, though their interest is great at home. As I expect to hear from you in answer to this, give me your opinion of the state of my finances.

[The regiment returned home in 1807.]

January 1808 Canterbury
Dear Thomas,
You should have been informed of my arrival in England through the proper channel, had I not been bent upon seeing Harry before I wrote; we were not allowed to communicate in any manner whatever with the shore, during the few days we remained in quarantine in Portsmouth; on the 6th instant when released I grant you, I ought to have written, notwithstanding the reason I have given above; but as every man who sincerely acknowledges his faults and promises future amendment is entitled to ask forgiveness, I humbly implore yours.

Harry is six feet ten inches high, everyone confesses remarkably well formed and handsome, dresses well, soldierlike in every sense of the word. So entirely altered that after a day of his company I had not the least recollection, nor was there the least resemblance in him of the simple modest Kotzebue [his family nickname], who spent a few weeks with us at Rotherham during the troublous time in 1806. His conversation delighted and surprised me, his superior knowledge in every topic made me listen to him without any reply, so confident was I of my inability to cope with him in any way, in fact instead of advising him I must ask his advice in future on every subject. His character seems to be finally formed and of the very best material. I believe him to be as virtuously sound principled and as gentlemanly a man as I ever saw and to the utmost of my knowledge he is thoroughly acquainted with the duties of his profession. Perhaps his modesty never allowed him to inform you of his having had the sole charge (payment and command) of a company for a long time past; this is not all, he has frequently been appointed to command the advanced guard of his regiment on a field day in preference to many of their captains, which in itself is no trifle. I may say Harry has sown his wild oats now [he was 17], he was once a dashing character, kept a horse, idled away his time in spending more than his income and on trifles; in short was a lounger, in debt with the Paymaster, these were his only faults.

I found now that he was going on rather too economical a plan, never drank wine at the mess, almost refusing himself what was necessary for his health. I prevailed upon him to take his share of wine at dinner to save appearance and convinced him that he was in better circumstances than he was aware of.

[His next letter largely dealt with the family struggles to retain their family home.]

21 March 1808 Canterbury
You well know, the interest I have always taken in regard to Harry, from his being in great measure put under my charge and direction in the earlier period of his military career, and from his invariable good conduct and excellent disposition I feel an attachment to him which a close acquaintance and strictest friendship for many years back has been continually increasing. As far as it interests myself [His brother Thomas had put forward a scheme to retain Brush House[171] in the family] I am inclined to think it would entirely ruin my prospects in the army. If after paying £1,000 for my company, nearly £300 debt, contracted during my minority and the expense attendant on the sale of my estate, [if] I were to sink the residue in the manner my brother [John] proposes, it would not allow me an interest sufficient with the pay of captain to enable me to support the consequence attached to the situation. Some few unacquainted with the rules and customs of a military life suppose that a captain in the British service may live very comfortably and maintain his rank on his pay. But the officers of our regiment are of a different stamp; as to drinking, gaming &c (even were they inclined) they would have very few opportunities of indulging themselves in this way: their time is employed in attending to the comforts of the men and in keeping up the drill system of the regiment. Their expenses arise from their being always well dressed and with some few exceptions, in the culture of their minds. Believe me no fool would be suffered to keep a command here, neither would he feel comfortable in doing it.

But to return to the subject of Brush House, my brother seems determined to keep it to the last moment; family pride is everything with him, many and various, able and convincing, of course, are the arguments he makes use of 'No king without a kingdom', 'No Booth without Brush House'. Yes, any particle of consequence we have as a family is actually derived from those who have gone before us. It is saying very little of them who have gone before us to suppose that they derived all their consequence in the world from having in their possession the estate of Brush House. I would much rather they had

171 Brush House was the family seat, it was situated at Ecclesfield near Sheffield.

derived their consequence as a family from some service performed to the state, either in a civil or military capacity. Then that consequence might have been of great service in improving the fortunes of their descendants; for instance, you might have been Secretary of State and I Adjutant General of His Majesty's Forces. Every gentleman will conduct himself as such, of this, no person questions the truth. That we are all gentlemen with rather comfortable fortunes, thanks to the labours of those who have gone before us and to the liberal education they have enabled us to profit by is true. But as to any great consequences in the world that we have inherited from our ancestors by the possession of Brush House, I have never been able to find it out. In my humble opinion (convinced of the impossibilities of retaining Brush House on any reasonable terms) rather than sink our fortunes in providing that trifling consequence that the possession of this estate gives to the family, it would be better to employ them together with our own exertions in obtaining that kind of interest and consequence in the world that would one day enable us to acquire fortunes adequate to the building of a mansion really deserving the name of the family seat of the Booths and by these means bequeath to our progeny a consequence worth inheriting and as much interest in the world as would still enable them to increase their fortunes; but whatever might be the consequence I could never refrain from laughter should anyone pompously hold forth to me upon the 'family, pride and consequence' of the Booths, and the great sacrifices that ought to be made for their preservation.

[A few days later Charles wrote again on the subject.]

I again repeat one of the principal enquiries I made, as it is one in which I feel most interested, viz, what difference is it likely to make in my income or annual allowance, after I have obtained the age of twenty-one years? I could ask a thousand more questions connected with the former, being very much alarmed, lest my income next year should not suffice to pay my ordinary expenses during that period. My stock of necessaries 'especially linen' begin to wear a shabby appearance, in consequence of which, and for the purpose of discharging all small bills up to this time, I did yesterday draw upon Downe Thornton & Co.[172] £30, in addition to the £57 4s 4d before drawn since 1 July 1807; you say that I shall not be able to raise money enough for the purchase of a company before the latter end of next year. I am sorry for it, perhaps I may lose my turn for purchase of the next vacant company.

172 Down, Thornton & Free of London was a banking firm established in 1784.

The officers are now giving into the Agents their names for purchase mentioning where their money is lodged. If it should come to my turn to purchase a junior officer will have the preference, as he gives in his name, whereas I cannot raise the money. After deliberating in this manner for some time past, a thought has lately struck my fancy viz Mr J W[173] would, my case being duly presented to him, advance me £1,000 for the purchase of a company, should it become vacant and be my turn for purchase before I could otherwise raise the wind from the sale of my land. If he would do this, he would certainly be acting in a gentlemanlike and considerate manner. If he would not, as I have great reasons to believe, from his very particular regard for me, he would but realise the opinions I have always had of him, as a niggardly revengeful old rascal.

19 April 1808
To his brother Thomas
If it was not for your superintendence of the family affairs, what would become of all our fine projects, prospects &c? but I am silent on this score, lest you should imagine I mean to flatter, so averse are you to being praised, when it is ever your due. I heard from Henry this morning, he says and I am sure he is right in his conjecture, that he shall have his company in the 43rd before I get mine in the 52nd. Do you know that Lieutenant Haverfield[174] purchased over the heads of 21 lieutenants? There are but 10 above Harry who can be supposed to offer themselves as candidates for the next vacancy. Yet, it is neither ten to one nor yet four to one that he will not have the opportunity of purchasing the company, for most of his senior officers are Scotchmen (with lots of cash to spare, of course). What a most annoying circumstance it would be to Harry if he was not able to purchase, should it come his turn; rather than this should be the case I would wish that the money lodged for the purpose of my company should be appropriated for the purchase of Harry's. Then should it be my turn for purchase soon after this period let Harry (if at the time enabled to raise as much) furnish me with the means.

[Charles was now sent out with a recruiting party.]

20[?] April 1808
To his brother Thomas

173 Who this may refer to is not known.

174 William Haverfield, 43rd Foot, became a captain on 31 March 1808.

It was not my own wish, rely upon it, but that of old Barclay, that sly penetrating ruler of ours. He proposed to me at first, what he called a pleasant excursion to Chatham to receive volunteers from the West [York] Militia, hinting to me at the same time that I was the most proper person to go on this service as I had always a plentiful supply of the ready [money]. I opposed this strenuously, you may be sure, [I] told him I was as poor as a rat &c and all would not do. I was informed in pretty plain terms by the Adjutant[175] that I was to proceed on this service instantly and that it would require my utmost exertions &c and a trifling sacrifice of cash, but this last he observed, I could say nothing against, as I have not purchased either of my commissions in the regiment and further that the general always expected that officers, not having purchased their commission in the regiment, would particularly exert themselves in inducing the militiamen to volunteer into the line. I urged my nine months on this service in York, I was soon told that this was considered as 'on leave' for they knew pretty well that I had been at home during most part of that period. As to my being short of cash, they dared to say that I could procure it in any quantity from home, in the meantime Barclay offered to lend me what money I chose to borrow. Seeing that I was obliged to surrender, I did it with as good a grace as possible, left Canterbury on the 9th instant and returned in triumph on the 17th with 8 volunteers and only £10 out of pocket. Old Barclay well pleased and he had good reasons, for there are six parties returned from the same service (Barclay himself at the head of one) without a single man, Scotchmen these six officers alluded to and not willing either to sacrifice much to the good of the service.

[Charles went with the 1st Battalion from Ramsgate to Sweden. He embarked on the *Hazard* transport.]

To his brother Henry
Early May 1808
Fortunately for us, the wind was directly in our teeth on the 2nd instant and our bucks hastened to Deal to lay in stock for our voyage, which we got safely on board that night and a most glorious living we shall have for the next three weeks as our stock will cost us at least £10 each before we land, yet £12 received before embarking will more than suffice to pay for this. I am very well off altogether, having about a credit of £20 with our Paymaster, besides £12 or £13 which I have

175 The adjutant was Lieutenant Abraham Shaw, 52nd Foot.

not drawn from Downe & Co. of my allowance from 1 July 1807 – 1 July 1808.

[Charles arrived in Flemish Roads, Gothenburg]

To his brother Thomas
19[?] May 1808
If it is really intended that a large force shall reinforce us in Sweden, I should think that the 43rd 1st Battalion would be employed. General Moore was offered by the Duke of York the choice of two regiments. He chose his own of course. Some are of opinion that the 43rd Regiment is under the displeasure of HRH for its conduct in Zeeland,[176] but this is mere supposition, yet some of the officers of a certain regiment have had the ill nature to say the contrary.[177]

July 1808 Transport Portsmouth

Dear Thomas,
Do not think that I mean to forget to tell you that the gallant Kotzebue [Henry] one of the best soldiers in His Majesty's Service is going to accompany us, his merit is so well known in the 43rd that he has been appointed to act as Adjutant to the 2nd Battalion of his regiment now about to join this expedition, they are in our brigade, nearly the whole of the 95th Regiment go with us.

[Charles was upset at missing the *Battle of Vimeiro*.]

As usual we are again disappointed, it is my belief that our 1st Battalion will never have an opportunity of distinguishing itself.

Lugo [9 January 1809?]

[Charles was only at Lugo during the retreat to Corunna, it was therefore strange that he found time to look around the church and convents.]

Dear Thomas,
I never omit on any occasion visiting the different churches and convents, the latter are generally converted into quarters for the men in the towns, where there are any, to the no small annoyance of the

176 It is unclear what criticism the 43rd had drawn in Denmark.

177 It is likely that he talks of the 52nd, who had a reputation for being very staid and thinking themselves better than the rest of the army.

friars and padres, who are the most damnable vagabonds upon earth, swarming in every town like bees and guzzling upon the vitals of the poor inhabitants who contribute nearly their whole to these vile fellows. Notwithstanding, their church ceremonies are somewhat grand. The service is chanted in Latin and I have frequently thought when I hear a good bass voice, what a noble friar you would make if you had but the back of your head shaved and have frequently gone out laughing at the idea; I mean from your strong voice. I have never yet been able to get into any of the nunneries as the doors are nearly constantly locked but frequently pay the nuns a visit through the iron gate. They are fit to go mad when they see a British officer and the old abbesses are sometimes obliged to remind them of their duties. Some of them are most elegant and beautiful women, those I mean who I have seen pass through the convents to the church which is the only opportunity.

[Henry returned to Portugal with the 1st Battalion in June 1809, but the next letter we have comes from the Lines of Torres Vedras, after the Battle of Busaco.]

Camp near Arruda [dos Vinhos], about fifteen miles from Lisbon, 9 November 1810
Never did a military man commit so great a blunder as Massena in attacking the position of Busaco. Without any previous reconnaissance of our force or the nature of our position, he attacked what was far from being its weakest points with a force unequal to make the slightest impression. We lost certainly some brave fellows, but compared to their loss (especially in killed), ours was a mere trifle. In the part of the line occupied by the Light Division and about 200 yards immediately to its front. two columns of the enemy, supposed about 5,000 each, were met by the two left-hand companies of the 43rd and the right two of the 52nd. The front of their columns alone, chiefly composed of officers, stood the charge; the rest took to their heels, throwing away their arms, pouches &c. Our men did not stand to take prisoners; what were taken were those left in our rear in the hurry of pressing forward in the charge. The flanks of the 43rd and 52nd in their charge met only the enemy's skirmishers who had by superior numbers driven in the 95th Rifles but a few seconds before the charge of the division. These poor fellows were all glad enough to give themselves up as prisoners, our men not being allowed to fire a shot at them. The advanced part of the charging line, the four companies first mentioned, after throwing themselves into the midst of the enemy's retreating columns, killing, wounding and in short felling to the ground lots of them, were with

great difficulty halted and then commenced from the flanks of the whole division the most destructive flanking fire that I believe was ever witnessed. Not a tenth part of their whole force would have escaped had not the four companies, by precipitating themselves too far in front of the general line, exposed themselves to the fire of their comrades and thus prevented more than 300 firelocks on each flank of the division from being brought into action. The flanks and in fact every other part of the division (except the four centre companies), had to pass over in the charge some very steep rugged ground, where, not meeting with anything but the enemy's skirmishers, they pushed on head-over-heels, until the descent became almost perpendicular. At this time they were halted and had a fine view of what was going on in the centre.

I was in the left wing of the battalion and am sure, though we were not five minutes in the charge down the hill, it cost us more than half an hour to get up into our first position again. I have often had described to me what is called a 'hot business,' and where confusion it is said 'reigns triumphant on all sides'. If this be true, then I have only to say that I have never been in a general action, or what is termed 'hot business'. It must indeed be a terrible sight if it exceeds what we experienced at Busaco, where, to all those who had their eyes open and not poking their way with a bayonet, everything appeared to be carried on with the greatest possible regularity, considering the ground we had to act upon. Orders to be sure, could only be communicated by sound of bugle, or by the stentorian voice of a company officer. Great was the screech set on foot by our fellows during the charge. Poor Barclay[178] was shot twice in front of the four companies, at a very few paces from the enemy; he was cheering the men at the time.

You will see by the 'Gazette' that the 52nd took General Simon, two or three field officers and some of inferior rank. Someone has had the audacity, rascality I should say, to contradict this in the newspapers; if this gentleman is wise, he will not give the slightest hint of his name to any of the Light Division. It was said too, that he was actually engaged with the division on that day. General Simon was both wounded and taken by the same person, a private soldier of the 52nd.[179] He had been much in advance and on the right of their column in coming up the hill, and at the time he was wounded was reconnoitring in their line of skirmishers. Harry I reckon, as having narrowly escaped on several

178 Lieutenant Colonel Robert Barclay was severely wounded at Busaco and he died of his wounds on 3 May 1811.

179 Private James Hopkins, 52nd Foot, was credited with the capture of General Simon and received a pension of £20 per annum as a reward.

occasions during the retreat. At Busaco, he was in Captain Lloyd's,[180] the left-hand company of the 43rd, in one of those 'who met the head of the French column in the charge'. His captain, who was close to him at the time they reached the enemy's columns, was on the point of being bayoneted, but knocked down the fellow attempting it. Harry must have had a [close] shave or two, as he could not prevent himself from being in the very thick of them, but he speaks only of the actions of others.

At the Coa near Almeida, his was one of the companies that covered the retreat of the division across the bridge; and had it not been for the gallant manner in which this detachment, principally 43rd behaved, most of the division would certainly have been taken prisoners, or forced into the river, where they must inevitably have perished. Lieutenant Hopkins,[181] in command of this company, had been wounded in the early part of the day, whilst in conversation with Harry respecting their unfavourable position. Harry, of course, took command of the company for the rest of the day, which was by far the most trying part of it, having been amongst the last of the few who escaped over the bridge after the retreat of the principal body of the covering party. Had any person of interest been inclined to have taken proper notice of his conduct, and that of a few others on that day, and represented it properly to Lord Wellington, a company would have been the least he could have rewarded them with.

The day of the retreat to our present position, Harry's (Captain Lloyd's) company was on the rear-guard on the most stormy disagreeable day I ever witnessed. The enemy had come upon us rather unexpectedly whilst snug at our dinners at Alenquer.[182] Considerable confusion ensued on our leaving the town, for the enemy's riflemen were actually entering it before the 43rd had assembled. Harry was in rear of all with a section of the company and obliged to blaze away in all directions in order to keep them in check, so great was their impudence and spirits at seeing us retreat in so confused a manner. The town withal contained excellent plunder, and what they most wanted, shelter for the day.

[Towards the end of 1810 Henry of the 43rd was sent to Lisbon sick and his brother Charles went there to look after him for a few months.

180 Captain Thomas Lloyd, 43rd Foot.

181 Lieutenant John Hopkins, 43rd Foot.

182 The incident at Alenquer was potentially more embarrassing than the Coa. No sentries were placed while the Light Division rested in the walled town of Alenquer. They were surprised and nearly surrounded, but did escape without serious loss.

He was back with the regiment by late spring and constantly marching, but was well.]

Saugo [El Sahugo] on the Sierra di Gata, 19 August 1811

We are knocked about from North to South and East to West as usual, without the slightest prospect of ever finishing this tedious campaign. However, we keep up our spirits; there are even some who have grown fat upon contentment and amongst the latter, thank God, I can number myself; my constitution, I really believe, growing every day stronger.

[Charles wrote to Henry, who had returned home on sick leave about his situation.]

Saugo [El Sahugo] near Ciudad Rodrigo, 17 September 1811

My dear Henry,
To enter at once on the subject; I admit of yours being a hard case, but not of so singular a nature as not to allow of its being managed with honour, credit and ultimate success, keeping you at the same time on the strength of the 43rd Regiment; though in opposition to the opinions of Thomas and the doctor, for whose opinions on all other subjects I have such a deference that I should adopt them without presuming to examine them. I must be understood as setting out with a supposition that your health is not such as to oblige you to be absent from your regiment for more than six months. But before I bring arguments on either side I think it scarce necessary to mention that I dissent entirely from your opinion when you say in your letter (debating with yourself), viz could I ever remain at rest or satisfied in the 2nd Battalion. No, most assuredly not. Could I ever forget that the officers of the 1st Battalion were fighting for my promotion? Could I remain at home for so great a length of time, whatever might be the cause and still continue to hold my place in the 1st Battalion actively employed on service? No, it would not only be unreasonable but dishonourable, at all events repugnant to my feelings. I am sorry Harry, but I cannot admit the justice of these remarks. As to your opinion of the dishonour of an officer of a 1st Battalion on service remaining at home with the 2nd Battalion on plea of sickness or urgent necessity, I can only say by way of showing instance to the contrary that Colonel McLeod[183] was in England on

183 Lieutenant Colonel Charles McLeod, 43rd Foot, was killed at the storming of Badajoz.

sick leave, not so urgent a case as yours, during the advance of the army from Santarem to Gallegos and I believe for some time after the battle of Fuentes d'Onoro, in short, left Lisbon before you and did not return until the French were chased out of Portugal and even from the neighbourhood of Rodrigo and though now with his regiment he scarce ever does a day's duty with it, yet he is not thought a dishonourable, sculking, faint hearted fellow; on the contrary it is well known that he has behaved with credit to himself in action and from the goodwill and alacrity with which he does his duty when able, all agree that he is the last man to sculk or ever think his duty a bore. This is your case, with the exception that McLeod has had the good fortune to re-establish his health sufficiently to venture out again into this climate, which I am sure he must again quit for England if we shortly, as hourly expected, recommence active operations. Dalzel[184] too, now on sick leave in England and likely to remain until well. Duffy[185] was absent from his regiment in this country on plea of sick leave to England, but joined just in time enough for the last action that took place in the retreat of the French at Sabugal; he was by no means reflected on, on the contrary, all wished him joy of the brevet he got in consequence of the action. Old Morrison[186] was in England on private affairs for nearly two years and never in any action in which the battalion had been engaged; yet he scarce joined his battalion before his promotion to a company was notified to him. No reflection cast on him neither. Colonel Gifford[187] I might mention as an instance of the length a man may go to on the score of leave and with safety too, when urgent business requires it. You have had others, too, on leave to England for considerable periods with just pleas of absence and nothing dishonourable ever imputed to them. Captain P Campbell[188] who you will know to be as honourable a man and as courageous a Scot as ever lived, is now at home on private affairs, but he left us after the action of Sabugal, wounded but long since perfectly well, yet no dishonour to him. Black[189] our 4th lieutenant absent on private affairs in England, never present in any action in which we have been engaged in this country since our first landing, has thought it convenient to secure his stay in England by getting the appointment of Adjutant of the depot at Lewis in Kent. Nothing said

184 Captain Robert Dalzell, 43rd Foot.

185 Captain John Duffy, 43rd Foot.

186 Captain William Morrison, 43rd Foot, was missing from the peninsula almost all of 1809–10.

187 Lieutenant Colonel William Gifford, 43rd Foot.

188 Captain Patrick Campbell of the 52nd Foot.

189 Lieutenant George Black, 52nd Foot.

to his discredit. Now all these are honourable characters and men of equally as fine feelings as yourself and will get their promotion the same as if they had been fighting here. Be not too punctilious. Swim with the stream as others do. By out-heroding Herod you will (let the intention be ever so good) draw upon yourself ridicule instead of applause.

Wait not for any further opinion, only let me hear that you have decided coolly and deliberately one way or other, without taking into consideration any false notions about honour. Health, health is the only thing worthy of your consideration.

[A short scrap from the siege of Ciudad Rodrigo was next.]

El Bodon, 15 January 1812
No officer was allowed to volunteer his services at the storming of the Fort (San Francisco) or your humble servant would have been one. If there is any more volunteering at the storming (of the city) I should like to get my company this way in preference to waiting another seven years. Don't say anything of this to the female part of the circle.

[After the storm of Ciudad Rodrigo, he wrote complaining that Lieutenant Gurwood[190] got the 'Forlorn Hope' having put his name forward one month prior to Charles and gained his captaincy for it]

[Fuente]Guinaldo, 19 February 1812

Gurwood was a month beforehand with me in volunteering [for] the 'Forlorn Hope' or I don't know what would have been the case. I sent in my name for the storming-party, but Young[191] who was senior was taken.

[The next snippet was written only thirteen days before his death, we find him in the midst of severe work and weather in the trenches before Badajoz.]

Badajoz 22 March 1812

I don't care for the hard work a pin, nor for the climate, nor the danger, for thank God, I have a constitution to bear ten times as much as I have already suffered and the will to bear it.

---

190 Lieutenant John Gurwood, 52nd Foot.
191 Lieutenant George Young, 52nd Foot.

[His last letter spoke of all the inconsequentials of life.]

Badajoz, 24 March 1812
My expenditure will, I have no doubt, amount in your opinion to downright extravagance in comparison to my former money transactions and if we continue in this country a year longer it will increase in proportion, in short, amount to obliging many to quit this country and perhaps the service altogether. You may easily conceive the difficulty of supplying ourselves with the necessaries of life, when we are obliged to pay three times the former (last year's) price for provisions. The country is entirely eaten up by the army, our rations are for the most part from England or America. Bread long since and even meat now has ceased to be supplied by the country people. The only comfort we can boast of is a small Portuguese tent which is just sufficient to prevent the rain from washing us away though not sheltering enough to save us from a sound drenching every night. I cannot say every night, for we are only one night out of the three in camp, the rest of our time is employed in the trenches for acting with covering parties to those employed there. I just give you an instance of the duty; I returned from the trenches to my tent yesterday at 5 am and returned at 5 this evening, to continue until seven tomorrow as a covering party; chief part of the time firing at the besieged loading their guns. Our guards in the night are close under the walls of the town watching opportunities of picking off their men from the guns.

If Harry has not embarked already, tell him that Colonel McLeod does not expect him, nay even advises his remaining in England for the next six months. It is my opinion that Colonel McLeod will refuse H[enry]'s application to join, at all events I shall do my best to prevent it.

[Charles volunteered for the storming party at Badajoz and was killed on 6 April 1812.]

9. LIEUTENANT GEORGE GAWLER
ACCOUNT OF BATTLE OF NIVELLES 1813

George Gawler joined the 52nd Foot as an ensign on 4 October 1810 and he became a lieutenant on 12 May 1812. He served in the peninsula from July 1811 and served there through to the end of the war, seeing action at Badajoz, San Millan, Vitoria, the Pyrenees, Vera, Bidassoa, Nivelle, Nive, Tarbes and Toulouse. No journal of his *Peninsular War* years has been found, but an account by him of the action known as the Battle of the Nivelle was published in Moorsom's History of the 52nd Foot. It is reproduced here:

The morning of the 9 November 1813, found the different regiments of the Light Division in their usual positions at and in front of the pass of Vera; holding La Rhune to their right front with a strong detachment and having their pickets at the very base of the ridge, in the plains of France, towards St Jean de Luz and the country to the eastward of it.

In the dusk of the evening the columns fell in and moved by wild passes across the lower slopes of La Rhune to within two and a half miles of La Petite Rhune. Pickets were thrown out (Captain William Rowan's company for the 52nd) and the men laid themselves down in their blankets.

A full hour before daybreak the 2nd Brigade fell in and advancing, formed a line of contiguous quarter distance columns, just behind the summit of the last lateral ridge of the Great Rhune. Between it and the French fieldworks on La Petite Rhune there was only the enormous ravine, which commencing at the little isthmus that connects the two Rhunes, runs for five or six hundred yards nearly perpendicular to the

An officer and private of the 52nd Foot by Hamilton-Smith 1814.

Lieutenant General Sir John Moore, Colonel of the 52nd Foot.

William Rowan, 52nd Foot.

Charles Rowan, 52nd Foot.

John Gurwood, 52nd Foot.

George Gawler, 52nd Foot.

Lieutenant John Gurwood, 52nd Foot, leading the advance of the Forlorn Hope at the Storming of Ciudad Rodrigo.

Private John Jack, 52nd Foot.

Private Shadrack Purton, 52nd Foot.

Military General Service Medal with 14 Bars (centre) and Regimental Medal commemorating his Volunteering for the Forlorn Hope at the Storming of Badajoz of Private James Morris, 52nd Foot.

Regimental Medal for the Forlorn Hope at the Storming of Badajoz.

Sir John Colborne.

Battle of Sabugal by Colonel James.

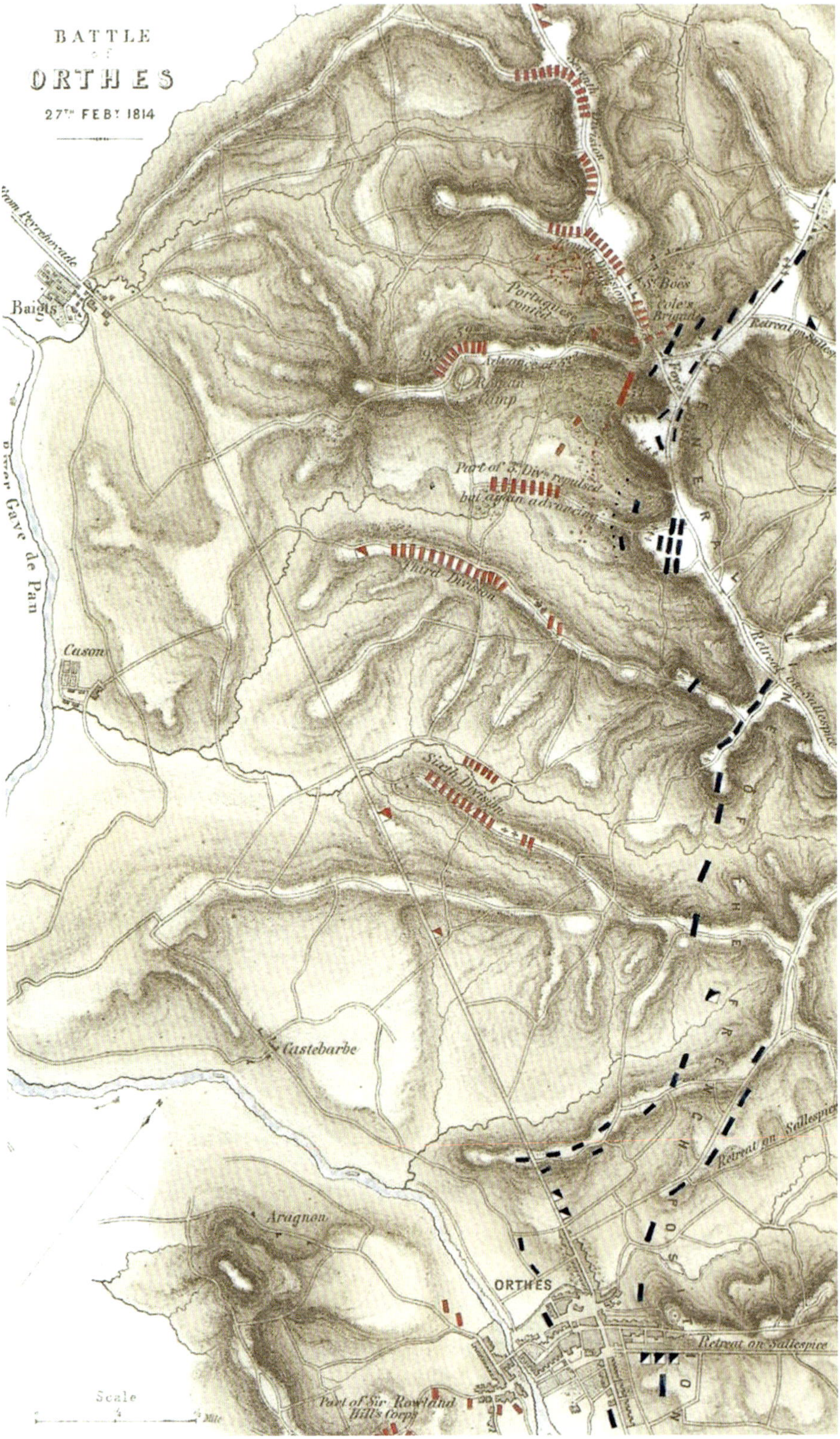

Battle of Orthez by Colonel James.

face of the Great Rhune and then rounds off towards the north and towards that part of the French position near Ascain.

The sky was almost cloudlessly clear; the twilight rapidly brightened and the mighty outlines of the mountains had become distinctly marked, when the flash and echoing report of a mountain three-pounder on the extreme point of La Rhune gave the signal to advance. The columns sprang from their concealment and a few small French pickets, on the face of their mountain, commenced a dropping fire.

The right brigade went directly at the French works by the isthmus and its western slopes. The 2nd Battalion of the 95th kept up the communication between it and the 52nd. The latter regiment hastened straight down the slope in its front, but as soon as it had crossed the rocky watercourse at the bottom, brought up its right shoulders and pushed rapidly on, in a line nearly parallel to the watercourse on its left and to the French works, about 500 yards off, on its right.

The enemy, either in the darkness of the mountain shadows did not see, or perceiving, had not the presence of mind to attempt to check this bold flank movement of Colonel Colborne's own devising. The 52nd gained the line of the extreme flank of the French works, brought up its left shoulders, scrambled up the rocky slope and stood in rear of the enemy's right, on the plateau of the Petite Rhune.

At this point a scene of extraordinary magnificence burst upon the view. The sun was just springing in full glory above the horizon and lighting up the boundless plains of the south of France. The Pyrenees stretched away to the eastward in an abrupt series of enormous sloping walls and the long lines of white wreathing smoke near their bases showed the simultaneous advance of the whole allied army.

In the foreground, to the right, the 1st Brigade of the Light Division had done its work and was rapidly pouring over the entrenchments. The French defenders of the last of their Pyrenean summits were rushing into the huge, rough punch bowl which is bounded by the eastern and western spurs of La Petite Rhune. A large portion of the Light Division, in packs-of-hounds order, followed down the slope for twelve hundred yards in pursuit, but our men were so thoroughly winded and the fugitives, on their part, so fresh, that the results were insignificant. An officer and forty or fifty men who garrisoned their extreme right redoubt, actually crossed close along the front of the leading company of the 52nd (Captain William Rowan's) without any loss of consequence, so thorough was the exhaustion from the tough struggle up the very rugged mountain's side.

The 52nd collected on the right rear of the now abandoned French redoubts of La Petite Rhune. The line of the French main position, commencing upon a comparatively low range of hills, was in front of the regiment, with an intervening rocky watercourse, which it would seem, was deemed impassable by our enemies.

The 52nd moved by threes to the small open ravine and wood in their front, under a smart fire of artillery from the ridge which was next to be assailed. In front of this wood the watercourse was crossed by a small and narrow stone bridge, on the opposite side of which was a road running close and parallel to the watercourse, with a sheltered bank towards the enemy.

The officers and men of the 52nd crept by twos and threes to the edge of the wood and then dashing over a hundred yards of open ground, passed the bridge and formed behind the bank, which was not more than eighty yards from the enemy's entrenchments. The signal was then given, the rough line sprang up the bank and the enemy gave way with so much precipitation as to abandon, almost without firing a shot, the works on the right of the advanced ridge, under no doubt, the apprehension that their retreat would be cut off if they remained to defend them.

The 52nd soon paid dearly for this (with the exception of the passing of the bridge) easy victory. Full eight hundred yards beyond this advanced ridge was the main ridge of the enemy's position and on its most prominent summit was a large and strong redoubt, garrisoned by a battalion of the French 88th Regiment, under its old and veteran *chef*. No supports appeared near it and it was determined that the 52nd, single handed (which it had been from the time of leaving the position on La Petite Rhune), should make the assault. Moving off therefore in column at quarter distance, left in front, the right wing took a long spur that led to the redoubt and the left wing the next to it, which was so far to the left as to menace the enemy's rear.

The calculation probably was, that the garrison, like those which had been attacked before, would retire rather than risk the occupation of its line of retreat. The veteran *chef de bataillon* [battalion commander], however, remained firm to his charge and his men to their ramparts. The 52nd, moving up the long-exposed slopes in massive formations, suffered fearfully. The great strength of this main redoubt became evident and that it was impossible to surmount its nine or ten feet walls if its defenders stood firm. Happily for the honour of the old corps, there was between the two wings the head of a rounded ravine; into this they obliquely moved and lay down within twenty yards of the edge of the ditch.

After taking breath for a little while, Colonel Colborne could not refrain from another attempt. The word was passed to stand up and move on, the leading ranks sprang into the ditch, but no mere human courage and activity could get further and the mass steadily *stepped back* to its cover.

At this moment an interesting episode occurred. Baron Alten,[192] seeing from the lower ridge the desperate nature of the effort, endeavoured to send an order to prevent further attempts. It was confided to the Brigade Major, Harry Smith.[193] Trusting to the shifting character of the mark of a horseman in motion, he tried the desperate venture; but it was impossible: no single living creature could reach the 52nd under the concentrated fire from the forts. The horse was soon brought down and Captain Smith had to limit his triumph to the carrying off of his good and precious English saddle, which he performed with his accustomed coolness, to the amusement of observing friends and enemies.

The hairbreadth escape of another fine fellow deserves to be recorded. Sergeant Mayne[194] who had volunteered into the 52nd Regiment from the Antrim Militia, was among the foremost to spring into the ditch of the redoubt. Unable to climb the ramparts, when his comrades fell back, he threw himself on his face. A Frenchman rising on the parapet, reversed his musket and fired. Mayne had stuck the bill hook of his section at the back of his knapsack. The tough iron flattened the ball and unhurt by the blow, he lived for many years to tell the remarkable tale.

The precarious position of the 52nd was not of long duration. Colonel Colborne's coolness and ingenuity had not forsaken him. Making a bugler sound a parley, he hoisted his white pocket handkerchief and rising, walked to the gate of the redoubt. To his summons to surrender, the old chief replied indignantly, 'What! I with my battalion, surrender to you with yours!' 'Very well' said Colonel Colborne in French, 'the artillery will be up immediately, you cannot hold out and you will then be given over to the Spaniards' (some of whom were appearing in the distance). The word 'spaniards' was all powerful. Officers and men pressed round their commander till he gave his reluctant assent. In a few seconds the 52nd stood formed in a double line at the gate of the redoubt, to give to the fine old fellow his required satisfaction of marching out with the honours of war. A detachment of the 52nd, under Captain William Rowan, took them down the hill towards Sarre and gave them over to the British cavalry.

---

192 Sir Charles Alten commanded the Light Division.

193 Captain Harry Smith, 95th Foot.

194 Sergeant Francis Mayne, 52nd Foot.

10. LIEUTENANT EDWARD NORTHEY
EXTRACT OF LETTER REGARDING THE ACTION AT SAN MUÑOZ

Edward Northey joined the 52nd as an ensign in July 1811 and became a lieutenant on 1 October 1812. He served in the peninsula from October 1812 until the end of the war, seeing action at San Millan, Vitoria, Sorauren, Vera, the Bidassoa, Nivelle, Nive, Orthez, Tarbes and Toulouse. Unfortunately, we only have this snippet from one of his first letters home from Spain; the present whereabouts of Northey's letters is not known.

[June 1813?]
Immediately after we had crossed a small branch of the River Yeltes Lord Wellington gave orders that the Light Division, in which is the 52nd, should go towards the left & skirmish with the enemy's infantry, which skirmish soon became very hot & which I am grieved to say, soon proved fatal to Captain Henry Dawson,[195] who was shot in the breast whilst at the head of his company, marching in line just as he was giving orders to them to extend; *he died instantly* without uttering a word as the ball went immediately to his heart. He is very much missed by all his brother officers who had the highest opinion of him, as an officer, a gentleman & a friend. He was buried on the spot.

195 Henry Dawson was killed at San Munoz in November 1812.

11. CAPTAIN HENRY DAWSON LETTERS[196]

Henry Dawson saw quite a meteoric rise in his army career, having joined the 43rd Foot as an ensign in June 1805 and transferring only one month later to the 52nd Foot. He then became a lieutenant by purchase in the same regiment in November of that year. He became a captain in the 52nd in May 1812. He served in the peninsula from August 1808 to his death in November 1812 with only a single six-month period absent from the peninsula after Corunna. He served at Corunna, the Coa, Busaco, Sabugal, *Fuentes de Oñoro,* Ciudad Rodrigo, Badajoz and San Millan. He was killed at San Muñoz during the retreat at the end of 1812. Unfortunately none of his correspondence exists before 1810. What we do have are paragraphs from the letters, not the entire letters.

Val de Mula 12 July 1810
At 12 o'clock at night of the 10th instant, 2 companies of the 52nd Regiment (the company I belong to was one) received orders to march to Fort Concepcion where we [were] met by 5 companies of the 95th. It was the intention of General Craufurd to surprise one of the enemy's picquets. There were also employed on this enterprise 6 squadrons of dragoons. The whole affair I am sorry to say turned out very indifferently. The enemy occupied Villa de Arganan with 50 dragoons & had 300 infantry hidden in some cover, of which we had very imperfect information. We were never brought into the action, unluckily, otherwise we should have been able to have coped with their infantry. However, the dragoons charged upon the town & in their way came in contact with the infantry, which fired a volley on

[196] A copy of his correspondence is held at the Museum of the Oxfordshire Soldier, Reference SOFO 6001 & 6008.

our dragoons as they came near them. At this instant a squadron of our dragoons made their appearance at some distance, but which at first was taken for French & in consequence they left the infantry to charge this supposed French squadron, which appeared to be coming out of a wood, but finding their mistake, they returned immediately & succeeded in taking 45 French dragoons, the whole of the infantry escaped.[197] I am sorry to conclude this affair with such a serious loss on our side. Poor Colonel Talbot of 14th Dragoons[198] and 20 men belonging to the 14th/16th Hussars were killed & 20 wounded. We have made every preparation to retire behind the Coa. Fort Concepcion is to be blown up when we begin to move to the rear.

Junca 19 July 1810
The post which carried my letter of the 12th had scarcely left us before we received intelligence of the surrender of Ciudad Rodrigo having held out 17 days as we hear. The town is in compleat ruins. The French have been very busy in reconnoitring our right flank & this morning a strong patrol of them came in contact with some of our dragoons at Villa [Vilar] Formosa, who proved too strong for them & drove them back; it caused an alarm in camp & of course we had a general turn-out and remained under arms till all was quiet. We marched on the 16th from Val de la Mula [Vale da Mula] to this place & where I think we shall remain. It is reported amongst us that our general has received positive orders from Lord Wellington to remain in our present position till the French invest Almeida, which I do not think will be done for some time. The deserters from the French report that Massena has gone back to Salamanca & that a great part of the army had also retired. I am afraid it is a deep game they are playing. It is said a great force is collecting near Placentia [Placencia], it may be their intention to enter Portugal in three or four different places at once, in that case we shall retire without firing a shot, or else if we delay our retreat upon Lisbon must be cut off.

Camp near Almeida 22 July 1810
Yesterday the French compelled our cavalry to leave Val de la Mula [Vale da Mula], on their advancing in the morning we blew up Fort Concepcion and came ½ a mile on this side of the village of Val de la Mula [Vale da Mula], our cavalry have their picquets immediately in front of theirs, about 1½ miles in front of our present position, which is

197 This refers to the Action at Barquilla.

198 Lieutenant Colonel Neil Talbot, 14th Light Dragoons, was killed.

close to Almeida, we had 3 men & 3 horses wounded only. The people in Almeida are terrified beyond all conception. However, they must stand a siege & I hope it will be a good one, they have great faith in their English governor Colonel Cox.[199]

Time will not allow me to give you a proper account of myself. On the 23rd went on picquet; 24th were attacked by an immense force of French and were driven across the Coa and Pinhel, we are now on a height above Alverca near Freixedas. We have lost in our division near 300 men killed, wounded & missing. I was returned taken prisoner but just arrived in camp today 25th; in time to have an NB put to the return for Lord Wellington. The general has been so good as to order the dragoon to call in camp for us. Thank God I am well in health & in good spirits.

Celorico [da Beira] 29 July 1810
I hope that you will have received the letter which I wrote you on the 25th as it will have relieved you from any reports which may have reached you respecting myself, as I know several of the officers wrote to England mentioning that I had been taken prisoner. On the morning of the 24th, as soon as daylight, Captain R[obert] Campbell who commanded the infantry picquets, one company of 52nd, one 95th reported to General Craufurd that there appeared a number of French cavalry advancing in front of us, we immediately stood to our arms & were placed so as to protect 2 guns of the horse artillery, we had also in advance with us 500 cavalry. We immediately threw out a few skirmishers and before they were driven in upon us, 4 more guns came to us, from superiority of numbers we retired, keeping up however a very heavy fire and joined the division in their position, who were waiting ready to receive the enemy. Although we had retired 2 long miles firing the whole way, only 3 men were wounded of the 95th & a few of the cavalry. As soon as the picquets had retired upon the division we were divided and sent to different places that required strengthening. With a section of the company, I was placed on the outer ditch of a small tower to protect the artillery who were placed about ½ a mile from Almeida, on the left of our position. I saw nothing of the battle of the division except where the artillery were engaged. General Craufurd had given particular orders for the artillery to stand to the last, they certainly did their duty & served their *shrapnels* in beautiful style. The force of the French before they attacked the division was upwards of 10,000, besides what they had in their

199 Lieutenant Colonel William Cox, Portuguese Army, Governor of Almeida.

rear to support them. The artillery & my little party that consisted of 1 sergeant, 20 privates kept our ground, till the whole of the division were driven over the hill, we then received orders to this effect. 'The artillery & cavalry will retire immediately across the river as quick as possible', and the officer (turning to me said) 'make the best of your way to your regiment.' To join it I saw, was an impossibility, 'You must attempt it' was my orders. It was impossible for me to keep up with cavalry & flying artillery, therefore I made the best of my way to some vineyards and made three attempts to get to the bridge [on] the Coa below Almeida, but every time always found the French between me and the party of the 95th who were quite on the left of the division almost 20 times my number. After a little consideration I determined to retire among the rocks below Almeida, which I did unperceived & after having collected my party & a few stragglers of the 43rd & 95th, in all about 30 men, I went by the banks of the Coa to a bridge below Cerico Vallas [Cinco Vilas] & succeeded in passing it unmolested. On my arrival at Calvahal [Carvalhal de Atalaia] on the 25th, where the division was quartered, I found the returns of our loss just going to be sent off. General Craufurd ordered them to be made out afresh and to take out our names as prisoners. Thank God for my escape. Yesterday we retired to this place. The French patrolled this morning past Pinhel. My opinion is that we shall retire through Portugal immediately. The Light Division may have frequent skirmishes, but that no general action will be fought until we get to the fortified position near Lisbon.

Camp near Celorico [da Beira] 9 August 1810
General Loison occupies our old quarters at Junca, and deserters say, that there are in the neighbourhood of Almeida 30,000 men. I cannot account for their inactivity, they have not broke ground before Almeida, nor even crossed the Coa, except with patrols & foraging parties. Why they have not brought up the whole of the force, which they had before Ciudad Rodrigo. It was reported at one time that they were obliged to retire for want of provisions. The French desert enormously, no less than 15 have come in in the last 3 days, the cavalry completely equipped, we give them every encouragement, allow them to sell their horses and valuables by public auction & generally they commence their march to Lisbon with 50 to 100 dollars in pocket.

Freixedas 22 August 1810
We marched on the 19th to Logioza [Lajeosa do Mondego], on the 20th to this place, we are ignorant why we are moved or even where the French are, except small parties.

St Pahao [São Paio da Farinha Podre] 19 September 2 leagues from the Punte de Murcella [Ponte da Mucela].

We marched on the 16th from Nave[?] to Murcella [Ponte da Mucela], 17th to Saragossa [Carragosela], 18th to Venda do Porco and on the 19th to this place.

Camp near Coimbra, 30 September
We are now close to Coimbra. I am very well & have escaped all the dangers of the action of the 27th near to the Convent of Busaco. It was a glorious affair for our cause. The loss of our army I should think to be about 1,200, that of the French about 4,000.

The 52nd & 43rd had the good fortune to make a charge, which was most grand. General Simon's Brigade about 4 or 5,000 were opposed to us, we remained very quiet behind the summit of the hill till they came close to us, General Craufurd pulled off his hat and said 'Remember Sir John Moore & Revenge his death'. We gave 3 cheers & made our appearance, ran down the hill and the French very soon showed their tails. Our two right hand companies came in contact with them with the bayonet. The halt was immediately sounded & we opened a most destructive fire upon them and laid at least 400 dead before us. The left-hand man of my company shot General Simon through the mouth & took him prisoner. Colonel Barclay[200] wounded under the right knee and in the left foot, Captain Napier slightly in the breech,[201] Lieutenant Wood[202] slightly on the top of the shoulder, 3 men killed & 7 wounded.

I should have wrote on the 28th, but we have been standing to our arms or marching ever since. We arrived on our present ground about an hour ago. If the French will not press us too hard, I will write whenever we move. The officers from England have just joined us.

Arruda 20 October 1810
They retired from Busaco through Boton [Botão], Coimbra, Condexia [Condeixa-a-Nova], Pombal, Boavista, Batalha, Condiceros [Candeeiros?], Alcoentra, Carrigada [Carregado], Cadafos [Cadafais], Alemquer [Alenquer] and arrived on the 10 of October 1810 at Arruda [dos Vinhos].

25 October 1810 Carvalha, on the heights above Arruda [dos Vinhos]
You suppose us to be in a perilous situation, we think it quite the reverse. The accounts the French deserters give us are very good, that

200 Lieutenant Colonel Robert Barclay, 52nd Foot.
201 Captain George Napier, 52nd Foot.
202 Lieutenant Charles Wood, 52nd Foot.

they have no meat, no bread, how can they subsist themselves? The have built a bridge of boats over the Tagus above Santarem, to draw supplies I suppose from the Alentejo, as well as to secure a retreat. The French since we have arrived have allowed us to remain very quiet, not so with some of the other divisions, at or near Sobral they made an attack & drove in some of the Duke of Brunswick's corps, but received a most glorious check from the Portuguese, who murdered every man they could. The 71st regiment had an opportunity of making a charge, in which they succeeded. The Portuguese peasantry under the command of General Silveira, Colonel Trant & Wilson and a number of others who come from the Tras-os-Montes, have succeeded in retaking Coimbra & 5,000 men & murdered 800 in cold blood. They have possession of Pombal & Leiria, so as to cut off their communication with their rear, blown up the bridges of Coimbra & Ponte de Murcella [Ponte da Mucela].

If Lord Wellington means to attack them, depend upon it, we shall not know it five minutes before we march. All the English troops have been working like dray horses to make our position stronger & it will be the greatest disappointment than an army ever felt, if the French do nor attack us.

21 November 1810 Camp halfway between Cartaxo & Santarem
I have just time to say that I am well & in good spirits. Whilst we remained in our position at Arruda, we had most dreadful weather & I am sorry to say it continues so. The French on the morning of the 15th marched from their ground with the rearguard of their army and were followed up very close by our dragoons during the day of the 15th & on the evening the infantry commenced moving forward & came up with them on the 16th, but we had only a little skirmishing. 17th marched to Cartaxo, nothing occurred during the day, except that we found a number of the French in the woods. 18th arrived on our present ground, in front of their position which is immensely strong and I hope for heaven's sake, that we shall not attack it, there is not a doubt, if it was attempted, but that we should succeed, but our loss would be of great magnitude, of course, that is not the game for Lord Wellington to play.

24 November 1810 Valle [Vale de Santarém]
From our remaining so quiet we may suppose that it is Lord Wellington's intention merely to watch the enemy closely, if they retire to follow them up, if they advance to retire to our old ground,

the latter I think most probable, as they are said to have received a reinforcement of from 12 to 18,000 men. This is of great service to the French, where they are at present, or in manoeuvring with us, but if we should again retire to our former position, it would require as many more to attack us with any prospect of success. I have heard it is said that it is possible to turn our position, then thank God, the position of Bucellas [Bucelas], which is stronger than that which we may be obliged to leave, is close in our rear. I believe it is the general opinion that the position of Bucellas [Bucelas] is impossible to be taken. I hope Massena may not prove too deep for us, we have already frustrated two of his attempts to entrap us. When we first came here, he sent the main body of his troops a few leagues beyond Santarem leaving about two corps and a half concealed, only allowing a very few indeed to be seen, we were in the very act of moving off our division to attack, when Lord Wellington received some fresh information & the attack was countermanded. When he found that he would not advance upon him, he brought back the whole of his army, but we were even with him, ours were all close at hand regularly arranged. Our advanced videttes are within pistol shot of each other & what is more, we have not had one unnecessary alarm. General Silveira it is said has attacked General Drouet's advance guard, killed 300 and taken 8 officers prisoners & a few men. There is a long report about it, but coming from a questionable channel, I cannot hardly believe it. Time, nor orderly's stop for no man, I had only ½ an hour allowed me when I commenced writing, an orderly of General Craufurd's has offered to take our letters to headquarters.

15 March 1811 Camp 2½ leagues from Ponte de Murcella [Ponte da Mucela], 1 league beyond Miranda do Corvo

I hope this will be the first intelligence of Massena's retreat from his position at Santarem, he commenced it on the 6th and on that morning we marched on the grand causeway to Santarem, I found the place entirely destroyed. However, by hard marching we came up with them on the 10th at Pombal, attacked them & drove them beyond the town. On the 11th we again attacked them in a very strong position & succeeded in gaining it, but they took up another, which Lord W[ellington] turned on both flanks, in the finest style imaginable. The grandest sight that I ever saw, was our army advancing from the woods in 3 or 4 different lines in extent about 8 miles and the enemy retiring in the greatest confusion.

12th Had some skirmishing and succeeded in taking Condeixa [-a-Velha].

13th Continued a general skirmishing, from right to left about 7 in the morning & continued till night, drove them till we could see no longer, finding that they could not go by Coimbra, they have taken the road to Ponte de Murcella [Ponte da Mucela].

14th A very heavy fog & to our misfortune could not follow them till near 11 o'clock in the day, but when he did advance & passed their camp, we found ammunition waggons innumerable burnt & destroyed. Every village we have passed has been burnt to the ground, I suppose with the intent of burning their dead, as well as to deceive us in the immense quantity of baggage as well as of every other equipment they have been obliged to abandon; we came up with them about 4 in the afternoon, found them cooking, we drove them from their woods & from their dinners, which were great prizes to those who were fortunate enough to get them.

15th Encamped on the very ground the enemy occupied last night, we can so easily overtake them, that we are to halt today. Report says that they cannot pass the Ponte de Murcella [Ponte da Mucela] and that they are taking to the mountains to pass by Guarda. Our loss has been very great. I know that Lord W[ellington] sends off a dispatch at 2 this afternoon. I refer you to that, as I know not exactly the number of killed & wounded. But of the 52nd we have poor Gifford killed,[203] Captain Napier slightly wounded, Captain Mein slightly,[204] Captain Jones severely,[205] Lieutenant Cross slightly,[206] Ensign Lifford severely[207] & Winterbottom slightly,[208] 12 men killed and 74 wounded. The weather is very bad, raining every half hour today. I thank God for having protected me in the hour of battle & for giving me health & strength to undergo what we have done.

25 March Navahinos [Nabainhos?] and Edom [Nabais?]
The 2nd Battalion had joined them on the 23rd. His brother Charles looking remarkably well and pleased with the novelty of campaigning.

203 Lieutenant Theophilus Gifford, 52nd Foot.
204 Captain William Mein, 52nd Foot.
205 Captain William Jones, 52nd Foot.
206 Lieutenant John Cross, 52nd Foot.
207 Ensign Richard Lifford, 52nd Foot.
208 Ensign John Winterbottom, 52nd Foot.

26 March. Marched to Celorico [da Beira]

28 March. To Barracal [Baracal], the French are at Freixedas. Part of the 95th and cavalry engaged near there in the afternoon, I am sorry to add that Lieutenant Stewart of the 95th, acting Brigade Major[209] to us, was killed.

29 March. Went towards Freixedas, after we had shown our force, the French evacuated it, we then kept on the sierra towards Guarda, and arrived just in time to overlook 2 divisions of the French leaving Guarda in the greatest hurry imaginable, took up our quarters for the night at Valenca de Bom[?].

30 & 31 March.
The enemy's rearguard passing Sabugal. We hear today that Almeida is evacuated. Part of our cavalry are in Sabugal. We are in villages 2 leagues from thence, the 52nd in Edom [?]. We may now say that there is not a Frenchman in Portugal. Marshal Beresford is past Campo Maior.

1 April 1811
How impatient I am to see Lord Wellington's dispatch, I hope it will be an excellent one and the Light Division cut no small figure in it. His lordship in his general orders desires the commanding officers of the 43rd, 52nd, 95th Regiments, each to recommend a non-commissioned officer for an ensigncy as a mark of his esteem as well as approbation of their conduct during the last 10 days. It is said that we shall not march today. We are in perfect readiness as the dragoons have moved forward towards Celorico [da Beira]. Yesterday it was reported that the French had on this side of Celorico [da Beira] 30,000 men, of course they must have moved to the other side of the Mondego as the cavalry are in motion. You must be much surprised to learn that we have not fired a shot since my last, although our division has been as close to them as it was possible. The fact is, that the remainder of the army could not be brought up to our support, being short of provisions. No fault of Lord Wellington's arrangements, but that of the Portuguese who had received orders to form magazines & stores in case of a march, to supply their own troops only, but which they had neglected, so much so, we were 3 days and a half without a morsel of bread to eat, as he was obliged to feed the Portuguese, as well as our troops, till fresh arrangements were made. The French seem to be evacuating the

209 1st Lieutenant James Stewart, 95th Foot.

country without making a single struggle. No wonder, they see our army in the finest state of discipline & their own perfectly disorganised, at least for the present; besides their sick & killed & those found dead in the road, we have taken from 14 to 1,600 prisoners.

7 April, Albergaria [La Alberguería de Argañán] 1811
Lord Wellington by a masterly manoeuvre succeeded on the 2nd in driving the French, all except a few over the Coa; which few he allowed to remain. On the 3rd in the morning, we left our picquets in front of the enemy in the neighbourhood of Sabugal & marched the Light Division with the cavalry & horse artillery by a ford 2 miles up the river. After fording the river, which was only disputed by a few roundshot, we took possession of the first heights & were marched directly to the attack, which lasted only about an hour, but the hottest fire I suppose that ever was experienced for the time. The French advanced in column thrice to the charge, but were driven back by our brave & steady soldiers, thank God we remained masters of the field, but not I am sorry to say without severe loss. 3 officers killed, 5 wounded & 150 men killed & wounded. Of the 52nd Captain P[atrick] Campbell & Lieutenant Gurwood[210] wounded. 3 rank & file killed; 1 sergeant, 17 rank & file wounded. Lieutenant Arbuthnot 95th,[211] brother to our major, killed by a cannon shot. The French ran off in the greatest confusion, leaving 300 dead on the field, 1 howitzer taken by the division, about 200 prisoners, most of General Loison's & young Soult's baggage.

Yesterday, the cavalry and 2 troops of horse artillery advanced upon Almeida, surprised batteries of French at Junca, drove them with shells out of the town, cut them up very severely. 2 of the battalions retired by Fort Concepcion, the other was obliged to take refuge in Almeida, being cut off from the others.

28 April, Gallegos 1811
The French never halted till they got to Salamanca. They have left Almeida garrisoned by 1,500 men, and which I think are in a perilous situation. Our left flank is Barba del Porco[Puerco], where General Dunlop's Division is stationed; the Light Division in the centre. The right are where the Guards are posted, I believe at Albergaria [La Alberguería de Argañán] & Forcalos. Directly in our rear are General Picton's & Pack's Divisions, in constant readiness to turn out at a moment's notice & from the few officers doing duty, its rather severe

210 Lieutenant John Gurwood, 52nd Foot.

211 Lieutenant the Honourable Duncan Arbuthnott, 95th Rifles, was killed on 3 April 1811. His brother was Major the Honourable Hugh Arbuthnot, 52nd Foot.

for those who are effective. The enemy have been extremely alert since the 20th, they moved out of Ciudad Rodrigo on the 21st to cover some provisions they were expecting, we were out all night after them, but were not fortunate enough to fall in with them. They again sallied forth on the 23rd and attacked me at the bridge of Marialva, where I was posted with 30 men, fortunately we were just relieving (Lieutenant Eeles[212] with 30 men of the 95th came to relieve the party then on picquet), which increased my party to 60 and another officer. On receiving intelligence of their approach I proceeded with 20 men over the bridge to a small height that commanded the road from the village of Marialva, with the intention of covering the cavalry picquet that was in front and of retiring upon the bridge. I succeeded to the best of my wishes, checked their cavalry completely, who were obliged to retire behind a hill till their infantry came up, they soon dislodged me from the height and I retired as fast as I could over the bridge, the remainder of my men were posted on heights commanding the bridge and where I had ordered them to stand as long as possible. On seeing about 3 or 400 men moving down in front of me in skirmishing order, I began to be rather fearful of our safety. Our fire was so well kept up that they came to a check for some little time; at this time some of my men on the right were falling back from the very heavy fire of the French, I was just in the very act of ordering the whole to retire, when to my great joy I saw Captain Dobbs[213] with his company coming to my assistance, and although they had succeeded in gaining the bridge with about 40 men across it, they were obliged to retreat and left us in full possession of our post. We are not acquainted with their loss, I know for a certainty that we killed a lieutenant colonel. Our loss was Ensign Pritchard[214] of my company and 17 rank & file wounded, the number of French that were on the opposite side were about 1,500 infantry & 75 cavalry. This little affair lasted nearly 2 hours.

Yesterday the 27th, they had the impudence to sally forth again with about 3,000 men as a reconnoitring party, they attacked the same picquet but were again repulsed. I do not know the particulars as I was not present. We sent two or three companies to their assistance, which as they usually do, behaved most gallantly. Our loss was 10 men wounded. The report of the day is, that Almeida has no provisions, I give credit to it, as Colonel Delancey Quarter Master General[215] is my authority. Lord Wellington returns to headquarters at Alameda

---

212 Lieutenant Charles Eeles, 95th Rifles.

213 Captain Joseph Dobbs, 52nd Foot.

214 Ensign Samuel Pritchard, 52nd Foot, was wounded.

215 Lieutenant Colonel William Delancey.

[Le Alameda de Gardon] from the Alentejo today. Charles is not yet quite so inured to hardships as myself, he has had a very violent cold & been blistered & physicked, but is nearly recovered.

Fuentes d'Onoro 8 May 1811
We are now labouring under the greatest anxiety possible. The French are either retiring or removing their ground. They seem to be moving on the road upon which they advanced and are showing about 7,000 men within cannon shot of our advance picquet, which I think is to cover their baggage & stores, as also to form their rear guard. I wish I had time to write you an account of our movements for the last seven days. Some regiments of the line have distinguished themselves most gallantly in defending the village of Fuentes d'Onoro, but neither time nor place will allow me. We retired from Gallegos [de Argañán] on the 2nd instant, got to our present position on the 3rd & maintained it. Left flank, Fort Concepcion, right flank on the 1st instant Nave de Haver, and from which we were obliged to fall back on their attack on the 4th instant, but not any considerable distance. The Light Division have not been engaged in the position, we have been kept as a reserve.

Gallegos [de Argañán] 27 May 1811
Advices from Albuera inform us that previous to Marshal Beresford having completed the trenches in the investment of Badajoz, the French made a sortie & attacked our working parties, our men like brave & gallant fellows flew to their arms & drove them back, but from too great impetuosity followed them too far and got cut up most dreadfully from the cannon of the town, we lost 30 officers & above 400 men. Further advices from thence induced Lord W[ellington] to proceed thither with all his Staff and though we have not the correct accounts of the action of the 16th, which I understand Lord Wellington says was the most brilliant that ever took place, I shall mention what we have heard. That Marshal Beresford with 7 or 8,000 English,15,000 Portuguese & Spaniards,[216] was attacked by the French consisting of 25,000 infantry and 3,500 cavalry with the determination of relieving Badajoz. When the action had commenced Marshal Beresford found that some adjacent heights on one of his flanks ought to be occupied. Colonel Colborne was ordered to take possession of it with the 3rd, 66th [&] 88th Regiments and were immediately surrounded by an immense force. The Fusileer [sic] Brigade was ordered to rescue them & did it most handsomely but with very severe loss. The total loss is said

[216] The combined British–Portuguese & Spanish army numbered about 35,000.

to be 30 officers killed, 180 wounded & 4,000 men killed, wounded & missing; that of the French supposed to be 10,000,[217] having left the field in our possession and their wounded in hospital behind them and retired to Llerena on the road to Seville. The whole of the army here, the Light Division, 1st, 5th & 6th Divisions have been on the alert all this week and were pushed forwards a long day's march on the high road to the Alentejo but received orders to move back to our old quarters.

San Miguel 10 June 1811
The guns did not open upon Badajoz as soon as was expected nor until the 2nd instant & on the 5th it was thought it would have surrendered in consequence of a practicable breach having been made, but last night we heard that the 51st Regiment had attacked the Fort of St Christopher [Christoval] & were repulsed with the loss of about 200 men, I am not so sanguine as I was about the fall of Badajoz. With respect to ourselves, when Lord Wellington went to the Alentejo, Sir Brent Spencer[218] was left in command of the army near Ciudad Rodrigo. On the 1st of June Don Julian sent information that the French were in motion near Salamanca & he believed concentrating. Every department, both civil & military were ordered to prepare for a move. On the 2nd the French having concentrated 22,000 infantry & about 18 squadrons of cavalry, moved on towards Ciudad Rodrigo, where they arrived on the 4th. All was quiet & we were commemorating the day, for which every preparation had been made and dancing with the natives, when to our great annoyance, orders were brought to us at 12 o'clock at night to march at ½ past two. Some retired to sleep, others kept it up till the bugle sounded to fall in. We marched a mile from the town & formed the brigade on a height where we remained till the reports of the cavalry patrols came in [that] all was quiet in our front & we returned to our quarters, to remain accoutred and baggage packed. In the middle of the day, they pushed over the bridge of Ciudad Rodrigo 2,000 infantry. From information we had received, we knew they intended to advance upon us on the morning of the 6th. Our division was formed on the heights of Naver de Haver at 7 in the morning, 2 leagues in the rear of Gallegos [de Argañán], leaving our cavalry on a plain flanked by two woods in our front. W Crosbie[219] who is very well, will I suppose send you an account of our cavalry manoeuvres, I know his troop & Captain Purvis's[220] made a charge & cut through those who

217 The losses on both sides were nearer 7,000 each.
218 Lieutenant General Sir Brent Spencer.
219 Captain William Crosbie, 1st (Royal) Dragoons.
220 Captain Charles Purvis, 1st (Royal) Dragoons.

were opposed to them, came threes about & cut back again, although their flanks were entirely surrounded, I believe they lost 14 men. That afternoon we continued our march to the heights in rear of Alfaiates. On the 7th marched over the ground where the action of Sabugal was fought, everyone had something to say about what he had done and what he had seen. I am persuaded the greatest satisfaction we all felt, was that every man had done his duty. Having crossed the Coa, we took up our abode for the night in the woods 2 miles above the river. To get us across the Coa was all the French wanted, as it gave them in some degree possession of the Puerte de Banos & the Pass of Perales, by which way they are moving with the intention, it is supposed, of reinforcing those near Badajoz. On the 8th we marched to Penamacor, we now suppose that we are on our route to the Alentejo. 9th to Sao Miguel [de Acha] rather low in spirits, in consequence of the news I have already related to you. 10th the day is so far advanced, I think we may halt here the remainder and our next days march be probably to Castello [Castelo] Branco. Charles as well as myself enjoying very good health. I am now acting as Adjutant.

Portalegre 18 June 1811
We hear that Lord W[ellington] has raised the siege of Badajoz in consequence of the movements of Marmont, who is moving by Placentia [Plasencia] to join Soult, this we cannot prevent. Also that part of the army near Badajoz has taken up the position Beresford fought on. Our little force under the command of Sir B[rent] Spencer is collected here, about 15,000.

In Lord Wellington's despatch, I perceive the little affair of the 23 April is mentioned. *Every* officer's name appears in it except mine! It would have given me pleasure to have seen Lieutenant Dawson's name there, your letter however is quite sufficient for me &c &c.

Many of the officers of the division have spoken to me on the subject, since the appearance of the Gazette. Without wishing to attach more credit to myself than others are inclined to allow me; I was engaged an hour before Lieutenant Eeles of [the] 95th came to relieve me and being my junior officer, I posted him to protect my right. As all was quiet, when the colonel of our regiment visited the picquet in the morning, Captain R[obert] Campbell, my captain, went with him to breakfast, long before the action commenced, and joined us just as it was finishing, having left his company under my command. Both of the above are mentioned in the Gazette, Captain Dobbs who is junior to Captain R[obert] Campbell, brave fellow, ought to have been mentioned in the strongest terms possible, but it is merely said that he behaved gallantly. You shall judge for yourself. He was posted in the first instance at Molinos dos [Caseria Villar de] Flores to watch a ford over the Agueda. On hearing the firing in the direction where I was posted, he immediately proved the ford not to be passable & marched his picquet to my assistance, taking upon himself the whole responsibility of quitting his post. The cavalry picquet which I said was in my front, passed the bridge with me.

[NB added by his father:] I believe it is not usual to mention subalterns in the Gazette, except when in command. Captain R[obert] Campbell ought to have and was supposed to have been present and any notice of Lieutenant Dawson would have been a severe censure upon Captain R[obert] Campbell. Though Lieutenant Eeles was junior to Lieutenant Dawson yet he was the only officer with & in command of the party of the 95th.

Monte Reganca [Reguengo] Camp 25 June 1811
Since my last, we have been constantly on the move except the 3 days & we halted at Portalegre and arrived yesterday late on our present ground. Our present position extends to Elvas on our right and Campo Maior lays 5 miles directly in our front. I have received your letter of 27 May & am highly pleased &c &c. I showed it to Colonel Ross[221] who said he thought a recommendation from General Craufurd would have more influence than from him & that he would speak to the general for me. When Colonel Ross asked me to act as Adjutant, till the arrival of Winterbottom,[222] he at the same time asked me to live with him & I find all the comforts of it. Charles is now in Captain Sheddon's[223] company & he could not be in a better one in any respect.

Mamoa [Meimoa] near Sabugal 6 August 1811
The whole army has retired as we thought into summer quarters & we expected to have remained quiet for 2 or 3 months, as it was distributed as follows:

1st Division at Portalegre; Headquarters, 2nd & 4th Divisions under General Hill occupying Estremoz, Evora & Vila Vicosa; the Portuguese attached to that part of the army at Crato and its neighbourhood; 7th Division under General Houston[224] at Nisa; 5th under General Dunlop[225] near Portalegre; the Light Division Castelo de Vide; General Pack's

221 Lieutenant Colonel John Ross, 52nd Foot.
222 Lieutenant John Winterbottom, 52nd Foot.
223 Captain John Sheddon, 52nd Foot.
224 Major General William Houstoun.
225 Major General James Dunlop.

Portuguese Brigade at Pove [Póvoas e Meadas] & Montalvao. We had marched on the 21 July from camp at Monte Reguanga [Reguengo] and arrived on the 23rd at Castelo de Vide. On the 29th we were again on the move & have never known the day before where we were to proceed to the next, but suppose we are to go to Sabugal tomorrow and shall probably soon occupy our old quarters in the neighbourhood [of] Ciudad Rodrigo. Provisions are likely to be very scarce, on this last march we have been two days without bread and we are obliged to draw succours from Tras os Montes from the reduced state of this part of the country. We are expecting a convoy of 1,000 carts from thence, the French are said to have retired from their ground on the Guadiana by Seville & the bridge of Almaraz. Marmont is at present at Placentia [Plasencia].

Martiago 11 August 1811
So secret are our movements, instead of going to Sabugal as we expected, we marched on the 7th to Quadrasuites [Quadrazais]; 8th to Aldea de Ponte [Aldeia da Ponte]; 9th to [Fuente]Guinaldo and arrived here yesterday. The country people are extremely glad to [see] us. It is too evident how cruelly the French have treated them, burnt every village, collected all the grain, compelled the inhabitants to thresh it by taking some of the principal people prisoners as hostages for its being done & levied contributions to a considerable amount. The whole division is gone out today with Lord Wellington towards Zamora, I conclude to reconnoitre Ciudad Rodrigo, which is said to be garrisoned with 1,500 men & that the enemy have not any others nearer than Salamanca. Charles is quite recovered and is left in charge of some sick of our division at Sabugal.

Saugo [El Sahugo] 21 August
We are all sorry to lose Colonel Ross, he is going to India as Adjutant General to General Brownrigg. Colonel Colborne was one of poor Sir John Moore's most particular friends & I believe will be of more service to the regiment than Colonel Ross ever had it in his power to be. He promised fairly, but I believe he never spoke to General Craufurd about me. Though Colonel Colborne is senior to Arbuthnot[226] in the army, he is junior to him in the regiment and consequently will command the 2nd Battalion. It is still supposed that the 2nd Battalion will be sent home. I have already spoke[n] to the commanding officer to allow Charles to remain out [in Spain] & I have no doubt I shall succeed.

226 Lieutenant Colonel Hugh Arbuthnott, 52nd Foot.

I have entirely given up my project of going into the Portuguese service in consequence of fresh orders having been given out, of which I do not quite approve.

Camp near Soito 29 September 1811
Giving a short account of the death of my nephew Captain William Crosbie of the Royals at Albergaria [La Alberguería de Argañán] on the 26 September of a nervous affliction on the brain[227] and of his having [been] buried on the 27th.

In consequence of a note Henry received from Colonel Clifton[228] he went over to settle his cousin's affairs.

Cassillas de Flores and Fuenteguinaldo 6 October 1811
Before this arrives, you will have heard of the advance of the French, of their having relieved Ciudad Rodrigo and driven us some considerable way into Portugal, but I hope it has not disconcerted you, or even made you change your opinion, it is impossible for me to give you an exact account of the movements of the army as they were on such an extensive scale, or anything more than what took place with the Light Dragoons, and those at the time immediately connected with it.

Previous to the 20th of last month we heard of the enemy collecting in force at Salamanca, for the purpose of throwing a convoy of provisions for 6 months into Ciudad Rodrigo. We all knew it was not his lordship's intention to hinder the convoy going to Rodrigo or even to molest the enemy, having gained his object by making them concentrate, but he had taken every precaution in having his army well placed in case they should advance upon him. Two divisions were on the Gallegos [de Argañán] side of Rodrigo on the high road to Almeida to protect the left. Three divisions on the high road in front of [Fuente]Guinaldo as far as El Bodon, their right on the River Agueda, one division guarding the pass at Perales. The Light Division across the River Agueda divided and occupying the strongest heights from the river to the serra & to prevent the right being turned. The army remained nearly in this order till the 25th when the enemy advanced on the El Bodon road in 3 very strong columns supported by cavalry and cannon. His Lordship ordered the troops on that road to retire, which they did in a most masterly style across a plain of six miles in extent in close column of regiments although surrounded by French cavalry who made several very dashing attempts to put them into confusion,

227 He died of an overdose of opium.

228 Lieutenant Colonel Arthur Clifton, 1st (Royal) Dragoons.

but without success. I must refer you to the Gazette for the particulars of this day. The 2nd Battalion 5th Regiment & 77th deserve the greatest credit. The enemy by 4 o'clock in the afternoon were at least a league in our rear & about which time we received orders to withdraw our picquets and to retire by the nearest roads, by Los Agallos [Agallas] to Espidoza [Cespedosa de Agadones] where the division would unite. At daylight the next morning we continued our march by Saugo [El Sahugo] & Robledo & passed the river half way to Penaparda & brought up our left shoulders for [Fuente]Guinaldo where we arrived about 4 in the afternoon on the 26th. You may conceive our situation when the army had picquets on the road we were to march Saugo [El Sahugo] & Robleda, but they retired as we approached. On the evening of the 26th we all commenced our retreat from [Fuente]Guinaldo to Casillas de Flores, Foscales [Forcalhos] to Alfaiates and where we gave them some sharp skirmishing on this day the 27th. On the morning of the 28th the whole army was moved into position behind Soito, where we were to have fought any number they might have brought against us. They refused the offer and returned the same road they came, but *vice versa,* we pursuing them. Our quarters here are miserable, the houses destroyed by the French. Headquarters of the division at [Fuente] Guinaldo. Obliged to leave off [writing].

I finish this, 2 o'clock in the afternoon at [Fuente]Guinaldo where I have been ordered. The 2nd Battalion are at Puebla de Azaba. Charles has had a slight attack of the ague, hope it has left him, as the attack expected yesterday, did not return. The French have always moved when we did, following our example; advanced when we moved, avoiding an action. Our loss in this retreat and advance has been inconsiderable, that of the French immense. Some of our officers who are quartered here have been all over the plain that our army retired over on the 25 September, dreadful havoc, men & horses now laying on the ground for vultures & ravens to feed upon, they found only two English horses among the whole.

Zamorra [Zamara] 8 November 1811

I have been lately so much employed by General Vandeleur[229] who commands the 2nd Light Brigade, in gaining information in the villages in front, that I really have not a day to myself for this last month and also by General Craufurd who very kindly told me to my face that he wished *me* to undertake to procure some carts from the arsenal at Almeida & that he thought it would be necessary to *humbug*

229 Major General John Ormsby Vandeleur.

the governor not a little. However, I succeeded completely to his wishes & found politeness & civility were better than having recourse to other methods.

Our living is most expensive, everything is extravagantly dear and as we are so much on the move, I have two good horses & carry my own baggage & am independent of the officers in whose company I am. The day that Lord Wellington reconnoitred Ciudad Rodrigo, I was officer of the Baggage Guard. On the night of the 27 October, General Hill by forced marches succeeded in surprising part of General Girard's Division,[230] between Caceres & Merida.[231] He was luckily favoured by a very dark & rainy night and actually marched round the town unperceived. The rain was so very heavy that the firelocks would not go off & they most undauntedly commenced the attack with the bayonet sabre. Their reward complete success, took 1,500 prisoners, including General Brun [Bron],[232] Prince d'Aremberg,[233] the chief of the Staff, several chiefs of battalions & 40 other officers, all their baggage & stores, the last contribution of Merida and an immense quantity of plunder. The remainder have retired to the mountains without arms, they talk of a dispersion of 15 to 20,000 men; General Murillo[234] with a Spanish division in pursuit of them. In short, one of the most brilliant affairs that has occurred; highly to the credit of Lord Wellington in having planned it, equally so to General Hill in the ability with which he executed his orders, our loss but trifling.

Los Agallas [Agallas] 18 December 1811

Since my last, we have moved, but to no great distance. General Vandeleur still remains at Martiago. The French have been moving with 2 or 3,000 infantry & 2 pieces of artillery from Salamanca towards Miranda [de Azan] & to the villages in the neighbourhood merely to get provisions. I was sent last week to Guadapero with a party of dragoons and the inhabitants complained bitterly that Don Carlos d'Espagna[235] pressed everything for his troops & that they were actually starving. I offered money for bread, wine and spirits for the dragoons who were with me, but could not succeed and we travelled the whole day without anything to eat, yet the men do not grumble.

230 General Jean-Baptiste Girard.

231 This refers to the Battle of Arroyo dos Molinos fought on 28 October 1811.

232 General Andre Bron de Bailly.

233 Colonel Prosper Louis, 7th Duke of Aremberg.

234 Spanish General Pablo Morillo.

235 A French officer in the Spanish Army, General Carlos de Espana.

30 December 1811
The French are said to have sent a considerable force from hence towards Valencia to overwhelm General Blake.[236] Our army have 100 men per regiment working daily near their own cantonments, making gabions, fascines &c for the last six days; preparing most probably for the siege of Ciudad Rodrigo. It is said that the garrison has only 5 bullocks & about 60 pigs which they have stolen from the inhabitants, who speak confidently that we are to open our entrenchments in the beginning of the year and that the garrison are terribly afraid. However, we ourselves are in total ignorance.

El Bodon, 15 January 1811
Charles wrote to you yesterday. Thus far we have gone most prosperously. Last night the Germans attached to the 1st Division took an outwork in which there was one gun, they did it certainly in a brave and soldier-like manner, but they had no sooner gained their object, than they turned to plundering and allowed all their prisoners to escape. Tomorrow our division return to the trenches, may God preserve us both through all our dangers, which in my opinion are over in a great measure, as it is impossible for the enemy to annoy us in the degree they did before we opened upon them and a breaching battery within 200 yards of the place will soon be erected. Our loss has hitherto been trifling; I have not seen the Returns, but report says about 200 killed & wounded in the 7 days; but of which the Light Division has lost 50. If it should hold out 7 days longer, in my opinion, a general action will take place. An intercepted letter of Dorsenne's[237] says. The outworks of the city I expect will prove a second San Christoval, at least will hold out for 5 days. (He should have said 5 minutes, he did not know the Light Division were to *storm* it, but expected we should have made regular approaches. He also says that the English cannot commence before the 12th & that he will be down shortly with a convoy of provisions).

Fuenteguinaldo 12 February 1812
Note by his father – The letter he wrote to me on 24 January which was returned to him, having been opened at headquarters, as the direction, from the badness of the ink, was quite obliterated.

[It is] ridiculous to forward it now, as you must have seen the Gazette. It must have astonished you to have heard that Ciudad Rodrigo had fallen in 11 days from the opening of the trenches. The Light Division

236 Spanish General Joaquin Blake y Joyes.
237 General Jean-Marie Dorsenne, Count Lepaige.

had the honour of commencing the siege, on the morning of the 8th we marched from El Bodon. Before we could break ground, we were to take a fort on the breaching hill, which the French expected would hold out 4 or 5 days at least. The storming party consisted of rather better than a company of each regiment commanded by Colonel Colborne & Major Gibbs.[238] The senior captains went with their company, they fell in at dark and about 8 o'clock at night marched to the ground they were to start from. The ensuing half hour was a most anxious one, we were all looking towards the place from a little height, when the signal was given. I really believe the anxiety of the spectators was greater than of those actually engaged. All round the fort was in a perfect blaze, the enemy threw fire pots into the ditch & then commenced with hand grenades, supported by musketry. Our brave lads leaped into the ditch, got over the palisades, then gave 3 cheers, placed their ladders against the wall and stormed into it and cheered again, which was answered by the whole division. Spades, pickaxes &c were immediately put into our hands & before morning we had sufficient covering for the next division. On the 19th the Light Division received orders to meet the 3rd, General Picton's. His Lordship was determined to make an attempt that night. Lieutenant Gurwood 52nd volunteered [for] the forlorn hope. He was knocked down by a hand grenade to the bottom of the breach, he mounted again & received a slight wound in the head which stunned him for some minutes & had a second roll, a third time he succeeded in getting [a] footing on the breach & was supported by 300 volunteers from the different regiments & went in with him. The main body moved with them & mounted directly in the rear of the stormers. The enemy ran in all directions, my God what a happy moment. I suppose we were not more than 10 or 15 minutes at most in getting in. The officers who volunteered [for] the storming party of the 52nd were Major Napier, Captain Jones,[239] Lieutenants Young,[240] Royle,[241] Hamilton[242] [&] Knox,[243] an equal number of the 43rd and 95th.

The 3rd Division stormed the large breach & we the small one, the carnage at first was great, but luckily did not last long. To describe the scene which took place afterwards, is more than I am equal to. Firing into windows, bursting open doors, setting fire to houses, in

238 Major Edward Gibbs, 52nd Foot.

239 Captain William Jones, 52nd Foot.

240 Lieutenant George Young, 52nd Foot, he became a captain on 20 January but may not have heard yet in mid-February.

241 Ensign Job Royle, 52nd Foot, did not become a lieutenant until March.

242 Lieutenant Douglas Hamilton, 52nd Foot.

243 Lieutenant the Honourable John Knox, 52nd Foot.

fact sacking the town, stripping the inhabitants of their gold chains, earrings, trinkets & valuables of every kind, getting drunk and doing everything that soldiers are capable of after having carried a town by storm. Lieutenant Gurwood took the governor to Lord Wellington, who immediately made him a present of the governor's sword, with a promise that his gallant conduct should be represented to H[is] R[oyal] Highness & a promise of promotion.

Conceive poor Charles' mortification during all this operation, being prevented by a severe ague, which he caught in the trenches from going with us, or rather which brought it on again. But doctor's orders must be obeyed & he was obliged to submit. He has had several severe attacks since, but by bark & attention to his medical attendants, is getting better. The officers and Staff of the 2nd Battalion are certainly to go home, but the necessary arrangements I think, are made for Charles to remain with the 1st Battalion. He wishes to enter into the Portuguese [service], about which I have written to Charles Rooke[244] to use his interest with Marshal Beresford. We hear that Valencia and all Blake's army [are] taken. The Spanish officer's say the men will escape & that they regret the loss of the army more than anything else. Tarragona however has fallen into our possession & they say the whole garrison was put to the sword.[245]

Castelo de Vide, 11 March 1812
We marched on the 26 February & arrived here by easy stages on the 7th instant. Headquarters at Quinta St Julian one league on this side of Elvas. Our battalion now 1,200 or 1,300 on paper, 921 effective fit for duty.

Camp near Badajoz, left bank of the Guadiana, 24 & 25 March 1812
Charles is going on duty now, and as I am just come off, I will give you a little of my opinion. We were very unfortunate in our commencement, as the weather became bad the very evening we began to open our works, but considering everything has been against us, our entrenchments are in a very great state of forwardness, we have already finished one battery of 5 guns and four others will be completed tomorrow night, the first batteries are merely to play on the defences of the town, which when silenced will afford us an opportunity of making our breaching batteries. It is generally supposed the Battering Train will be playing on the town between the 28th and 30th and that we shall gain full

244 Captain and Lieutenant Colonel John Charles Rooke, Assistant Adjutant General.
245 A false rumour.

possession of it on or before the 15th of April. Marmont they say, can only collect 50,000 men, *they* will avail him nothing. His Lordship it is understood really wishes they would attempt to relieve Badajoz, as our force is if anything, superior to that number. A peasant to whom the governor Philippon[246] had entrusted his account of the sortie on the 19th for Marmont, brought it to General Picton. He had exaggerated not a little, but seemed perfectly aware that things began to wear a dismal aspect. I am afraid that we shall have great sickness after all this bad weather; literally we have not had one day or night without very heavy falls of rain. Charles I am glad to say is very well, myself never better.

25th All last night on the covering party in front of our batteries, we lost only one man killed, two wounded. The engineers finished five of the defence batteries during the night & which opened in fine style at ten this morning. The town and batteries are in a perfect roar. We have been generally on duty 10 hours out of 24. The French are said to be on the move.

Camp near Badajoz 26 March 1812
Last night we attacked the Fort of Picurina, which was taken in the usual style when English soldiers are employed, I write to say Charles who was in the attack is safe. The fort commanded all our works & at ½ past 8 last night was ordered to be attacked by parties of the 3rd Division who were in the trenches, supported by those of the Light Division also there. Part of the latter who were ordered to carry fascines & ladders thought proper to mount & show the way. We can only answer in an affair like this for what happens immediately about ourselves. Captain Ewart[247] commanded a part of the advance with Charles and Ensign Nixon.[248] Ewart slightly wounded in the fleshy part of the arm above the shoulder, Nixon in three different places and I am afraid mortally.

Camp before Badajoz 3 April 1812
Note by his father – He had received my letter informing him of his brother William's death.
Everything is going on in the finest style possible, the breaching batteries opened on the 31 March and are at this moment playing away as hard as they can, requiring however to be occasionally repaired as

246 General de Division Armand Philippon.
247 Captain John Ewart, 52nd Foot.
248 Ensign William Nixon, 52nd Foot.

the town has damaged them a good deal. Two of the breaches out of the three are very far advanced & when the engineers pronounce them practicable without the least doubt of success, then are we to storm. For my own part I am never too sanguine, but I have such confidence in British soldiers, that they have only to receive the order & if it is in the power of earthly beings to perform what they undertake, they will accomplish it & especially when led on by such officers as we at present possess in our service. There are some reports of Soult's coming to relieve Badajoz, he had better be quick, or he will be a day too late. The 5th Division are gone to join General Graham, who in conjunction with General Hill will have little short of 40,000 men. The French cannot bring more. At all events one of the three divisions which are at present besieging, can be spared if it should be necessary. Ewart I am happy to say is so well that he moves from Elvas to Estremoz today. Ensign Hall[249] doing well, Nixon pronounced out of danger, Charles is better than I have known him since he came out and is in good spirits, better than I could have expected.

Badajoz 8 April 1812
Badajoz is now in our possession, but I am sorry to say with most severe loss on our side. Poor 52nd, Charles is very slightly wounded in the calf of the leg with a slug & is doing very well; I did not escape, but so trifling the wound, I would not allow myself to be returned wounded. I sincerely hope they will reach you before any idle reports, or even the Gazette. The plans of attack were most admirable; there were 3 breaches made which were attacked by the 4th and Light Division, they appeared perfectly practicable, but were found when attacked, to be utterly impossible. Three times were we driven down, every implement of destruction was used against us, chevaux de frize made of swords, chains across the tops of the breaches, under which were planks filled with hooks and nails & behind the breaches were entrenchments & works of every description. Not only shells of every kind were thrown over upon us, but barrels of powder which blew many a poor fellow to atoms, immense bags filled with iron & stones were also thrown down the breach, which from their weight, swept everything before them. By one of these I was hurt, when attempting the second time to rise [up] the breach, but not so much as to hinder my doing everything that can be done for Charles' comfort. The 3rd Division attacked the castle by escalade and succeeded & entered it with 3,000 men, Philippon had only 120 men in the castle, so little did he

[249] Ensign George Hall, 52nd Foot.

expect an attack in that quarter. The 5th Division made the same kind of attempt on the other side of the town, on the bastion of St Vincente, who also succeeded after some little difficulty. They remained in the castle and on the ramparts till morning, when everything was settled and the town given up to plunder. I cannot give you an exact account of our loss, not even of the 52nd, but it is supposed to be 19 officers killed & wounded, about 20 sergeants killed & wounded, about 50 rank & file killed & about 230 wounded, about 320 in all. Captains Jones, Madden[250] & Poole,[251] Lieutenants Booth[252] & Royle killed; of the wounded Lieutenant Colonel Gibbs likely to lose an eye, Major Mein shot through the thigh, Captain R[obert] Campbell shot through the arm, Captain Merry leg splintered by a cannon shot,[253] Lieutenant McNair,[254] Kinloch,[255] Davis,[256] & Royds slightly,[257] Lieutenant Barlow severely,[258] Lieutenant C[harles] Dawson slightly[259] – a slug in the calf of his left leg, Ensign Gawler slightly,[260] Adjutant Winterbottom slightly.

Lieutenants Harvest[261] and Taggart[262] of [the] 43rd both killed, [Lieutenant] Thomas Wilkinson of [the] 43rd wounded slightly in the trenches, doing very well, Ewart also very well considering. Charles Rooke has just been here to pay us a visit looking remarkably well. Charles wishes to add a few lines that you may have something from his own hand. It is just reported that the loss of the Light Division in killed and wounded is about 70 officers & 1,000 men.

Portalegre 16 April 1812

Since I wrote you on the 8th, we have been in the most horrid confusion from the shock which the poor 52nd had received & having the affairs of our poor friends to settle before we commenced our march, but what was really most required was to get our men into some kind of order, which I must confess was not done, but with the greatest difficulty. Charles I am happy to say is doing well. I rather foolishly thought that I should have been able to travel with my regiment, but was soon

250 Captain William Madden, 52nd Foot, was killed.
251 Captain Clement Poole, 52nd Foot, was killed.
252 Lieutenant Charles Booth, 52nd Foot, was killed.
253 Captain Augustus Merry, 52nd Foot, died of his wounds on 9 April 1812.
254 Lieutenant James McNair, 52nd Foot.
255 Lieutenant Charles Kinloch, 52nd Foot.
256 Lieutenant Francis Davies, 52nd Foot.
257 Lieutenant William Royds, 52nd Foot.
258 Lieutenant George Barlow, 52nd Foot.
259 Lieutenant Charles Dawson, 52nd Foot.
260 Ensign George Gawler, 52nd Foot.
261 Lieutenant Horatio Harvest, 43rd Foot was killed.
262 Lieutenant Charles Taggart, 43rd Foot was killed.

convinced to the contrary, obliged to haul my wind and cast anchor in this happy port (Portalegre). I am now with my leg up, well poulticed, very little pain & in high spirits. Had I known this would have been the case, I would have laid up with Charles, I am only 36 miles from him and as soon as I can sit on horseback, I will ride over to him. You will see by our having moved so soon after having taken Badajoz, that the French were not idle, they had moved from the north as far as Castelo Branco with part of their advance guard, but are now returning with a little more speed, the Light Division in full chace [sic]. Report says that they moved into Castelo Branco last night. Our cavalry in front of Badajoz gave a good account of some French gentlemen a few days back, they all attacked their rear guard in a most handsome style, took 300 prisoners & killed nearly as many more. The 1st, 6th & 7th Divisions are here, 4th & 5th Divisions between this place and Castelo Branco, Light Division in the advance. General Hill with the 2nd Division in front of Badajoz in conjunction with the Portuguese army. We are moving up to the north, it is evident, but what is to be done puzzles us all. Poor Gibbs obliged to go to the rear, Major Hunt has recommended me to Captain Merry's vacancy. He died poor fellow from not allowing his leg to be amputated.

Portalegre 27 April 1812
I hear Charles is in comfortable quarters, good medical attendants, in good health [&] spirits, but the slug is still in his leg & bleeds very freely on the least motion, it is not as trifling as it was at first considered. He is still in his bed, but expects to be able to sit up in about a week. As for myself, my leg from the exertion of coming here with the regiment, had put on such an ugly appearance as to alarm me & my doctor, but by good care & paying proper attention to his advice, I have been able to walk about a little and to ride for an hour today, and do not find my leg the worse for it. I have not heard from the regiment since their departure from there. The Light Division were on the 22nd at Penamacor. Cavalry patrols have been as far as the Coa today, report says, that the enemy have crossed the Agueda and are in full retreat towards Salamanca; that his lordship's headquarters are at [Fuente] Guinaldo. I hardly know how to credit it, the people here seem to be as ignorant as brutes & so perfectly indifferent about what is going on in their own country.

Estremoz 6 May
On the 3rd I quitted Portalegre & arrived here yesterday having travelled 16 leagues & no worse for it, though the wound is not closed.

I hope to be able to join in a fortnight. I found Charles much better, than I expected. Colonel Gibbs has lost his eye, Blackwood[263] I am afraid will lose his arm. All others doing well.

Quinta Esquiras, Estremoz 20 May
I am so much better that I hope to be able to join my regiment in about 3 weeks. Every day makes a material difference in Charles for the better, yesterday he walked out of doors for 2 hours on his crutches and is no worse for it, the Medical Board say the slug is in an awkward place & will require time to shift from the back of the muscle. We have about 20 of the Light Division here who are well enough to hobble to the marketplace to see each other & to hear the news. A letter from our division this morning mentions that Major General Charles Baron Alten has taken the command of it. I understand he is a gallant and good officer, fit for the command of light troops, if so we are sure to like him. Poor Craufurd, he might have his faults, but it may be some time before we have as active an officer at our head. I was rather a favourite with him than otherwise, I have been told by Major Napier that he has heard Craufurd say 'send for Dawson & he will be able to do what we want'. I do not mean this as praising myself, for whenever I was sent for by him, I went as an officer on duty & happily succeeded in performing anything he wished, as one. Captain Ewart marched from hence to join the army with 600 men under his command a few days ago. The commandant here says he will send as many more in a fortnight, I hope I may be one of the officers, as I am quite miserable from my regiment (my sword home), it is the first time that I have been from it in this country and I hope it will be the last.

Quinta Esquiras, Estremoz 3 June
The orders of today, have given me 14 days for recovery, a week I should suppose will be sufficient for my leg to be well enough for me to be able to report myself to the commandant as able to join. The next board I am persuaded will order Charles to England, his nasty complaint, the ague is returned upon him, his wound is nearly healed, but I am sorry to say he cannot straighten his leg. Both Maling & Walker, surgeons of our regiment[264], blame me for having advised him to remain in this country. England may be more favourable for his recovery & I am satisfied that he should go home. Report says that the 1st & 6th Divisions are on their march to join Lord Wellington in the

263 Lieutenant Robert Blackwood, 52nd Foot.

264 Surgeon John Maling and Assistant Surgeon Thomas Walker, 52nd Foot.

north and that it is his intention to advance upon Salamanca. General Hill it is said is returned to Almendralejo.

Castelo Branco 14 June 1812
I left Estremoz on the 9th instant, my wound very nearly healed. I could not remain there any longer, hearing the Light Division was going to move. The headquarters report says are at Tornemais[265] and some of the troops on the other side of Salamanca, where I hope to be on the 24th & in the state in which my leg is at present, without being any worse for the journey. The commandant at Estremoz[266] has behaved particularly civil to me, in allowing me to go from the depot without escort or detachment, of which I was afraid being the senior subaltern there. Lieutenant Rideout 43rd[267] also got the same indulgence and we are travelling together. As I suspected the Medical Board have given Charles orders to go to England and he is now on his road to Lisbon. The commandant will have made all arrangements for him.

265 Wellington was at Cabrillas to the west of Salamanca on 14 June 1812.
266 Major Arthur Heyland, 40th Foot.
267 Lieutenant George Ridout, 43rd Foot.

12. LIEUTENANT CHARLES DAWSON LETTERS

Charles Dawson, the younger brother of Captain Henry Dawson, joined the 52nd Foot as an ensign in June 1809 and became a lieutenant in June 1810. He served in the peninsula in the 2nd Battalion from March 1811 to January 1812, and transferred to the 1st Battalion to remain in the peninsula in February 1812 until June of that year. He returned to the peninsula in November 1813 and remained there for the rest of the war. He saw action at Sabugal, *Fuentes de Oñoro,* Ciudad Rodrigo, Badajoz (where he was severely wounded), Nivelle, Nive, Orthes, Tarbes & Toulon. He also fought at Waterloo, where he died of his wounds. A copy of his correspondence is held at the Museum of the Oxfordshire Soldier, Reference SOFO 6001 & 6008. What we do have are paragraphs from the letters, not the entire letters. He arrived at Lisbon on 5 March in the *Pompee.*[268] The 2nd Battalion 52nd embarked on 26 January 1811 at Portsmouth, in the *Pompee* & *Argo.*[269] They sailed on 30 January and put into Torbay, from whence they sailed on 15 February. They were quartered in the Convent of St Dominique and expected to march in a few days to join the Light Brigade, with which the 1st Battalion 52nd then was.

Navaies [Vila Franca das Naves] 25 March 1811 about 3 leagues from Celorico [da Beira]
The 2nd Battalion left Lisbon on 12 March, went by boats to Vila Franca [de Xira]. Marched on 13th Alcoentre, 14th to Rio Mayor [Maior], 15th to Carvalhais, 16th to Lyria [Leiria], 17th to Pombal, 18th to Condeixa, 19th to Miranda do Corvo, 10th to Ponte da Mucella, 21st to Galizes,

268 HMS *Pompee* of 74 guns.
269 HMS *Argo* was a 44-gun frigate.

22nd to Pinhancos where they joined the 1st Battalion. 24th to Vinho, 25th to Navaies [Vila Franca das Naves], 3 leagues from Celorico [da Beira]. Henry very well.

Albergaria [La Alberguería de Argañán] 8 April 1811
Our battalion I am sorry to say, saw very little of the French at the affair of Sabugal, as we were attached to 2 pieces of artillery. We had a few shots flying near us but did not lose a single man killed or wounded. As it was the first engagement I had witnessed, several of us after the affair was over, walked over the field of battle, the sight was horrid in the extreme. Lord W[ellington] I understand was very much pleased indeed with the Light Division beating back the 2nd Corps d'Armee, commanded by General Reynier consisting of about 15,000 men.

Gallegos [de Argañán] 29 April 1811
We are informed by a French deserter that the French received a reinforcement yesterday of 7,000 men viz 3,000 cavalry, 4,000 infantry and 8 guns from Salamanca supposed to be the Imperial Guards, if they think fit to attack us, we are ready to receive them. The fords are still reported to be impassable. Henry went out this morning at 3 o'clock with his company, on outlying picquet to Marialva [Marialba] ford about 1½ mile in front, we have a cavalry picquet in front of that and our videttes can see all the way down to Ciudad Rodrigo. Lord W[ellington] arrived yesterday & immediately went on to the front. Our poor 2nd Battalion I am afraid cannot remain long in this country, their spirits are sinking from the Walcheren ague, we have about 150 sick to the rear since we came into the country. Yesterday I was sent with a fatigue party of 100 men to erect breast works at Carpio [de Azaba] ford, about 1 mile to the right of Marialva [Marialba] ford. We built up 4 of stones & earth, which will protect the men in some degree.

Gallegos [de Argañán] Sunday 12 May 1811
Henry wrote to you on the 8th from near Fuentes d'Onoro. I can now inform you of our movements from the 2nd instant, on which day we were roused out of Gallegos [de Argañán] by the French who came out of Ciudad Rodrigo in force with the intention as was generally supposed to relieve Almeida.

The Light Division ordered to the heights before Alameda [La Alameda de Gardón] and remained there till the evening when we moved off to the right and took up our abode for the night in a wood to the right of Gallegos [de Argañán]. On the 3rd at daybreak we moved on towards Fuentes d'Onoro and took up our position on the heights in its rear, where we remained anxiously expecting the advance of the enemy, whose drums we heard very distinctly & thought them near, but as they did not advance opposite to us, but showed themselves to their own right, we were pushed on to the left as a reserve to General Campbell's Brigade who were stationed on the heights directly in the rear of Alameda [La Alameda de Gardón].

Nothing occurred that evening. On the morning of the 4th, the division were agreeably surprised (I think I may [say] so from the manner in which he was received), by the appearance of General Craufurd, who had been expected for some days. The whole division received him with 3 cheers, [from] each regiment separately as he arrived on their right, we then moved more to our left and remained quiet until evening when we took ground again to our right and commenced the gypsy style of sleeping very comfortably under rocks. On the 5th, a short time after daybreak we moved off to our right, as we understood the enemy had commenced skirmishing. We marched past the Guards & Highland Brigade toward Nave de Haver. The light regiments 51st & 85th of the 7th Division, were in a wood skirmishing with the enemy, when we came up we sent part of the 95th to relieve them, as they had lost a great number of men. We halted upon a plain opposite to a large wood where the French were and had the pleasure of seeing our artillery upon some heights on our right, playing in upon them in grand style, they were however shortly after obliged to retire, as the enemy's cavalry & artillery were quickly advancing; then commenced the engagement. We had an opportunity of seeing the enemy's cavalry charge the Chasseurs Britanniques who were in line, they gave them a pretty warm reception &c as to make them turn tail, after firing the front rank came down to the kneel and the rear rank to the charge. They did not try them a second time, the 16th Light Dragoons afterwards charged them, supported by the 14th and Royals. As soon as the 16th came up to the first squadron of the enemy, they opened out and let them in and then closed again, which threw the 16th rather into confusion, but being well supported by the 14th and Royals, they cut their way out without much loss. The Royals made three very pretty charges indeed & have been fortunate in not losing many men & not an officer. We certainly were not able to cope with them in cavalry, they were at least 5 to 1 & the greatest part fresh horses, whilst our horses have been harassed about with little or no corn to eat. After their cavalry had charged ours, we expected they would have come down upon us, so we formed into 3 hollow squares and waited for them, but they did not advance as far but got in amongst our artillery.

Captain Hulton of the Royals[270] rallied his men and with the assistance of the horse artillery men, drove them away. All this time their cannon were playing upon our squares, but were not able to hit the exact place where we were, as there was a small elevation of ground that covered us; their shot went rather close over our heads.

This having been the *first* time I had stood to be shot at by cannon, I must confess that I did not much relish it, but after a few shots had passed, it became more *familiar* to me. At this time the enemy were bringing up more artillery upon the long trot, it was thought advisable for us & for the artillery to retire. We moved off in squares as regularly as on a field day, this manoeuvre of General Craufurd's I understand was generally admired, as we were safe from cavalry if they had attacked us, our artillery took up their station on some rising ground. We moved off to our left, supposing that their infantry would advance, but not finding them anxious to move forwards, we moved towards Fuentes d'Onoro, in rear of the Guards & Highland Brigade; the enemy's guns were pointed & firing in that direction, as our artillery was upon the hill before the Guards. We passed by some rocks where almost every other shot pitched within 3 or 4 yards of those who passed. Not a man of the division was hurt. We halted upon a hill not far from Fuentes d'Onoro, the enemy perceived us and saluted us with a few shot which made us retire, when halted we found that we were still within range & were obliged to retire further still. Our division was kept in reserve. We have not heard the particulars of the loss of each regiment, but the total is reported to be 1,700 British & 250 Portuguese killed, wounded & prisoners; the loss of the French about 3,000. The regiments at Fuentes d'Onoro were the 24th, 45th, 71st, 79th, 88th. During the skirmishing the enemy attacked the right of the town & another part in front. The right composed of Portuguese & Germans gave way and allowed the enemy to get into it; upon the rear of our troops, who were then between two fires. The enemy took several and killed a great many, the 79th & 88th charged in a gallant style & drove them to the lower end of the town; the enemy returned with fresh troops but could not get possession of it, they were driven back with great loss. We remained on the hill till all the cannonading & firing was over, which began before 6 o'clock in the morning & did not cease till ½ past 4 or near 5 in the evening. Towards evening we moved nearer to the town, the 43rd was sent into the town, to keep possession of it. The French remained quiet at the town end. On the 5th we expected they would

270 Captain George Hulton, 1st Royal Dragoons.

make a second trial, but no and also on the 7th, when they made a great show of waggons laden with provisions & ammunition from Rodrigo, which led us to suppose that they would attack us on the next day, but instead of attacking us on the 8th, they withdrew their videttes and sentries & moved off towards their own right, leaving in our front the 6th Corps d'Armee and the whole of their cavalry, as we supposed as their rear guard. On the 10th they moved off entirely. Our cavalry followed them & saw the infantry pass Ciudad Rodrigo towards Salamanca. Our division moved on shortly after the cavalry & had to halt until we received their reports, when we moved towards Gallegos [de Argañán] and took up our old quarters. Our company was on outlying picquet at the Carpio ford on the Azava [Azaba], saw nothing all night. 11th all was quiet & we thought the French had all gone to Salamanca, but we found the cavalry were not, for this morning they appeared in our front and roused us out of Gallegos [de Argañán]. Ewart & myself were very comfortably just sat down to breakfast, when the bugle sounded the Assembly. We were forced to pocket our breakfast as well as the affront. The division retired again to the heights before Alameda [La Alameda de Gardón], but did not remain there long before reports came in that they had retired & moved towards our right where our 1st Brigade was quartered. Brenier[271] had heard of Massena's retreat and on the night of the 10th he with the garrison of 1,500 men got out of the town of Almeida, blew up the fortifications & almost the whole town to atoms. We have not yet heard from headquarters who is to blame. I am inclined to think the French may move towards the Alentejo, as Lord Wellington has ordered the 7th and 3rd Divisions to march from hence to reinforce Marshal Beresford.

Camp at Monte Regania [Reguengo] 25 June 1811
We have heard that Marmont has withdrawn his army across the Guadiana, having previously detached 1,500 men after General Blake's army, which is in Catalonia. We had a tedious march of it from Villa Velha, where we crossed the Tagus, the artillery commenced at daylight and the baggage of the division was not over until dark at night. Report says all 2nd Battalion men are to be drafted into the 1st Battalion and the junior officers & Staff to be sent to England, except our 2nd Battalion as our 1st Battalion is 800 sergeants, rank & file effective, but of our 2nd Battalion we have now 60 sick in the rear.

271 General Antoine Brenier de Montmorand, governor of Almeida.

Arronches 11 July 1811
At sick quarters to avoid the night air, bowel complaint. The French are sending out foraging parties every day and patroles towards Alburquerque & Campo Maior, they are at Montijo. W[illiam] Crosbie[272] only ½ a mile from him and comes to sit with him. He has seen Charles Rooke, dined with General Hill & Clement Hill[273] who were very kind and civil to him.

[La] Encina 7 September 1811
Here we are still very quiet, about 3 miles from our 1st Battalion at El Sahugo and 1½ miles from Martiago, where General Craufurd remains. I have been dreadfully off with the sick at Sabugal. The doctor himself ill & gone off to Celorico. The Assistant Surgeon could get no answer from the doctor. No commissariat to assist us in provisions & I was obliged to get the sanction of the Juiz de Forno to go into the country to press what sheep & bread we could get, the men were without provisions for 2 days. Nearly 3 weeks in this situation, when the sick were ordered to go to Celorico, I was obliged to go out to press cars which I got in two days, sent them off and started for the division with 11 men who had recovered. Henry has been absent for the last 8 days, he has been to the rear to bring up money for the 1st Battalion, he is just arrived and very well. We have lost our Brigadier General Drummond,[274] he left saying only 4 days to go to Fuenteguinaldo, where he died. Major General Vandeleur is to have our 1st Brigade.

Martiago 22 October 1811
Our summer quarters have not been quite so settled as we expected, generally on the move and always in front as the advanced guard. We are now the most advanced brigade of the division & the only brigade across the Agueda. Our 1st Battalion is at Zamarra, 95th at [La] Atalaya, 1st Cacadores & ourselves at Martiago & chiefly to protect the villages from being plundered by the garrison of Ciudad Rodrigo. This is a pleasant village and a tolerably good market, some things brought from Rodrigo & some from the mountains, the villages in the mountains afford us the best things, as all the elder peasants when the French make their appearance, send the younger ones into the mountains, with all their valuables and as the French do not meddle with the villages out of their road, as soon as they make their departure, the paysans return

272 Captain William Crosbie, 1st Royal Dragoons.

273 General Sir Rowland Hill and his brother Captain Clement Hill Royal Horse Guards.

274 Colonel George Drummond commanding a brigade of the Light Division, died on 8 September 1811.

with their goods & are always glad to see the English. Henry is gone to Almeida by order of General Craufurd to get carts for the use of his division to carry provisions. I have lately recovered from a nasty attack of the ague; which lasted 3 weeks, attacking me every 3rd day.

Martiago 5 November 1811

You will have heard that the governor of Ciudad Rodrigo was taken about 3 weeks since & we have been upon the move to intercept the new governor, who was expected with an escort of 4,000 men & some live bullocks for the garrison, but we were it seems, one day too late, they all got in unmolested. Henry has rejoined his regiment, he has been living at headquarters like a fighting cock, dining with General Craufurd, with Colonel Barnard[275] 95th, Colonel Macleod 43rd[276] alternately when he returned from Almeida with the carts. General Craufurd sent him orders to remain at headquarters till he should be desired to join his regiment, in short he was everything but on the general's Staff and I really think as General Craufurd has taken so much notice of him (for he has frequently called on him to go with dispatches and so reconnoitre in the mountains as Henry can talk the language tolerably well) that should General Craufurd want an officer for the Staff, he would stand a good chance of getting the situation, than which nothing would give me greater pleasure. At Almeida met a Mr Taylor of Brasenose College, who was out of provisions & obliged to Henry for a dinner & made himself very agreeable as he seemed to know a great deal about our family. We have at present a great many amateurs with the army who assist only in eating up our provisions, corn &c &c.

Martiago 2 December 1811

We are again all quiet after having had another wild goose chase after a French convoy of provisions for Ciudad Rodrigo. Our whole army moved up, but the French thought it prudent not to attempt to supply the garrison. I am sorry to say that our commissariat is not as well conducted as it ought to be. I can answer for the Light Division. Our poor fellows have not had any bread for some time, not until the last 3 days & then only half rations and at a time when they have no money, 3 month's pay due to them & have been obliged to feed themselves upon chestnuts & acorns. The inhabitants refuse to bring bread to market as the commissary prefer it and pays only by paper, a receipt for it.

---

275 Lieutenant Colonel Andrew Barnard, 95th Foot.

276 Lieutenant Colonel Charles McLeod, 43rd Foot.

The men have 1½ or 2lb of meat when they have no bread, but without salt or potatoes & they would prefer ½lb of bread. Our 2nd Battalion naked and have been excused outlying picquet. We cannot muster 30 shirts amongst them, no stockings, coats & pantaloons patched like harlequins, but we are expecting cloathing [sic] every day. Finished at Zamarra where he had recovered to dine with Henry, who was quite well.

Martiago 10 December 1811
I send you a sketch of the country [not extant] near Caceres, where General Hill surprised the French under General Girard,[277] I copied it from one sent to Captain Ewart[278] by an officer who was present & may be considered correct. Colonel Colborne has joined us & taken the command of the 1st Battalion.

Martiago 31 December 1811
Henry & myself are employed as superintendents over the gabions & fascines, it is not to be *sneezed* at 4/- a day when finished. I hope they will be used in besieging Ciudad Rodrigo though there will be many broken heads, yet that town is of too great importance to us to allow them to have it when we have the least chance of getting possession of it. Don Carlos & Don Julian[279] have pressed & sent to Fuentes d'Onoro 1,000 carts and animals. For what purpose? Henry came over to dine with me.

El Bodon, 14 January 1812
Our quietness has been greatly disturbed since my last, disturbed by a movement at which I rejoice, as I may perhaps never witness a movement of the same nature again and of its completion, I hope to be able to inform you in a short time. You cannot be ignorant of what I mean, as Ripley[280] wrote to his father by the last packet informing him of Lord W[ellington's] intentions to take Ciudad Rodrigo. He could not have chosen a better time for it, as the French Army are greatly dispersed for their winter quarters, and Suchet's corps has been sent after Blake. Lord W[ellington] must succeed either in taking Ciudad Rodrigo, or in forcing the enemy to concentrate to relieve it. Report says they are coming under Marmont and Count Dorsenne. Rodrigo is a well-built fortification, very strong, supposed to be practicable to

277 General Jean-Baptiste Girard.
278 Captain John Ewart, 52nd Foot.
279 Spanish guerrilla leader Don Julian Sanchez Garcia.
280 Lieutenant William Ripley, 52nd Foot.

breach only at one place, it is built on high ground, the River Agueda on one side and round the rest of it the glacis is built so high that it screens the walls from being breached, the place where we intend to breach it is exactly the same where the French did when they took it from the Spaniards. On the 8th instant we marched at daybreak, crossed the Agueda and marched as near as we could, keeping out of range of shot, to Rodrigo, where we found a very convenient hill to encamp under. When the French took Ciudad Rodrigo they built a very pretty fort on a hill (San Francisco) about 800 yards from the town which commanded it and might protect it from assault; where they mounted an 8 pounder, a 4 pounder & a howitzer and a garrison of 50 or 60 men. Lord W[ellington] thought it necessary for us to take this fort before we broke ground and wishing it to be a duty & no volunteering, the senior company of each regiment in the division were ordered out and marched off, commanded by Colonel Colborne, with Major Gibbs 52nd who was to lead the storming party at dusk and at 9 o'clock we heard them commence, in 5 minutes we heard a cheer and in less than 5 more, we heard 3 more cheers. This was answered by our division, when we concluded that the fort upon which the French had placed the greatest confidence, in its lasting out 3 days, was most brilliantly taken in less than 10 minutes. Our loss much less than could have been expected. Of the 52nd Captain Mein slightly, a flesh wound through the thigh; Lieutenant Woodgate[281] his subaltern, hit in the upper part of the thigh with a hand grenade; 5 men killed, 5 wounded. Mr Hawkesley 95th,[282] since dead, Mein & Woodgate doing well, these the only officers wounded. Captain Mein was the first man who put the ladders up & the first in the fort & Woodgate was close to him, but knocked down by his wound. They took 2 officers and above 40 prisoners. As soon as this was effected, the 3rd Cacadores broke ground to the right of the fort. The division was employed afterwards by reliefs to make entrenchments. Our company was not employed that night. The fire of grape, roundshot & shells was tremendously great indeed, but we were very fortunate in not losing many men. The next day, H[is] M[ajesty's] Household troops and the rest of the 1st Division relieved. You may conceive me not at all glad, for the nights are now amazingly cold, hard hoar frosty nights, obliged to our pipes, tobacco & spirits for what warmth we can get, no wood near the place. The 3rd & 4th Divisions are at present employed. On the 12th we again took up our old station. The 1st Brigade went into the trenches in

281 Lieutenant John Woodgate, 52nd Foot.

282 Second Lieutenant Rutherford Hawksley, 52nd Foot.

the morning and we relieved them at 5 in the evening. We remained in until 2 o'clock in the morning, levelling the parapets & building platforms for the guns to work upon. Our entrenchments are made as follows, the entrance or covered way is about 8 feet broad and 3 deep, all the earth being thrown up on the town side as a cover, afterwards an angle is carried in for a certain length, at which end a parallel to the town is made, in which parallel the battery is formed, this is 3 times the breadth of the others, higher & built with gabions, fascines & sandbags. The parapet of the battery is about 18 feet in breadth. We were rather annoyed by their throwing lights to see where we were working, these lights are so constructed that they cannot be put out, but must burn out, they sometimes burn 15 or 20 minutes. The batteries are now 550 yards from the town, they are to be carried on by angles & parallels until they get quite close, but as the first battery are finished they opened their fire this evening at 4 o'clock. Our Battering Train consists of 38 24-pounders, 4 18-pounders, no howitzers. Now we have commenced our fire upon them which will attract their attention we shall continue our work, in erecting other batteries and I think in 8 days or less we may have a breach large enough for 50 men to go abreast and it is reported the Light Division is to have the honour of storming the town, in which I have no doubt but they will succeed. We again resume our station on the 16th from which I hope both Harry & myself will return as well as we hitherto have done.

El Bodon 20 January 1812
Ciudad Rodrigo was taken last night by storm, but not without severe loss. Thank God, Henry, myself, Ewart, Ripley are quite well. General Craufurd desperately wounded, not likely to recover. General Vandeleur wounded slightly. Colonel Colborne is I am sorry to say severely, Major Napier lost his right arm, Captain Dobbs killed. Lieutenant Gurwood headed the forlorn hope and escaped with a slight wound, he took the governor to Lord Wellington, who presented him with the governor's sword. Owing to the ramparts having been mined, the 3rd Division lost a great many men. I hope this will be in time.

El Bodon 29 January 1812
Henry wrote to you on the 21st instant, to which I added a PS [not extant]. We are now perfectly quiet, have orders to hold ourselves in readiness to march, expecting Marmont down, as some of his advanced infantry & cavalry have been seen at Tornedos [Tornadizos] by Don Julian's people. Marmont is reported to have been at Salamanca with an army of 40,000 men, but as Ciudad Rodrigo is now in our possession,

I think he will consider it more prudent to remain where he is. I still much regret not having been at the storming of Rodrigo, though I was at the siege and attribute the return of my ague to the damp trenches. I have been in the town since, but had not time to see more than just the part of the ramparts where the breaches were made, they are getting on with the repairs very fast & expected they will be finished in a day or two. The bustle & confusion that was in the town after it was taken, is more than my pen can describe, plundering, men getting drunk, setting fire to houses, &c &c &c. It was wonderful that the whole town & everybody in it was not blown to atoms, several of the party were. Soldiers made a large fire in the great magazine, where it was fortunately discovered soon & the fire extinguished. Our loss has not proved rather severe, our officers all doing well. Henry quite well, I am just as the ague takes me, ill every third day & very weak after it.

Fuenteguinaldo 3 February 1812
We have removed to this place for more room & hope we shall remain quiet till the winter is over, and I do not expect to see a Frenchman till they show themselves at Badajoz, where it is now all the talk that we shall shortly be. Speaking of sieges, what grievous accounts we have had from Tarifa and of His Majesty's eagle bearers, the 87th. This spring, summer, I think there will be something great to be done. It has been mentioned today from headquarters that our 2nd Battalion is to be sent to England about [the] 24th. I will contrive to remain here if I can. Henry has succeeded to Captain Dobb's company in the 1st Battalion.

Fuenteguinaldo 25 February 1812
We have been engaged all day in drafting the men of the 2nd Battalion to the 1st Battalion and we have unexpectedly received orders to march tomorrow towards the Alentejo, we suppose to take Badajoz. Ripley goes home with the 2nd Battalion, by whom I have sent you a snuff box taken at Ciudad Rodrigo and Henry has sent to my mother a gold chain taken out of Soult's baggage at Sabugal. I have arranged to stay with the 1st Battalion by exchanging with Lieutenant Cross,[283] who is going home on private business. Colonel Rooke advised me to write to Lord Wellington about going into the Portuguese service, which I did, and got in answer that His Lordship regretted he could not comply with my wishes, owing I suppose to the numerous applications which have been made.

283 Lieutenant John Cross, 52nd Foot.

Camp near Badajoz, 21 March 1812
We arrived here on the 17th instant [&] began the entrenchments on the same night, our works are getting on in an admirable style. We expect to open a battery on a fort in front of Badajoz in a day or two & expect it will fall in a very short time. Fort St Christoval it is said is to be left to itself until the town is taken. There are also two other forts to protect the town, which it is not intended to molest, one in the rear of St Christoval, the other directly opposite, on the other side of the town. The garrison have not as yet annoyed us as much with shot & shell as we were at Ciudad Rodrigo. On the 19th however, they made a sortie on some of our new works and to our shame, be it said, they succeeded in filling up part of the trench and carried off 150 pickaxes & shovels. However, they were driven back again after ½ an hours' sharp engagement. Their number it is said, amounted to 1,400. Ours I should think, about the same number, if not more. They lost 7 officers and 200 men killed & wounded. Captain Cuthbert,[284] adc to General Picton was killed, Colonel Fletcher, Chief Engineer slightly wounded, one or two more officers and about 100 men killed & wounded. The garrison is supposed to consist of 5,000 men & Monsieur Philippon has hoisted the French flag on the top of the citadel, but I hope he will be stripped of his honour in less than 3 weeks. We think we have a right to consider ourselves highly affronted in being made mudlarks of a second time, when there is anything going on in front, this we may attribute to the loss of our late general. Generals Hill & Graham are gone on towards Merida, to keep Marmont, Soult &c in check, while we are employed here, up to and over shoe tops in the trenches. For since we have been on this ground, we have not had a single day or night, not hardly 3 hours together, without heavy showers of rain. The first night we arrived here it was a bitter and a dreadful night, raining and blowing the whole time, the men [having] no cover but their blankets and but few officers with tents. Captain Ewart, to whose company I am now attached, fortunately got one before we started from Guinaldo. All the tents were blown down that night, by the violence of the wind and rain. Now all the army are encamped regularly in tents, which adds much to our comfort. Our guns are all on the road from Elvas and a fine train it is. 18 24 pounders, 20 18 pounders [&] 18 howitzers. I think we shall rather astonish them. It is said they least expected us to attack them at the place we intend to do & have mined a great part of their works, ready to set fire to them, should we succeed in getting possession of

[284] Captain Robert Cuthbert, 7th Foot, was wounded in a sortie by the garrison on 19 March and died of his wounds the following day.

the town. Lord Wellington, *the man of many names,* is determined not to spare one of them, if they do set fire to them. Last night our division broke fresh ground for a new battery, we were uncovered within 120 yards of the fort and not one of us touched, except one engineer officer who was pointing out the ground to us. Our covering party kept them pretty well from the guns, by firing constantly at their embrasures.

22nd
Last night I was on picquet, still bad weather. The garrison during the night and early in the morning commenced [a] very heavy cannonading and are still continuing it. Mr Hall,[285] Captain Ewart's other subaltern was wounded by a splint[er] of a shell this morning, not dangerously. General Graham has the command of the 1st & 6th Divisions in front, General Hill with his own corps. The 7th Division is at Santa Martha in front, our 2nd Battalion still at Lisbon.

Camp near Badajoz 26 March 1812
PS to Henry's letter
Henry has left room for me to add a few lines to say how thankful I am to a good providence for having protected me last night, from any hurt while so many around me fell. As I was a party engaged, I can inform you of what I was an eyewitness of. As soon as our party of the division arrived in the trenches, Captain Jones[286] 52nd Acting Field Officer, of the whole, ordered Captain Ewart, who was senior captain to move forward, to carry the fascines & ladders, and as we had not a sufficient number, we were completed from the 95th, the whole of the party consisting of 1 captain, 3 subalterns and 140 men. I had charge of the ladders with orders to place them against the fort as soon as we arrived; we moved forward down the trench and got into the high road leading to Badajoz under cover of low ground, until we got in a line with the fort, we then made a strait [sic] cut to gain the road between the fort & the town, receiving all this time the fire both of the town & fort & here we were impeded by a trench 7 or 8 feet deep, which however we crossed with little difficulty, the fire here became exceedingly hot. We ran forward to the fort and found a very strong palisading, which effectually stopped us, for a short time, the men with hatchets not being there to cut them down, the palisades so high, the ladder got entangled in them & only half over, too heavy for the men who brought them to get them quite over, we remained a few

285 Lieutenant George Hall, 52nd Foot.
286 Captain William Jones, 52nd Foot.

minutes in that state, our men got one of them clear and took it round to another part of the fort, planted it and got up with others who soon followed with cheers. What ensued you may easily guess, the fort was carried, the French ran, the garrison made a sort of sortie, but were soon driven back and we overtook the fort [&] turned their own guns upon them, it was thought at first to have been a weak fort, but when we came up, we soon found the difference, it took us half an hour to take it, the garrison consisted of 350 men. I cannot say their loss, but it must have been great, it is said, that only 3 escaped into Badajoz by swimming the inundation, our nearly 200 including officers. We immediately commenced breaking ground for there we intend to form our breaching batteries. My next letter I hope will inform you of our being comfortably quartered in Badajoz. General Graham it is said is in pursuit of Drouet who has with him 9,000 men. Marmont is making a feint at Ciudad Rodrigo, Soult in despair, Philippon in a terrible fright and greatly astonished at our successes, in short when once determined, nothing can withstand our *old patron*. Henry has now the command of Captain Ewart's company.

Badajoz 8 April 1812
[PS to Henry's letter shown previously]
I cannot allow this letter to leave us without assuring you of my being in good spirits. It will prove I hope of no consequence, I have certainly greater pain from the ball not having been extracted, it is to work its own way out. I expect to remove to Elvas tomorrow. Soult is at Merida with 25 to 30,000 men. Marmont has invested Ciudad Rodrigo with his army; his breaching battery consisting of *two* pieces of cannon. Colonel Barnard commanded the Light Division on the night of the 6th. Colonel Gibbs 52nd commanded one of the brigades.

Elvas 16 April 1812
I arrived here only yesterday, and expect to move on a spring waggon tomorrow to Estremoz. The ball brings still on occasions very severe pain, having as it is supposed bruised the muscle of the leg and remaining near the nerve, which it occasionally touches, it went in in the inner part of the left leg, 6 inches below the knee, and the leg is so swelled, the ball cannot be felt. Henry is gone with the division up to the north again to drive Marmont away.

Elvas 24 April 1812
I am still here in bed & likely to remain here for some days, my leg is excessively painful, but my health [is] good. Henry has been obliged to

remain behind at Portalegre on account of his leg, which he writes me is going on well and requires only rest. I think Henry stands a good chance of getting poor Merry's company as Lieutenant Black[287] has not been with us for the last 2 years. For me to attempt to describe the confusion at the storming of Badajoz would be folly. I can only say that from the unfortunate circumstance of the engineer officers who were to lead our division to our own breach, being killed or wounded. The division pushed on to the first breach they came to, not knowing which way to go & this happened to be the breach assigned to the 4th Division, who shortly after arrived and got so mixed with our men that the whole were soon in the greatest confusion, clubbed together, some bugles sounding the advance, others the retreat and our men finding it impossible to succeed in getting up the breach. In the midst of this confusion the garrison sent a fire or light ball, which nothing can extinguish into the ditch where most of our men were, there they had a full view of them and blazed away upon us in an extra manner. The men not liking to be under such a heavy fire ran to the ladders to ascend the counterscarp. I ran up also to get to the top in order to stop them, just as I arrived at the top, the shot struck me, I hobbled away as fast as I could until I got to the bottom of the glacis, where I found the most part of the division assembling ready to make another attack, from thence I was carried to the hospital where I soon got dressed. My leg contracted directly after the blood began to get cool & has been so ever since, but I think it will get straight again whenever I can begin to walk. The breaches were found to be impracticable and if the 3rd & 5th Divisions had not taken the town by escalade, we should have been obliged to have retired for some days. Our division did not get into the town till next morning when it was given up to the troops to plunder, which they did most effectually. I am sorry I was not able to see the world, as I understand they were considered to have been made impregnable, works behind works, every obstacle that could be constructed at the top and behind the breaches, mines &c. Marmont has been plundering Castelo Branco, ransacking & burning Penamacor and destroying every village on their march, robbing & murdering the inhabitants. I hope I shall be recovered in time to join the army on their road to raise the siege of Cadiz, which is now spoken of as the next thing to be undertaken.

Elvas 29 April 1812
Since my last I have not been able to collect any news, except that the French are all off on full tilt towards the Tormes & that our army is

[287] Lieutenant George Black, 52nd Foot.

to refresh itself for a short time. Our division now occupy their old quarters at El Bodon, La Encina, Pastores &c &c. Marmont it is said has retired across the Mondego. I am still lying on my back, though on the outside of my bed with my cloaths on, the slug still in the muscle of the leg which occasions great pain, I have begun poulticing again this morning, to cause suppuration. The Lisbon Gazette is arrived in which I observe I am returned severely wounded, you must pay no attention to it, as it is only a slight wound, though tedious.

Estremoz 6 May 1812
PS to Henry's letter shown previously
Henry has left me room to add a bulletin of myself, rather better today, the leg easier last night, though no sleep, more pain in the ankle than in the wound at present, I sit up at table during the day. I can manage to hobble from one room to another on crutches, the surgeons now say that my ankle is sprained, I cannot say when it was done. Henry looking very well, he commands at present the late Captain Poole's[288] company and has in general commanded the company of any absent captain. We have not at present any general to the division; Vandeleur has not yet recovered the shock of Ciudad Rodrigo. Colonel Barnard at present commands the Division and the 1st Brigade; Major Hunt of ours the 2nd Brigade.

Estremoz 13 May 1812
I have this day changed my billet for a much more comfortable one and can hobble about on my crutches. Henry has a billet on a house about ½ a mile from the town & spends the day with me, his wound is healing as fast as it can. Nixon is doing well, his wounds (on 25 March at Picurina) were gunshot, a ball through his body & the lungs, one in his leg, the other proved only trifling. It is now hoped that he is out of danger. I saw him in the fort after it was in our possession, but as there were a few Frenchmen who had got behind some cover, still firing upon the fort, he was ordered to go with some men to drive them off, which they did, and it was at that time that he was wounded. Hall was wounded in the trenches by the bursting of a shell, a piece of which lacerated his left thigh, but did not injure the bone, the wound is healing fast and he left this place for England yesterday. Ewart was wounded in the first or second discharge from the fort, the ball passed through his sword and lodged in his right arm above the elbow. He immediately left the field without sending word to me, who

288 Captain Clement Poole, 52nd Foot.

was next senior, so that I knew nothing of his having been wounded until all was over. I then collected what men I could to carry off the wounded. Lieutenant Stokes[289] of [the] 95th was the other officer with us. Here were men who were appointed to carry hatchets to cut down the palisades, I saw them precede us, but where they went afterwards I cannot inform you. It was intended that our party should carry the ladders for the others to mount up, but as we did not succeed where they were first planted, and they were carried round to another part of the fort. It is impossible for me to say who mounted first, but our men had declared they would mount them and certainly did with the rest, but all claim it alike. The party consisted of 500 exclusive of Captain Ewart's party. Neither of us are acquainted with Lieutenant Colonel Hardinge.[290]

289 First Lieutenant James Stokes, 52nd Foot.
290 Lieutenant Colonel Henry Hardinge, Portuguese Army.

13. LIEUTENANT FRANCES JOHN DAVIES EXTRACTS FROM LETTERS[291]

Born in 1791, Francis Davies joined the 52nd Foot as an ensign in February 1808 and gained promotion to lieutenant in January 1809. He later exchanged into the 3rd Ceylon Regiment to gain his captaincy in August 1813 and transferred to the 69th Foot at the same rank in February 1814. He saw action on the retreat to Vigo, Sabugal, *Fuentes de Oñoro*, Badajoz (where he was wounded), Salamanca, San Millan, Vitoria and Sorauren. For a brief period (March to July 1811) he served as an extra aide de camp to Major General Dunlop.[292] He transferred into the 1st Foot Guards in April 1815 as a lieutenant and captain (dual rank) and remained with the Grenadier Guards, finally becoming a full general in 1866, although he had retired on half pay in May 1841. He died on 4 December 1874.

Letters written to his mother (his father having died when he was a baby).

Canterbury, 16 March 1808
. . . As to my profession, I like it very much though we have such a deal to do, that we can hardly move out of the barrack square . . . We are obliged to be out by seven to see the men wash their eyes,[293] at a quarter before eight we go to drill for an hour, at ten we go for another hour, at one we go round the messes, at two we see the men wash their eyes. We have to get dressed by half past three, when we drill for

[291] Originally published in the 43rd & 52nd Light Infantry Chronicle. Unfortunately the whereabout of the original letters is not known.

[292] Major General James Dunlop.

[293] The regiment was suffering from an epidemic of ophthalmia.

another hour, and at five we go to Mess; so that the day is completely cut to pieces . . .

Lisbon, September 1808
. . . We are very unlucky, we have had as many pickets and have been laying on the ground as long as the others and after all had never had any fighting . . .

October 1808
. . . Henry[294] perhaps did not tell you that when Sir John Moore first saw the 2nd Battalion after the action, he thanked them all for their exertions, but more particularly Henry and his company, who were the most engaged, he is without exception the most lucky fellow I know . . .

27 January 1809
. . .You of course heard of the engagement which took place on the 16th.[295] I was unluckily sick on board one of the transports at the time, my feet were so sore that I could not walk. That day though we were successful in driving the French back was a most unlucky one for us, as we lost the best friend the regiment ever had[296] . . .

[Francis was posted to the 2nd Battalion and went on the Walcheren Expedition with it. He then remained in England until the battalion went out to Portugal in January 1811, joining the Light Division near Celorico on 25 March, in time to take part in the action at Sabugal.]

8 April 1811
. . . We have at length driven the French out of Portugal, except a few at Almeida, who we expect are by this time driven out. On the 3rd of April the whole army crossed the Coa at & near Sabugal, in the face of about 15,000 French drawn up on the other side; our division crossed about five miles to the right of the town (we were the right of the whole line) we expected great opposition in fording the river, but to our astonishment they only fired a few cannon shot which did not catch a man; they let us gain the first hill without any opposition, when our battalion was sent to the left to guard a gun which kept us out of the action, the rest of the division advanced and were very hotly engaged for about an hour when the French began to retire in great confusion. In the

294 His brother, Captain Thomas Henry Davies, 52nd Foot, transferred to the 1st Foot Guards as a lieutenant and captain in December 1809.

295 The Battle of Corunna.

296 He refers to the death of Sir John Moore.

meantime, the rest of the army were coming up but were not engaged. We had left the gun and were advancing but came up just too late, for as the French retired, there came on a most dreadful shower of rain which drenched us completely and prevented us from following them. We took one gun and about 300 prisoners. It was a most glorious thing for the troops engaged, a whole corps of the French army were licked by the Light Division consisting of about 5,000 men. When it was all over our division went into Sabugal to take a night's rest while the rest of the army watched . . .

[Francis Davies served for a period as aide de camp to Brigadier General James Dunlop in the 5th Division (his uncle), therefore he did not serve with his battalion at *Fuentes de Oñoro* and Ciudad Rodrigo. He returned to the 1st Battalion in time to go into action at Badajoz, where he was wounded in the leg.]

7 April 1812
. . . You of course know that last night we took Badajoz by storm after a most bloody fight, our regiment were the head of the column and suffered dreadfully. Out of 31 officers who went into action, we had 5 killed and 17 wounded. We have not yet ascertained the number of men, but I believe we have lost nearly half the regiment . . .

[He wrote again from his sick bed in hospital at Elvas.]

16 April 1812
. . . I shall not attempt to give you any description of the storming. I shall only tell you what happened to me. We advanced to the ditch under the heaviest fire everybody agreed that ever they had seen. Just as we got into the ditch I was hit, I reeled and fell down, I lay on the ground for a few minutes, when I found myself so well that I got up and went on to the breach, there I found a great crowd, the men could not get on, I stayed there for about ten minutes when I turned so sick with the loss of blood that I layed [sic] down at the bottom of the breach. That soon went off and I went on again, I was in the breach about a quarter of an hour longer, when the men finding that they could not get on, began to fall back. In going back I got a shot through my cap, which I felt graze my hair, another shot carried away the hook which is attached to the belt for fastening up the sword and another hit my scabbard. I lost my cap getting out of the ditch. When I got to the place where the regiment were forming, I found myself so stiff that I made the best of my way to the hospital. The French had fortified the breaches so that it was

impossible to get up and had it not been for the 3rd and 5th Divisions escalading we should not have taken the place . . .

[His wound kept him out of action for two and a half months.]

13 May 1812
. . . Thomas[297] got drunk several times at Lisbon, that I thought little of, but the day I arrived at Elvas from Badajoz, as soon as I got to bed, I sent Thomas out for rice for dinner & my batman with a note to the doctor to let him know where I was. They both staid [sic] out till long after dark and then came home so drunk that they could neither of them stand. The consequence was that I had no dinner, did not see a doctor for 36 hours & was very miserable all night. This I passed over as he was very penitent. The other day he came and asked me for two dollars to get his shoes mended. I gave it him with a great deal of good advice about drinking & he promised me he would never be drunk again. When I came home in the evening I found him laying in the back room so dead drunk that I could not awake him. The next morning I paid him his wages, gave him a little over & discharged him. . .

25 July 1812
. . . You will of course ere this have heard of the great victory of Salamanca, it is by far the finest thing that has happened since Blenheim. We had only three men wounded in following them after the battle, but I saw the whole from a high hill, just like a field day, it certainly was the most beautiful sight in the world, to see our fellows carrying everything before them with the bayonet. I shall not attempt to give you an account of it as you will see a much better one in the gazette . . .

26 September 1812
. . . There is going to be another issue of money, which is always great news for us. The army will then only be paid up to the 24 May . . .

Nave de Haver, 20 November 1812
. . . After all our conquests here we are brought up at the old place. Our retreat has been a very fagging one, as our division have had the rear guard all the way. From Madrid to Salamanca the French did not push us much, so that we always got to our ground before dark and kept our baggage with us the whole way except one night; but from

297 His servant.

Salamanca to this place the weather has been dreadful, rain almost the whole time & for the last three days we did not see our baggage, add to which the rest of the army straggled so much that we never got to our ground till after dark. On the 17th the enemy pushed us so hard that we were obliged to fight for the ground where we were to be bivouacked, which we succeeded in keeping. Our regiment was sent out and skirmished for about two hours pretty sharply. We had one captain killed[298] and two wounded and about twenty-eight men. We have in this year lost six captains killed in action. I suppose John Bull will grumble terribly at our leaving Spain, but notwithstanding our being obliged to evacuate all the country we had conquered, we have done a great deal this year.

Nave de Haver, December 1812
[His hunting for a few days numbered] 3 brace of partridges, 1 brace of hares, 2 couple of woodcocks, 23 snipes . . .

Nave de Haver, 15 December 1812
. . . We have made a partition of boards in our house & a window, and the men are now finishing a chimney. After that we shall have a very comfortable winter quarter. In fact into whatever place they put us, if the walls and roof are but good, we can always make it comfortable; we have quite rebuilt the village.

Nave de Haver, Christmas 1812
. . . There are plenty of girls here and we have dances almost every night. You would be surprised how well they get through the country dances, I am sure the peasant girls in England would not do it half so well. On Christmas day we had a grand dinner. As there were too many of us to dine all in one house we had two parties. To show you that we are not quite so miserable as you may suppose I shall give you a description of our dinner. In the first place hare soup at the top and vermicelli at the bottom, removed by a sirloin of beef and a fillet of veal, with various side dishes as maintenon,[299] cutlets, scotch collops, veal pie &c, & corned beef on the side table & a ham; second course roast fowls, hare and partridges, apple tarts, custards and jelly. We could get no plums, so that we were obliged to go without plum pudding & mince pies . . .

---

298 At the Action of San Munoz, Captain Henry Dawson was killed.

299 As maintainers.

Fuenteguinaldo, 14 January 1813
. . . I suppose you think we get *beastly drunk* every night, but you are quite mistaken, you could hardly dislike it yourself more than I do. I always eat and drink whatever & as much as I feel inclined, but that never leads me to excess . . .

Fuenteguinaldo, 9 February 1813
. . . Last Friday was a great festival here, on that day the women do whatever they please. In the first instance they go to the alcalde (who is the chief magistrate of the village) & take his staff from him & one of them is appointed alcaldessa for the day which is passed in dancing in the square. They made all the officers dance with them; those who to avoid it remained in their houses they brought out by force & they were marched up to the square between two of them, where of course they were obliged to figure away. They did not even spare the general[300] in fact anyone could laugh at the other, being all in the same scrape. It was very good fun . . .

Fuenteguinaldo, 16 February 1813
. . . We amuse ourselves all day in playing at rackets or football, shooting I have quite left off for the present, for besides there being very little game here, what there is, is now getting so wild that it is a great chance if you get one shot a day . . .

Ciudad Rodrigo, March 1813
. . . His Lordship was very affable and danced one dance with the governor's wife. To show you what a game old fellow he is,[301] he rode back to Freineda after the supper (which was pretty late) a distance of at least 16 or 17 miles.

6 April 1813
. . . This night is the anniversary of the taking of Badajoz, all the men have a dollar apiece advanced to them & by way of returning thanks for the narrow escape they had; mean all to get beastly drunk . . .

13 April 1813
. . . We had a long field day this morning, the general always takes us out on Tuesday, which is post day, it is very provoking . . .

---

300 General Vandeleur.

301 Wellington was only 43 years old.

16 May 1813
. . . They have just given us one month's pay (up to January), we are dreadfully off for money, I had not a farthing till I got this month's pay & I owe the best part of it in little bills to the tradesmen of the regiment . . .

6 June 1813
. . . We kept the King's birthday by a march of six leagues in a burning sun . . .

21 June 1813
. . . You will see by the papers the part we had in the action. We were more exposed to cannonade than musketry. The part allotted to us was the storm of one of the principal hills in the French position, which if they had stood as they ought to have done would have been a very tough job, but they were so frightened by the attacks made on their flanks that they did not wait for us . . . Two days before the Battle of Vitoria our division fell in (unexpectedly) with a French division on their march. One brigade of the French had gone by, the First Brigade went after them and skirmished with them; in the meantime our brigade fell on the rear brigade of the enemy, took upwards of three hundred of them, besides killed which was pretty considerable, with barely the loss of a man as they were in such confusion and in such a hurry to get off, that they had not time to stop to fire. We likewise took almost all their baggage, one general was killed and his aide de camp died the next day of his wounds. They were so frightened that another officer and myself without a single man cut off and took a mounted dragoon and four infantrymen. We tossed up for the horse and I won it . . .

14. LIEUTENANT JOHN GURWOOD
LETTER REGARDING TAKING THE CANNON AT SABUGAL

John Gurwood joined the 52nd as an ensign in March 1808 and was promoted to lieutenant in August 1809. He served with the regiment at Vimeiro, the Coa, Busaco, Sabugal and Ciudad Rodrigo, where he led the Forlorn Hope and captured the governor. He was promoted to captain in the Royal African Corps in February 1812, later exchanging to the 9th and later the 10th Light Dragoons. He later fought at Waterloo and eventually worked with the Duke of Wellington on publishing his correspondence.

Regarding the capture of the cannon at Sabugal

I was acting Adjutant at the time and am content to corroborate, from my recollection, the facts stated in the dispatch, to which I was witness, viz, the First Brigade, under Colonel Beckwith,[302] having advanced from the ground on which they had formed in line for attack, drove the enemy and might have taken from them a howitzer; but the brigade was overpowered and driven back, (having lost the howitzer) to the ground of their first formation, when they were joined by the 2nd Brigade, which formed on the flank of the 43rd. The whole then advanced under the command of Colonel Beckwith, assisted by Colonel Mellish[303] of the Staff of the division. The 52nd passed the enclosure and the howitzer was recovered from the enemy, who endeavoured to carry it off. The left centre of the 52nd on its advance came up to

302 Brevet Colonel Thomas Beckwith, 95th Foot.

303 Major Henry Mellish, Sicilian Regiment, Deputy Assistant Adjutant General to the Light Division.

the howitzer, being without horses at some distance in front of the enclosure; but immediately afterwards a fresh column of the enemy, supported by cavalry, charged the two regiments which were broken. The 52nd took refuge in the enclosure, when Captain Dobbs rallied his company and others and lined that part of the wall immediately opposite the howitzer (not a hundred yards from it), the remaining part of the battalion, under Colonel Ross, defending the other side of the enclosure, and in the act of jumping the wall, my horse was shot by one of the enemy's hussars that came up to and passed the gun and both fell inside the enclosure, the horse being killed. By the fire from this part of the wall the enemy were prevented from taking away the howitzer, thus a second time abandoned after its capture. A sharp fire was kept up on the French cavalry, which were driven back or destroyed; and the 52nd again advanced from the enclosure upon the enemy's infantry. Lieutenant O'Hara[304] had cut away a ham which hung from the axle tree of the howitzer.

304 Lieutenant Robert O'Hara, 52nd Foot.

15. LIEUTENANT ROBERT O'HARA
MEMORANDUM ON AFFAIR AT SABUGAL

Robert O'Hara was a lieutenant in the 52nd from December 1807 and he served with the 1/52nd at Vimeiro, the Coa, Busaco, Sabugal and *Fuentes de Oñoro* before becoming a captain in the 88th Foot in April 1811.

Castle Taylor, Ardrahan, Galway, 22 May 1843
I must protest against the statement in Colonel W[illiam] Napier's justification in reply to Colonel Gurwood's annotation in the Dispatches of the Duke of Wellington, relative to the capture of the howitzer at the affair of Sabugal. I was [a] lieutenant of the 1st Battalion, 52nd Regiment, in the company commanded by the present Colonel (then Lieutenant Love) both at the Bridge of Marialva and at Sabugal; and now, after a lapse of so many years, I can recollect facts, I trust quite sufficient to establish the correctness of Colonel Gurwood's statement. We (the 52nd) advanced in line across a ravine towards the enemy in a position on some high ground opposite to us. We had nearly reached the height, when I made a rush with part of [Captain] Dobb's company and took a large sized howitzer. A considerable body of French cavalry were posted below the height and were at first, unobserved by us. We retired to a stone enclosure which fortunately was very close (about 100 yards distant). We then with the remainder of the regiment, which had been under cover, threw a most destructive fire on the enemy, who retired with great loss and abandoned the gun. I beg briefly to add that I cut off the howitzer a ham and some spirits, which I gave to a soldier to take care of and whose name I remember to this day.

16. ENSIGN CHARLES PAGET JOURNAL OF CORUNNA AND WALCHEREN

Charles joined the 52nd Foot as an ensign in February 1808 and became a lieutenant in March 1809. In October 1813 he became a captain in the Royal York Rangers and transferred to a Captain on half pay in the 31st Foot on 25 December 1814. After the war he continued his military career, becoming a captain in the 90th Foot in October 1820, captain half pay in the 2nd Dragoon Guards in August 1821 and came off half pay while still with the 2nd Dragoon Guards in July 1832 and he retired by the sale of his commission on 27 July 1832. He died in August 1849.

He saw action at Vimeiro and Walcheren and then served in the peninsula with the 2nd Battalion August–September 1808; 1st Battalion October 1808–January 1809 and 1st Battalion October–November 1813.

The Corunna journal of Charles Paget has been published previously by Charles Esdaile as *With Moore to Corunna* in 2018, from a copy of his journal owned by his family. However, this is clearly a copy of the original, as the account is incomplete and there are portions that contain clear mistakes in the transcribing.

Strangely, I had come across a second copy of this journal at the National Army Museum (NAM 1985-04-101), where it is recorded as by an unknown soldier of the 52nd. This is clearly another copy of the original Paget journal, whose whereabouts are unfortunately unknown. This second copy is however a much fuller copy, correcting and completing much that is mistaken or missing in the published copy. It also includes his journal for the subsequent Walcheren Expedition, which is missing entirely from the Esdaile version. Having discussed this matter with Charles Esdaile, he has given me his full encouragement in publishing this improved version.

Journal in Portugal & Spain 1808 to 1809

16 July 1808
Embarked at Ramsgate 3 o'clock pm, arrived in the Downs[305] at 4 o'clock next morning.

17 July
Clear weather. Wind west, took my first watch.

18 July
The 43rd Regiment arrived in the Downs, went ashore & to the play in the evening.

19 July
The 9th Regiment 2nd Battalion arrived, 500 strong, dined at Three Kings.[306]

20 July
Orders to be convoyed by the *St Albans* 64,[307] Captain Austen,[308] wind contrary.

21 July
Went to Ramsgate, came back the same evening with my brother John.[309]

22 July
Blue Peter hoisted.[310] Got under weigh at 3 o'clock with twenty-two sail of transports, forming the Light Brigade under General Anstruther.[311]

23 July
Calm & fine, wind south-west. Signal made for all masters to repair on board the *St Albans.* Sealed orders given, which in case of separation, desired us to repair either to Weymouth Downs, Dungeness, Plymouth or Falmouth. Passed Beachy Head, Brighton &c &c.

---

305 The Downs anchorage lay about half a mile off Deal in Kent.

306 The Three Kings public house at Sandwich.

307 HMS *St Albans* of 64 guns was a very old ship, having been built in 1764. She had been converted into a floating battery in 1803, but was refitted as a 64 in 1807.

308 Captain Francis Austen, Royal Navy, brother of the Austen sisters.

309 Lieutenant John Paget, Royal Navy, of HMS *Ville de Paris.*

310 An all-blue flag known as a 'Blue Peter' was used traditionally to signal for sailing.

311 Brigadier General Robert Anstruther commanded a brigade consisting of a battalion of the 20th and 52nd Foot and four companies of the 95th Foot.

24 July
Very little wind, south westerly. Signal made to moor, anchored in 15 fathom water off the Isle of Wight.

25 July
Wind north-west. Rain in the night with lightning. Unmoored, squally. Signal made to tack! Going at 5 knots an hour.

26 July
Wind westerly & squally. Signal made to anchor, brought to, off St Alban's head.[312] Sent ashore 50 opthalmic [ophthalmic] men.[313] Weighed again, anchored in Weymouth roads.

[No further entries made until their arrival in Portugal]

18 August
Observed from the fleet a large fire on shore; which was kept up during the night & another opposite to it; apparently two or three miles distant. Men inspected preparatory to disembarkation; shirts &c in good order & ammunition served out, 60 rounds per man.

19 August
At 10 am, signal hoisted for landing the troops. Orders 'No man to land, except fit for the most active service & those with a shirt & a pair of socks folded in their greatcoats'. Landed in the *St Albans* long boat. Several apples, pears &c given us by the Portuguese. At 3 o'clock formed on the beach & marched up the heights by companies.

Brigade formed by divisions, on an Indian corn field, which was marched over the preceding day by the French, bayonets, pouches &c being found. Greatcoats put on & each man desired to sleep on his firelock in his respective place & officers by their companies. 'Found a striking difference between a comfortable bed & the open fields'. A friar present who blessed our undertakings!

20 August
Under arms at two o'clock this morning. Marched over a very delightful country, covered with myrtles, aloes &c. Saw several cottages which the French had plundered. Weather excessively hot & no water; that in our canteens being thoroughly warm; which obliged

312 A peninsula near Swanage in Devon.
313 An eye inflammation that is easily transferable.

nearly 300 men to quit the ranks.15 miles march! At 5 o'clock came up with Sir A[rthur] W[ellesley]'s army, but with difficulty, some French cavalry having endeavoured to outflank us, which was frustrated by the 40th Regiment being sent to our assistance. No dinner, neither washed. Hutted amongst the furze between the 2nd Battalion 9th & 97th Regiments.

21 August [*Battle of Vimeiro*]
Under arms at 2 o'clock, shots heard from the out picquets, every minute; as it grew later, the firing increased & the picquets were slowly retreating before those of the enemy. Brigade wheeled into line & marched to the top of the height, formed obliquely in the rear of each other. Distinctly perceived the French columns manoeuvring on the opposite hills & their riflemen[314] [skirmishers] (dressed in long white frocks) being detached from them, to the furze & woods. The enemy began a kind of independent fire on our lines, when the general sent to us to 'Remember Egypt'. Several men wounded fell out, Captain Ewart & Lieutenant Bell.[315] Five men of the 97th knocked down by a cannon ball, one killed. Men became impatient to fire, being now in the thick of it; the infantry of the enemy gained ground on the right, when three of our companies were ordered to the valley to oppose them. Reserved our fire till the enemy drew nearer, when it was opened with double fury; after three rounds we observed them running in all directions, upon which three cheers were generally given & the advance sounded, when below the companies extended & each had its separate duty. The 43rd, 50th &c making a most gallant charge on the left; the ground was covered with dying & dead Frenchmen; knapsacks, shoes &c &c. Got a vast deal of silk, cotton, pocket handkerchiefs, snuff box[es] &c from the knapsacks of the French. Plainly perceived their columns forming on the hills, which were absolutely hindered from retreating, from their immense baggage & plunder in their rear; as the prisoners told us after. The retreat sounded & the sight of the dying & the dead was most awful; blood, horses, wheels &c scattered throughout the hills. Our missing, killed & wounded amounted to forty, those of the enemy must have been twenty times that number; returned to our old ground. It was announced throughout the army, that Sir A[rthur] W[ellesley] wished us to pursue the enemy, but that it was not allowed by Sir H[arry] B[urrard][316] who arrived during the engagement.

314 The French skirmishers were not armed with rifles, but muskets.

315 Captain John Ewart and Lieutenant John Bell, 52nd Foot, were wounded.

316 Lieutenant General Sir Harry Burrard superseded Sir Arthur Wellesley in command of the army.

22 August
Flag of truce arrived & an armistice concluded for 48 hours. A false alarm, under arms at daylight. Went to the Convent at Vimiera which was made the hospital & the windmill where the artillery was posted & which was made the receptacle for the wounded soldiers who were lying in all directions, covered with blood & the flies, tormenting them & swarming round them, being without any medical assistance. Orders to take three days provisions.

23 August
At break of day began our march 8 miles through a most hilly country, covered with firs & vineyards. Halted & took our position, which from the kettles & half-dressed victuals we found there, suppose that the French had just quitted. Got some melons, honey &c, I found the boards of a cottage torn up by the French in order to look for plunder.

24 August
Men ordered to wash their shirts & stockings, when I washed myself & flannel waistcoat in a bye ditch. Got a fowl, some Indian corn & a quantity of grapes.

25 August
Sir John Moore arrived this day, inspected the troops; shook hands with me & asked after my friend Colonel Robinson.[317] Two flags of truce arrived & some conditions proposed.

26 August
Dreadful thunderstorm & severe lightning about the camp the whole of the day, so much so that during the night, the rain fell in such torrents that our huts were beat down upon us & the drops were so big, that it was impossible to light fires to dry ourselves & was obliged to go on out-lying picquet with a wet shirt &c &c. Eleven French & Swiss deserters arrived in the camp. Orders for one half of the army to march on the following day.

27 August
Very wet; part of the army marched to Torres Vedras (a part remained under Sir J Moore) a tolerable town & everything very dear. Reports of a convention being agreed upon, but the terms totally unknown.

---

[317] Lieutenant Colonel James Robinson, 91st Foot.

28 August
Walked to Torres Vedras & bought some soap, lemons, needles & thread & two drinks for a dollar & half. Hedges chiefly of myrtle, geranium & aloes; a shocking noise from the Portuguese cars.[318]

29 August
Marched a league beyond Torres Vedras & slept in a cart shed, in some straw. Got a quantity of grapes, apples & Indian corn; weather excessively hot & unpleasant marching from the dust.

30 August
Marched at break of day & toward evening halted in a vineyard; which I left to forage & was lucky enough to get some potatoes, onions & cabbages; which was made up with some beef for the dinner of the mess.

31 August
Halting day; spent in resting, mending my kit & getting fruit.

1 September
Marched 3 leagues farther & hutted at Chillicios [Cheleiros] under a stone wall; got some wine from the village.

2 September
Bathed & wrote letters to England. Lost my canteen.

3, 4 & 5 September
Remained on the heights.

6 September
Encamped on a hill close by the village of Porthiesaco [Portosalvo], having a delightful prospect of Cintra, the rock of Lisbon, Fort St Julien & Belem; with the British fleet at the mouth of the Tagus.

7 September
Walked to Fort St Julien, which is situated west of Lisbon 12 miles. It is famous for its immense strength, being situated on a strong rock which commands the entrance of the Tagus. It has a vast quantity of guns & is defended on the left by a strong mortar battery. The interior is composed of small houses & shops & garrisoned by some Portuguese soldiers & the 3rd Regiment of Buffs. Returning home, lunched with an

318 An abbreviation for carriages or carts.

American & a friar on some fish smothered with oil & pink vinegar & a bottle of bad port wine.[319] Dined with Cameron of the 9th Regiment.[320]

8 September
Bathed in the Tagus, after which we went to a coffee house, somewhat resembling a stable, being out in the open air & the ground covered with straw. Paid 2 dollars for dining on fish & oil.

9 September
Dundas[321] & self, went on board a brig to buy provisions & shoes. Bathed & observed the French flag flying on Fort Belem [Torre de Belém].

10 September
Remained at Porthiesaco [Portosalvo]. Orders to receive a month's pay.

11 September
Went to Belem in a boat, with Mr Maling,[322] which was garrisoned by French soldiers; who behaved in a most respectful manner & said they had not received pay for several days. Went over the fort & afterwards dined at an hotel with two Portuguese officers & returned in camp in the evening.

12 September
Mounted inlying picquet. The Russian fleet sailed out of the Tagus under Russian Colours; our transports arrived; except the *Robert*.

13 September
Went on board the *Robert* & *Alfred* 74.[323] Dined at Belem and walked to Lisbon. The cannon pointed down the streets, in case the Portuguese would rise on the French, who are a soldierlike & respectful set of men.

14 September
Superintended the landing of the baggage. Got my portmanteau to camp & walked to [Buenos] Aires.[324]

---

319 This refers to Douro wine, not the port liquor with brandy added.

320 Presumably Captain Hector Cameron rather than Lieutenant Colonel John Cameron of the 9th Foot.

321 Ensign Thomas Dundas, 52nd Foot.

322 Assistant Surgeon John Maling, 52nd Foot.

323 HMS *Alfred* of 74 guns.

324 A suburb of Lisbon.

15 September
French sailed out of the Tagus. Junot embarked 25,000, 5,000 disabled.

16 September
Walked to Fort St Julien & copied the following lines from the walls of a dungeon, which was written by a Frenchman confined therein.

Le charment objet que j'adore,
Brûle des même jeux, don't je suis
Enflamme, mais je sens, que je
Laime encore, mille fois plus, que je n'en suis aimé

[The charming object that I love
Burns with the same passions
Of which I am inflamed, but I feel
That I still love a thousand times more than I am loved.]

After having reconnoitred the above room, went to the Grand Mortar Battery, drawbridge &c.

17 September
Marched at ¼ before 8 in the morning to Queluz with the 9th [&] 43rd where there was a grand palace,[325] fitted out superbly by Junot. Outlying picquet this night, in a windmill 2 miles from the camp.

18 September
Headquarters 16 September 1810 [1808]

General Order – The following letter has been received by Lieutenant General Sir H[arry] Burrard from Lord Castlereagh, Secretary of State of the Foreign Department.

Downing Street 1 September 1808

To Sir H[arry] Burrard

Sir,
I received by Captain Campbell aide de camp[326] to Lieutenant General Sir A[rthur] W[ellesley] the dispatch of the 24th instant inclosing the report to you from that general of the signal victory obtained by his M[ajesties]

325 The Palace of Queluz.
326 Captain Colin Campbell, 75th Foot, aide de camp to Arthur Wellesley.

forces, under his order, when attacked at Vimiera by the whole French force in Portugal, commanded by General Junot in person. Having laid the same before His Majesty, I am directed by His Majesty to inform you, which signify to Lieutenant General Sir A[rthur] W[ellesley] that the disposition made by him, to receive the enemy & the skill & valour displayed by him in effecting their total defeat, has afforded His Majesty the highest gratification. The conduct of Major General Spencer[327] & of the other generals & officers, who so ably executed the orders they received & displayed so many instances of judgement & valour, is highly honourable to themselves & acceptable to His Majesty.

You will be pleased to communicate the satisfaction His Majesty feels in the deliberate & steady bravery with which his troops distinguished themselves. Reflecting at once the great honour, upon the character & discipline of his army, by which qualities alone, success in war can [not only] prematurely be obtained but hoped for. The delicacy & honourable forbearance, which determined you, though present in the action. Not to interfere with the arrangements previously made by Sir A[rthur] Wellesley & their progress of execution as being assured by His Majesty with approbation. I have the honour to be &c Castlereagh.

Relieved picquet at daybreak & lost ourselves in the fog. Went to Lisbon & bought several trinkets. Got from a Portuguese all Junot's proclamations. Visited the opera in the evening, at our entrance they played God Save the King & the flags of England, Spain & Portugal, were displayed in the centre. 1 dollar entrance. Went to the playhouse & returned to the camp that night.

19 September
Sir A[rthur] W[ellesley] embarked for England. Orders for the tents to be paraded. Went to Queluz & a concert in the evening of the Prince Regent's band.

20 September
Went to Lisbon, dined at Moore's Hotel,[328] went to the play & returned in the morning.

21 September
Received orders to join the 1st Battalion [52nd] encamped near Belem.

327 Major General Brent Spencer.

328 A well-known hotel in Lisbon, Commissary Richard Henegan stayed there too.

22 September
Went to Porthiesaco [Portosalvo] with my servant to get my luggage for the 1st Battalion, but on returning home, lost ourselves in the fog & were obliged to sleep under an old windmill, having got some chocolate & fish at a neighbouring hut.

23 September
Settled my accounts with the Paymaster[329] up to the 24th instant. Tinted some sketches.

24 September
Heard of the 1st Battalion going to Elvas, 200 miles from Alde Galigha [Aldeagallega]. At a great loss how to dispose of my luggage.

25 September
Joined the 1st Battalion which was under orders to march on the 27th. Officers only allowed to carry 25lb [11.3 kg] weight with them & one mule being allowed for a captain & [one for] 2 subalterns. Went to Lisbon with Dundas & bought a brace of pistols & a pair of shoes.

26 September
Rose at 8 o'clock & took a boat for Belem, got completely wet through in attempting to join the camp; it pouring a deluge of rain. Orders to march at 12 o'clock next day, men to carry four day's provisions, one day not cooked & tents to be struck up at 7 in the morning.

27 September
Marched at 12 o'clock, through Buenos Aires, [&] Belem to Lisbon. Embarked in the Portuguese boats but from their ignorance of the river, run aground several times & although it was but 15 miles they had to go, we did not reach it till 8 o'clock at night when we billeted the men; & afterwards got some fish, bacon & a quince to eat; slept with Shedden[330] in a straw bed.

28 September
Marched ¼ before 5 in the morning 24 miles over a vast extensive & hilly country. Bad roads & loose sand, occasioned numbers of our men to fall out of the ranks. Several waggons broke down. Washed my shirt & stockings in a little ditch full of bullrushes & laid me down

---

329 Paymaster Pierce Butler, 2nd Battalion, 52nd.
330 Lieutenant John Shedden, 52nd Foot.

to sleep about 10 o'clock on the bare floor of a house without a roof. Scarcely got a wink of sleep being tormented to death by bugs & fleas & covered with pimples the following morning. I dozed an hour here & then very little or no refreshed, we marched at 6 o'clock in the morning on the 29th.

29 September
Marched twelve miles to a village where there is a handsome palace fitted up for the Prince Regent & contains several beautiful paintings & no less than forty privies. It had been formerly occupied by the French. It was very visible, boards, paintings &c being daubed & written over in the French language.

[He wrote a further note expanding on the 29th.]

We had this day to march 12 miles to a town the name of which I forget. The country continues still flat & sandy, likewise quantities of fruits & shrubs, the bay leaf & fennel, firs innumerable. Halted twice, refreshed ourselves with a clear spring of water, about 2 came to the town & billeted the men in a palace made for the Prince Regent in the hunting season & an amazing beautiful place. The French had hold on it before & the natives made us to understand they had committed more depredations in this part of Portugal than anywhere else, they also tore the earrings from the women's ears & chains & committed their brutal lusts on some of the neighbouring convents. The officers occupied the higher rooms of the palace, of which there is an immense number, likewise upwards of forty necessaries, the 1st of which I have seen in Portugal, I therefore conclude that *princes* merely use them, however I determined also to do them the honour. This evening got some sugar plums & coffee, went to bed on the floor but from no covering & the hardness of the boards could not sleep much. I have now been in Portugal 64 days, 7 of which I have laid down without my clothes.

Indeed I forgot to mention having fallen in with a French deserter & a young man who was taken prisoner on the 21 August, the former enlisted in the 52nd & gave me a sketch of the French service.

He marched from Paris with Junot & the amazing difficulties he since underwent he told me nearly thus, that for 5 successive days they lived on nothing but the small kernel of the cork tree & that Junot when the troops were dying daily harassed by fatigues & ready to starve from marching the Pyrenees & Apennines. He said, 'soldiers push on, there is plenty of wine, bread & eatables in the village before you', they went & not a mouth full to be got, but they marched daily 36 miles at least & the surgeons went to the army in the morning as they were sleeping & felt the pulses of the men to see if dead or alive & that every day they threw away at least sixty souls from hunger & weariness, that those also who lagged on the march were cut down or tortured by Junot & that the difficulty he experienced then, he now had a bed of roses, he also added, Junot undoubtedly would be beheaded when he saw the Emperor Napoleon & the young man Mr Wells who was taken prisoner,[331] was treated well, dined with Junot & was taken by a Frenchman which he took for a Portuguese. Mr Wells is of the engineers.

30 September
Marched at 6 o'clock am over a lovely country with mountains in the distance, halted twice from the heat, the roads getting better, 16 miles march this day to a nice town named Montseora Nova [Montemor-o-Novo], heard that we were not all to go to Elvas but only a party of 200 men, 2 captains, 2 field officers & 6 subalterns & that the rest were all to be billeted in separate houses. About 12 o'clock we got to Montseora Nova [Montemor-o-Novo] & procured two convents for the regiment. The monks were to live in their cells & have their keys, these gentlemen seemed particularly fond of the soldier's wives. Got my billets which was this:

Porta de Sol, Mano et Pei & Sora de la Equartele apartment Tenente Samsson.

I was shown into a room, which though not good, I thought a blessing, it consisted of a good table, bed on the floor, 8 chairs, two pot de chambres, 2 dish[es] & leaden mug, one window &c. My landlady seemed a tolerable good old dame, she had two pretty daughters & some little brats, the old man devilish sulky, however I went to bed after buying 2 fowls for 3 shillings & slept most soundly, luckily no fleas!

31 September
Parade at ¼ before 5 between the two convents & immense deal of duty, 2 captains, 1 to each convent, 4 sub[altern]s besides two of the day &c. 7 men flogged this morning, mostly for drinking & quarrelling who should carry the camp kettle. The party for Elvas chosen out, report says they are to protect the French from this to Galingha Nova [Gallega Nova] and the XXth [20th] Regiment & Queen's [2nd] protect them here. General Paget whose brigade we are in remains here, many flying reports, some say we stay here three days, others the winter &

331 First Lieutenant John Wells, Royal Engineers, was captured at Vimeiro.

some a month; however report is a common liar, as yet I have found it. I will now give a light sketch of the English & Portuguese. The latter are a malicious bad set, they will cry out 'Vivre' &c as you pass but would see you hungry before they'd spare a piece of bread, are excessively stingy, mean & cowardly, that in the dark you may be poniarded in a moment, though they have a respect for an English officer, who were at first looked up to as demi-Gods, especially an English sailor, who they suppose almost invincible. They like dress & finery much and the first thing they demand is your rank. An English officer once in Lisbon was nearly stabbed by a Portuguese, but from our men being there, the natives nearly killed him. Often have I been hungry & begged a piece of bread for myself or a man & the Portuguese will not give it; one house out of ten on an average being full of lice, these houses were chiefly lath & plaster, very little cultivation & their pots are thrown out in the open street which is so offensive in Lisbon streets, a pocket handkerchief is absolutely necessary. In a word, the nation has as well as I can justly judge, all the bad qualities of Spain without a single good one. The latter are generous & brave; the former excessively stingy & cowardly. A shell at the battle I saw burst over a troop of cavalry's head & they immediately, shameful to say for England's allies turned their backs, however so it is & was it not for the French crossing Spain to enter this country, they must & would have Portugal, as the inhabitants of this country would be as happy with the French as us. Was it not for their priests who rule.

1 October
Mounted picquet this day, stayed at the convent in an old dirty cell, got bit terribly by the vermin, mostly fleas &c.

2 October
The French marched in here from Elvas, escorted by the 2nd Queens, they were a very nippish set, men seemingly much fatigued & ready to sell everything. A very handsome double barrelled fowling piece was sold for 20 dollars, Horses &c equally cheap. Our men escorted them three miles from Montemor-o-Novo where they encamped this night in a wood of fir trees,

3 October
Marched at 3 o'clock this morning; 12 miles which is equal to 3 Portuguese leagues, country hilly & many men fell out from the heat. Got billeted this night in a tolerable house, my landlord was very obliging & had 3 beautiful daughters who amused me much. Spoke to

Mr Hutchinson,[332] found myself much fatigued & very weak, alas! The Lisbon beauties, what tricks do they play upon us.

4 October
Marched at three o'clock this day, a march of 24 miles, which at this time I was not well calculated to perform, halted two hours on the road & arrived at Estremoz about 2 o'clock, where I got two bad billets & luckily got a third, much better, my landlord consisted of a grocer & an old hag of a landlady. I was shown up to a garret, 6 chairs a table & an image which they worshipped, it held in its hands roses & a little child meant I suppose to represent our blessed saviour, underneath was a small waxen figure to represent him in swaddling clothes, these & several other images in a large glass case which the family daily adored, thus was I profaned, the 2nd commandment in all the smaller houses of Portugal, either a cross or a picture is adored, in higher families a man nailed to a wooden cross. Oh! The superstition & ignorance of these poor souls, it is to be allotted to the monks who keep them in their state of ignorance.

5 October
Not being well rested myself this day.

6 October
Reduced to the necessity of speaking to the surgeon & writing different things.

7 October
Went out with my pistols, found them to be very bad ones. Mounted picquet this night at the convent, the monks behaved very civil & gave me sweetmeats &c.

8 October
Went off picquet this evening. Convents all clean & in good order, went to see the nunnery & had a peep of your old lady abbess, way of speaking most curious & sending messages. Slept in my new lodgings & got sadly bit by the fleas.

9 October
Was late for Divine Service today, a mess formed by the officers of the regiment. Weather rather cold, so clear & fine. Various reports relating

332 Surgeon Scroop Hutchinson, 52nd Foot.

to Spain & the shameful capitulation of the British general went to see the Castle of Estremoz in which is an amazing quantity of old arms taken in the battles with the French.

10 October Monday
I forgot yesterday to mention, the Portuguese ceremony of the Host. They got the permission of General Paget[333] to have 200 men, 6 subalterns & 2 captains to attend, then procession called *Te Deum*, 'twas something like the Lisbon one, only not so grand. It passed the monastery at 3 o'clock consisting of about 60 men with candles 5 feet high, in large purple habits, after was an image bearing a cross, as large as life, supported by 6 or 8 monks each having golden candlestick & candles. I could not make the people understand I wished to know who this image was, but have since heard it was a great Portuguese general who saved his country. As it proceeded, every person knelt & prayed before it; after this followed quantities of men, women & children with crosses &c & then came the Host, which is a kind of wafer shut up in a little box, covered by a golden canopy & supported by friars. To this mighty wafer all was adoration & respect, the procession staid [sic] out an hour & stopt Lieutenant Major General Paget's who availed it by taking a side. Heard of Sir J[ohn] M[oore] having command of the whole army in Portugal. Orders for the regiment to be well stocked with shoes & march 64 miles per week to keep them in practise.

11 October
The regiment marched 6 leagues this morning which is equal to 24 miles for practise. Staid at home this day writing &c as letters for England were ordered to be sent to the Orderly Room at the convent of the right wing.

12 October
The regiment ordered to be inspected by General Paget tomorrow, orders that the 97th Regiment should be attached to the Reserve till further orders. His Majesty has been pleased to make several promotions & Captain Hunt[334] to be major of the 2nd Battalion. Orders also that the regiments will send immediately returns of their want of ammunition. Lieutenant Laye[335] of the 1st Battalion was tried by a General Court Martial at Queluz for disobedience to his captain. The court were of opinion that the prisoner was Not Guilty & so therefore

333 Lieutenant General Edward Paget.
334 Captain John Hunt was made a major.
335 Lieutenant Thomas Laye resigned his commission in 1810.

honourably acquit him. Two soldiers sentenced to be hung for stealing a crucifix & two watches out of the house of Tailus Principe, men of the 9th [Foot] 2nd Battalion. Spirits to be served out to the men in wet weather. Officers to receive 200 days bat & forage money from the Deputy Commissary General at Barreiro. Lieutenant General Sir H[arry] Burrard having received His Majesty's command to place a large part of the Army in Portugal under the orders of Lieutenant General Sir J[ohn] Moore to be employed on a separate service. The following regiments compose the corps to be so employed and they are hereby directed to receive their orders from Lieutenant General Sir J Moore accordingly.

18th Light Dragoons, 3rd [Hussars] KGL,

1st Battalion 4th, 5th, 2 Staff Corps, 6th, 9th 20th, 28th, 32nd, 36th, 38th, 40th, 42nd, 43rd, 1st Battalion 52nd, 2nd Battalion 52nd, 60th, 71st, 79th, 91st, 92nd, 1st Battalion 95th, 2nd Battalion 95th, 1st Battalion KGL, 2nd Battalion KGL. These are divided into their respective brigades, we again compose General Anstruther's. Officers desired to furnish themselves with horses for baggage.

13 October

Fired my pistols today & hit once at six paces distance, out of 24 times. Weather as usual, remarkably cool & fine; inspected by General Paget at 4 o'clock this evening, went & talked to my old friends the nuns & took three sketches. The party from Galingha [Gallega] Nova arrived yesterday after having marched it in the same number of days as they before accomplished it.

14 October

General Orders

From the General Orders of the 11th instant,

The commanding officers cannot permit any woman with child, that hath a child, or that is not stout & equal to fatigue to accompany the regiment in the long march which is about to take place & who he strongly recommends the rest of the women to accept of the present opportunity of returning to England, in the manner of their proceeding to Lisbon & support there till a good opportunity offers of their going to England, will be hereafter pointed out. On their arrival in England they will receive their usual allowance to carry them to their respective homes. The commanding officer will therefore send in by tattoo this evening the names of those who remain behind & of those who do accompany the regiment. Companies to be inspected by the commanding officer for immediate & active service tomorrow at 1 o'clock. Men to be completed in white gaiters. Spent the whole of this day in writing to England. Weather very fine & cool.

15 October
Spent the whole of this day in lying in things for our ensuing campaign & long marches, got some flannel &c. Orders for the men to be to be supplied with gaiters and shoes. Orders to parade to muster for Divine Service.

16 October Sunday.
Had Divine Service in the morning. Wrote to England & took a walk to an adjoining hut, found myself not being well from a flux. Three Portuguese dined at the mess. Orders for me to mount picket tomorrow evening, at the right convent.

17 October
Staid on picket at the right convent all night & day, messes &c all regular.

18 October
Came of picket this day. Orders at Estremoz. As the division under the orders of Major General Paget is likely to move on at the shortest notice, commanding officers of corps are to pay the strictest attention to the following points which are found in the General Orders of the 9th & 11th instant and the Returns called for, are to be sent in with the least possible delay. The Regimental Surgeons have the same Returns of the sick with the regiments and also of those which we left in other quarters & last must be taken on the march, of the regiments of such convalescent men, that are not perfect to undertake a long march & not permitted to attend the regiments, but to remain in a place which will hereafter be pointed out for the hospital of the division, when a report will also be formed for the baggage, which regiments may find it necessary to leave behind. Returns of the horses & mules actually in possession of officers is also to be sent in & immediate steps are to be taken to provide any deficiency to the number stated in the General Orders of the 11th instant. Returns of the names of women & children who are to remain with the heavy baggage to be sent in for the purpose of being transmitted to the Adjutant General's Office in Lisbon & commanding officers are particularly recommended to impress in the minds of married soldiers, that the division in this part of Portugal are

particularly liable to pass through places where the women will be exposed to the greatest hardships at this advanced season of the year.

Regimental Orders, Mr Hutchinson is to send in as soon as possible, the Returns called for in the Divisional Order of this day. Commanding officer calls the attention of the married men to that part of the Divisional Orders of this day relative to the hardships their wives are likely to be exposed to on the march & as it is utterly impossible to have a man with them, or render them any assistance in regard to their falling, such to be recommended their strongly leaving, such as are not able to undergo the greatest fatigue behind. Powder horns to be given in with a report of the number. Got myself preparatory to marching, made a flannel waistcoat & long flannel drawers.

19 October
Procured soap, ink & all necessaries for our ensuing campaign. The weather continues here remarkably fine; got very thick with my landlord & lady. The former informed me we marched to Burgos, the distance of 480 miles from this part of Portugal & that the French army were at Pamplona. A lady staying in my billet & has been & still is excessively kind to me, her intrigues were very vicious I believe, she begged me to write to her often & gave me the following address viz Donna Anna Gertrudez Placida, she was a middle aged lass & up to romps as well as our English belles. General Paget sent his aide de camp to ask me to dinner. Dined with him at 8 o'clock. Sat till 10, drinking fine old port & claret, had a most excellent dinner.

20 October
Took a sketch of a neighbouring convent & wrote to Old England; weather remarkably fine. Colonel Lopez of the Spanish army arrived, he gives a very favourable account of matters in that country & likewise of the people intending to rid the country of French by Xmas.

21 October
Very long orders given out again concerning the women & the great hardships they will be subject to during the ensuing march; a subaltern officer left behind to take charge of them. Some reports of Sir D[avid] Baird[336] having landed. All my sketches lost by Mrs Walker.

22 October
Bought a stock of oilskin & some grog preparatory to our next campaign, saw also an English newspaper, not any news of consequence.

336 Lieutenant General Sir David Baird landed with reinforcements at Corunna.

23 October Sunday
Had a very gay party of ladies in my house this night viz Donna, Marianna, Beta, Valente the prettiest of the set & many others. Took a walk with Dobbs[337] to bathe & eat figs.

24 October
Sent off my luggage to the store by Mr Hair & a letter to England by Mrs Walker, also went out a shooting, but did not see anything except larks & other birds.

25 October
The German Rifle Corps arrived here & most of the army in motion except ourselves, went out skirmishing this morning, saw a hare & other game. My servant taken ill & not able to do anything. Orders that no officer is on any account to have a soldier for a batman, but a native of the country for whom rations will be drawn at a dollar per week. Spent this day in firing with my pistols, hit 3 times out of 20 at 6 paces distant. The following are some orders issued by Major General Paget to the soldiers under his command at Estremoz on the 26th.

Advanced orders.

Major General Paget is most happy to inform the advanced corps of the army, that the moment is arrived at which their efforts are to commence between them & the enemy. It is a very considerable extent of country, in many parts mountainous, rugged & very thinly inhabited. Under such circumstances considerable difficulties are likely to occur in the movement of a column, but he is well persuaded that it is only necessary to know, these must be overcome before the enemy can be conquered to inspire a degree of exertion, which must set all difficulties and hardships at defiance. Every arrangement that can be made for the supply of the troops on the march & for the conveyance of any men who may be sick shall be made, but still they must be prepared to expect serious deprivations. From the nature of the service in which we are engaged & which may prevent the possibility of leaving any of the regimental surgeons behind & it will become necessary to leave any men who from sickness are unable to proceed on the march with their battalions in charge of the magistrates & of such medical gentlemen as the country will afford. Upon this head however, commanding officers of corps have been furnished with the following instructions,

No. 1 As no doubt can be entertained that nine cases out of ten of sickness, arise from the immoderate use of the bad wine in this country,

337 Captain Joseph Dobbs, 52nd Foot.

soldiers are exhorted, as they value their health, as they value their honour, as they must feel ambition to be present with their battalions at the approaching conflict with the enemy, as they must feel reluctance at being left to the care of strangers, to abstain from the use of the most pernicious liquor.

No. 2 The advance corps will be prepared to march by battalions according to routes which will be sent to them.

No. 3 In order to have one day's provisions always in advance, the corps will march with 1 days biscuits & salt meat cooked for the 1st day's march, the provisions for the second day will be issued & cooked, the men eating the soup, but preserving the bread & meat for the following day & so on successively & commanding officers are desired most particularly to see this arrangement systematically established.

No. 4 Commanding officers to be very careful to procure good guides, they may be paid 400 reys per day.

No. 5 The corps are to march regularly at daybreak & when the moon will permit even before daybreak, as it is an object of the first importance to the comfort & convenience of the troops, to get the march over early in the day. It is recommended to halt for a few minutes, every 1 or 2 hours.

No. 6 An officer from each battalion is always to be one day forward with the returns of his corps, to make every exertion to have the supply in readiness for his battalion.

[No. 7 & 8 not in the orders]

No. 9 The sick of the several battalions are to be removed to Elvas according to routes which will be sent for them, they will be accompanied by an assistant Surgeon of each corps, with a requisite number of nurses selected from men least able to endure the fatigues of a long march. A month's subsistence is to be sent with the men, the Assistant Surgeon having delivered over the sick to the care of the medical officer appointed to receive them, will return to Estremoz & report their arrival to the Assistant Adjutant General.

No. 10 An officer from each battalion of Brigadier General Alten's brigade, with the pioneers & their tools with the mules & entrenching tools & a good sergeant, 2 corporals & 10 privates, good labourers of each battalion will repair to Estremoz & report their arrival to the Assistant Adjutant General, they are to march so as to arrive at Estremoz by the 29th instant. The mules & entrenching tools of the 52nd & 95th & 20th Regiments with similar parties are to be held in readiness to move when called upon.

No. 11 Paymasters to assemble at Estremoz to pay & receive officers 166 days bat & forage money & pay to the 24th of November, not being in want of immediate cash are requested to take bills in lieu of it.

Regimental Order. Major General Paget has so fully explained himself in the foregoing orders, that the commanding officer has only to call the attention of the officers & men to them.

Heard of Sir David Baird having landed & with him the 6th Regiment, wrote to my old friend Lasmbrecht.[338] Saw an English paper of the 25 September & heard of Sir J Saumarez's[339] action in the Baltic. The Army of Spain to compose 30,000 men. Intelligence from the Spaniards of the French receiving reinforcements of artillery & cavalry.

27 October
Nothing material this day.

28 October
My birthday. An English soldier stabbed by a Portuguese. Booth[340] of Captain Dobb's company.

G[eneral] Order of Sir John Moore
The commander of the forces, trusts that the troops on their entry in Spain will feel with him how much it is for their honour & their advantage to maintain the high opinion & cherish the good will with which that brave & high spirited people entertain towards the British nation. The troops upon the march will generally be quartered on the inhabitants. The Spaniards are a brave & orderly people, extremely sober, but generous & warm in their temper & easily offended by any assault or disrespect that is offered to them. They are grateful to the English & will receive the troops with kindness & cordiality, this the general hopes will be met with an equal kindness on the part of the soldiers & that they will endeavour to accommodate themselves to their manners, be orderly in their quarters & not stained by acts of intemperance. A people worthy of their attachment & whose efforts they are come to support in the most glorious of causes, to free them from French bondage & to establish in this nation, liberty & independence. Upon entering Spain as a compliment to the Spanish nation, the army

338 Ensign John Lambrecht, 66th Foot.
339 Admiral James Saumarez.
340 It presumably was not a serious stabbing as there is no record in the Regimental Casualty Returns.

will wear red cockades in addition to their own. Cockades are ordered for this purpose for the non-commissioned officers & privates & will be sent from Madrid, but in the meantime, the officers are requested to provide themselves & put them on when they pass the frontiers. H Clinton, Adjutant General[341] of the troops for Spain.

Dined at the mess & found part of my rum stolen, reports of our marching on Sunday. Did not keep the 28th.[342]

29 October

Passed through Estremoz. This day the public procession of Santa Isabella, a very paltry thing, all the rest alike. Orders by Lieutenant General Hope[343] to the troops. The pioneers with parties & entrenching tools of the 52nd, 1st & 2nd Regiments KGL will march tomorrow at 6 o'clock under charge of the senior subaltern officer to Monforte & there report themselves to Lieutenant Colonel Backworth [Beckwith] 95th Regiment,[344] these parties are to march with two day's provisions for the thirtieth & thirty first & forage of the mules for the same period.

No. 2 The 52nd Light will be in readiness to march at 6 o'clock on Monday morning, with two day's provisions. Much punishment this day, several corporals & privates having been tried.

30th October Sunday

Mounted picket this day, prepared myself for the march tomorrow, the following is a copy from a Portuguese officer of our supposed routes viz, Itineraire pour la marche d'Elvas jusqu'a Baionne.

Estremoz	Lieus [leagues]	
A'	Monforte	4
+	A Portalegre	4
1	A Castelo de Vide	2
0	A' Membrio	6
1	A'Alcantara	5
1	A Sorea Maior	3
0	A Moraleja	4
0	A [Fuente]Guinaldo	8
+	A Ciudad Rodrigo	4
0	A Sant Esprit [Sancti Spiritus]	3

341 Brevet Colonel Henry Clinton, 1st Foot Guards, was adjutant general.

342 His birthday was not celebrated.

343 Lieutenant General Sir John Hope.

344 Lieutenant Colonel Thomas Beck with 95th Foot.

0	A Sao Munoz [San Muñoz]	4
0	A Calzada de Don Diego	5
+	A Salamanca	4
0	A Babela Fuente [Fuentelapena]	4
0	A Tordesillas de la Ordur	5
1	Larnovadel Rey	3
1	Pordosillas	3
+	Valladolid	5
0	Duenas	6
0	Torquemada	4
0	Bilho Diego	4
0	Selhada	4
+	Burgos	4
0	Monasterio	4
1	Briviesca	3
0	Pancorvo	4
+	Miranda d' Ebro	3
+	Vitoria	5
1	Mondragon	5
1	Villa Franca	7
1	Tolosa	3
1	Hernani	3
0	Yrun [Irun]	4
+	Baionne [Bayonne]	6

31 October, Monday
Did not march this day according to the orders, the route not having arrived, I therefore spent it in procuring rum &c for a campaign. Orders to march tomorrow at 6 o'clock, warning bugle to sound at ½ past five.

1 November
At length the long wished for day is come. Marched from old Estremoz at 6 o'clock through an amazing number of boggy lanes & bye places, 4½ leagues. Light rains during the beginning of the day; arrived at Monforte & all got most shocking billets, all but two officers, this is a nasty town. Spent my time here in hearing the nuns singing & buying from them sweetmeats, in the convent there is 57, 14 out of which had taken the veil; several of them elegant & pretty girls, seemingly poor souls, heartbroken to get out, their forehead dress is most curious.

2 November
Halted this day at Monforte, which I spent in admiring the fine blue distance & the surrounding mountains. Found the master of the band & another man had deserted. Took up two men of the 60th.

3 November
Marched at 6 o'clock, 2 leagues for Arronches over a delightful country, met with a few swamps & stoppages in the road; I was greatly amused the whole of this day's march in admiring the distant & magnificent blue mountains, which divide Spain from Portugal each topping the clouds & the wonderful extent & distance of Spain far surpassed anything I ever in my life beheld. I attempted to sketch it, but found my pencil disgrace itself. Arronches is an excessive neat town and is very prettily situated; it is eight leagues from Estremoz. It has two good bridges on each side and is a fortified town. I got an excellent billet, but being on the main road deprived me of walking and making those observations I would have wished.

4 November
Marched from Arronches at 6 in the morning, a march of five leagues to Albuquerque. We passed the frontier this day which is divided from Spain by a small rivulet. The fine distant blue mountains surpassed anything I ever before beheld. Three leagues out of five entirely passes under and over mountains, amazing valleys and descents. We arrived in Spain about twelve o'clock and difference experienced was much; the language totally different in some degree like German and Dutch; the people in all our opinions excessively uncivil and disobliging (perhaps this is an erroneous opinion). We saw Albuquerque after much rain and wet about two o'clock situated on an amazing high rock commanding a view not to be expressed, mountains turning upon mountains & exceeding large vallies [sic], rocky & craggy; at 3 marched into Albuquerque & went to the officer's guard, which is a stable for mules & asses. Relieved guard at ½ past 5 o'clock & did not get into my billet till 8 or 9 o'clock, the people shutting their doors in our faces; such was our reception in the first Spanish town, I sincerely hope 'twill not continue. At last after going to the Juiz de Fora & procuring a gentleman called an Alquatil[Alcalde] I made my landlord the Spaniard open the door & gave me a tolerable bed, full of bacon & garlic, his name was Don Manoel; met [Lieutenant] Love in the street, who asked me to a ball. Danced till 12 o'clock & for the first time saw the Spanish ladies dance a fandango to the castanets. The ladies are excessive fine women & wear their hair (which is amazing long)

hung over their left eye. Their dancing appeared to me excessive rude, taking the man & hugging them round the waist. The bread is very good & white here, eggs hard to be got 2½d each, goat's milk equally dear. I did not observe much difference in the Portuguese & the Spaniards, the latter seem to have a more worthy idea of themselves, not touching their hats to English officers, though civil & cool etc, not appearing to me so generous as I have heard, easily offended I am sure they are, I can conceive jealous. I must say their unanimity is great, for they are determined to make sure of conquest; however, I can assert the English did not meet with that cordiality from the Spanish nation that they expected, however true it is; a John Bull will never find himself at home, he being some centuries more enlightened than other nations. This is a filthy town, but the people somewhat cleaner than the Portuguese, they live chiefly on pork, garlic & vegetables, things to us utterly impossible to swallow! Reports of a battle having been fought in which the enemy lost 18,000 men & the Spaniards 10,000.

5 November
Rested here this day & took a sketch of the castle & the adjoining & most beautiful country, likewise got rum to keep me up during tomorrow. As we had orders to march then, 6 leagues or 30 miles & the weather still continues wet & dreary; likewise somewhat cold.

6 November, Saturday
Halted this day at Alberquerque, took a sketch of the adjoining country & the castle which is situated on an amazing high rock, surrounded by an almost endless valley, the skirts of which were bordered by black distant mountains over which boars & wolves are constantly hunted, as a friend of my patrona brought in one. There was no rain this day; I tried to purchase some worsted stockings & other necessaries but found nothing but aguardiente in the town. Was alarmed at night from a Spaniard coming into my room, about some of the soldiers. Orders that the men were to keep in the ensuing days march to Almeida, close to their battlements as most parts was a total wilderness & roads not to be found & that there would be halts made for them to answer the calls of nature.

7 November
Marched at 6 o'clock this morning 7 leagues to Aliseda over a dreadful mountainous country, covered with heath in most parts & also lavender & myrtle, although the prettiness of the country did not make amends for the bad roads which was one sheet of rock in most

parts up to our knees in yellow water, resembling terra firma for above 2 leagues. We had not marched an hour from the latter town but it poured a deluge of rain & thunders, we were all wet as if walking through rivers, I supped constantly of rum but the cold & chill still permeated. We reached Aliseda about 6 in the evening where without dinner or anything else I turned into a tolerable bed, after having been dripping the whole of the day. Myself and Calvert[345] slept together; in the morning we were beastly dirty & not a clean thing or overcoat to change, my shoes also in a bad state.

8 November

Marched from Aliseda at 6 this morning 4 leagues to Brosus [Brozas]. Alas! As usual having deluges of water & wet to the skin, not a change & my rum all given to my servant the preceding night. Our march was mostly over deserted & massy mountains having before us a most delightful extent of country, which before I never before saw equalled. Reached Brosus [Brozas] at 2 o'clock & dried myself by a few embers, at the house of Antonio Ponare a monk. I had to thank God for the blessings of health, a thing which many of my brother officers were destitute of. Our landlord (the capuchin) told us, there had been a great battle between the French & the Spaniards & that the event was not known. This does not appear favourable and that couriers were arriving every day to quicken our marches, expected to halt three days at Alcantara & see the 20th Regiment. The regiment now sometimes marched half one way & half another. Yesterday two companies were lost by their guide & fell in with the other & again during the hard rain, much thunder this night & rain.

9 November

Marched from Brosus [Brozas] to Alcantara, 3 leagues which is a tolerable town & very well fortified, the back part is surrounded by mountains & has several convents in it; much rain on the march & wet through again as we all waded through a river up to our knees & more, the branch of the Tagus, I had now nothing to change & all dirty; dried myself by the fire & got a tolerable billet at the house of Antonio Valerio, the people were very civil & the townsmen glad to see us. Instead of staying here 3 days (stayed one) & another long march to have without a single halting day, till our arrival at Salamanca. Also heard here of a battle having been fought, evening not known, but of the Spaniards having 300,000 men & the French 50,000 only, but the former mostly rabble.[346]

---

345 Lieutenant Felix Calvert, 52nd Foot.

346 One of many false rumours.

The country was this day also covered with lavender; had no breakfast, till 1 o'clock & then got some chocolate. After having got a few things to rights & intending the next day, I went thank God to a good bed, not without wishing myself once more in that incomparable country Old England.

10 November
Intended to walk & sketch the Tagus which runs through his place (Alcantara) but from the bad state of my clothes was obliged to get a taylor [sic] to mend them & my cap. Some row last night with our men & the Spaniards.

Alcantara is an excessive old place, strongly fortified & a fine bridge near it, also an excessive high hill at the back. Orders to march tomorrow. Also bit in the most shocking manner by the mosquitoes &c, my face covered with bad pimples. Reduced to the necessity of leaving some of my luggage behind, not being able to carry it in a neat little box &c.

11 November
Marched at 6 o'clock this morning to Zarza [la] Mayor 3 leagues; the Bridge of Alcantara & excessively beautiful & would have made a fine drawing, but being obliged to buy worsted stockings, gloves & neckcloth, hindered me from taking it. The road is here excessively rocky & hilly, covered mostly the commons with lavender & myrtle. You have on this march a vast extent of country to view before you, mountains peeping above the horizon & tipping their heads on the clouds, indeed every day seems to increase the beauties of nature. The Spaniards begin to get more kind every day. Arrived at ½ past 11 at Zarza [la] Mayor & got tolerable billets, I took a sketch of it & the adjoining country. Found my feet begin to blister much. Saw several men who wore badges for thrashing us at Ferrol & also several Spaniards who spoke about the shameful capitulation. My landlord's name is Antonio Galado; indeed here all Antonios.

12 November
Marched at 6 o'clock through a deserted country, covered with corks & olives. We saw several eagles in the way; crossed the Tagus & waded up to our knees; at 12 arrived at Moraleja 4 leagues from our last place. The country [on] this march is beautiful, I mean the distance, for our way was all descent. Got a tolerable good billet at the house of Luando le Torre, she is a pretty girl & fine hair. Given me by a Spanish officer a Gazette of Madrid [dated] the 8 November, no news. Lost myself this night & was conducted home by a monk. Orders to march at

7. Moraleja is a pretty little villa[ge]. The Gata runs through it & there is fishing & a good bridge.

13 November
Marched at 7 this day; road at the beginning tolerably fair & country flattish, corks, olives & orange trees. The latter end, the roads craggy & mountainous. Arrived at nine o'clock at Perallis [Perales del Puerto] two leagues from the last; it is a dirty beastly hole, very small, though a good market of chestnuts, turnips, potatoes & such like, the Spaniards as well as the Portuguese live chiefly on vegetables. Orders for the right wing to march tomorrow & the left to remain here. Saw Colonel Offeney[347] here, who told me our next place was much worse than this & the roads dreadful. Got some cheese here from my dame & wet through getting some soldiers a lodging, 13 of them, the town being excessively small & a very few decent pigsties, the people full as bad.

14 November
Half of the regiment marched this morning & the other half remained. It rained much in the morning, we marched at 6. The road consists of mountains & woods, the beginning for a league tolerably fair, the remaining 3 entirely mire & rock, so that no artillery or cavalry whatever could pass. The sight was beautiful & for 2 or 3 leagues we saw the clouds floating under our feet in the most extensive & beautiful vallies [sic]. We passed two large woods entirely of oak & waded a river which I believe is the Tagus, not being able to get information. At 12 arrived at Penapardur [Penaparda], a very filthy brutal hole, was quartered on a peasant & he & self slept in the same room, call it pigstie, it is more applicable. Heard of the murder of the corregidor of Ciudad Rodrigo for being in favour of the French, supposed at least to be so. Much rain all this day. The Spaniards are now tolerably kind to us, though for my part I do not see their generosity. The more I see of them, the more I adore & praise, that country England, which no other in the world ever equalled.

15 November
Marched at 7 o'clock this morning to [Fuente]guinaldo 3 leagues. The road is tolerably good, running through a forest the whole way, it consists entirely of oaks & extends an immense way on all sides. We waded a river up to our loins & now found ourselves in the province of Old Castile, which is reckoned the most rich part of Spain. Got a

347 Lieutenant Colonel Wilhelm Offeney, 2nd Light Battalion KGL.

good billet here which Colonel Ross of the 20th[348] had quitted on the 13th. Reported our being 9 days behind the rest of the army through a mistake of General Hope's. [Fuente]guinaldo is a very decent little place, it stands on a hill, has a good church & commands a view of the almost never-ending forest; heard of Sir J Moore having been at Ciudad Rodrigo. Orders to halt here tomorrow for refitting.

16 November
Got the taylor [sic] to make me a pair of trowsers & a cover of oilskin for my cap, intended to get my jacket turned but had not time. Went out shooting with a Spanish peasant, saw some birds but could not get near them, was chased by a great dog home. Had a running match in the evening in the beautiful green on the right of the village where there is a chapel surrounded on all sides by crosses. Order to march tomorrow.

17 November
Marched at 7 o'clock to Ciudad Rodrigo, the capital city of Old Castile, 4 leagues excellent road from [Fuente]guinaldo. At 12 arrived at Ciudad Rodrigo & found the 20th Regiment there, who had orders to march the next day; looked out for Champigny[349] but did not find him. Heard of the French being reinforced by 60,000 men & these being at Burgos. Ciudad Rodrigo is a large town situated on the banks of a pretty river, over which there is a good bridge. It has a very neat fortification & plenty of tolerable shops; in fact I admire more than anything I have yet seen. Had a deal of trouble in getting my billets 6 out of which was disappointed in. Foster of our company[350] died in the convent here, where the men were billeted; heard Sir J[ohn] M[oore] has just left this.

18 November
Halted this day at Ciudad Rodrigo. The taylors [sic] all employed & could not get them. Foster buried at 3 o'clock. Got a knife blade & some lead for bullets, also a basin of goat's milk for breakfast. A little rain this day. Some of the 95th Rifles arrived this day, a very fine set of men. Orders to march tomorrow & to perform our march to Salamanca in 3 days, instead of four as was intended, from this something appears odd. Intended to sketch this town but the weather & my duty prevented me, as it always does in a soldier's life. My billet at last a d[amne]d bad one, stinking shockingly & my hostess weeping all day because her *patrona* was gone to Salamanca to procure food for the troops.

348 Lieutenant Colonel Robert Ross, 20th Foot.
349 Lieutenant Forbes Champagne, 20th Foot.
350 Private Joseph Foster died on 17 November 1808 at Salamanca.

19 November

Was on the baggage guard this day & was obliged to wait an hour behind the regiment for the hospital cars. At last started though with bad bullocks, the road at first is good but for a league or upwards afterwards it is very bad & from the incessant rain the whole of the day it was the greatest hardship to keep up & together but wandering on a march of 30 miles this day to a place called San Munoz with a mist before our eyes not able to see a bit & having no guide was puzzled to death to find the road. Towards 3 or 4 o'clock endeavoured to get bullocks at a village we passed but none to be met with. I therefore got Mr Maling to go forward. I was in a dreadful peril here, having given all my rum away to keep the wet from a soldier's wife. I had however the good fortune to get a little ham & bread here for a pisetta [peseta] though half-done it was good. General Paget passed the cars at the village, the entrance of which is a perfect bowling green. We started in ½ an hour with bullocks procured by Dr Maling but growing dark & 7 o'clock at night could not find our road, but acted entirely to chance & tracks of the commissaries cars, we saw a light & believed it to be the wished for town, but on approaching it found it to be peasants amusing themselves. I was in the rear now, my corporal acting guide, when I heard a dreadful crash, which was a car tumbled down a precipice with a woman & sick man on it, neither of them thank God badly hurt. I here was put to the greatest test to get it to rights, all with me except two rank & file being sick & ill in an unknown road, no guide, raining & chilly cold & surrounded on all sides by an almost endless forest of corks. At last through much exertion got it upright, but shortly our bullocks knocked up & here again a pretty job, but encouraged by a light in the wood & shoving the bullocks on, supposed we had reached the long sought for town, when travelling a league we found it to be nothing but men burning charcoal to sell & here again I determined to persevere & see the town if possible. About ½ a league further, beheld another light & thank God this proved the asylum of my regiment. I now carried all the opthalmic [ophthalmic] men & lame on the cars & just going into the town found before our feet a river to cross & no bridge, here again a wading match & after this another, however at 10 o'clock arrived thank heavens safe & sound after marching from 6 in the morning. I was, God knows, fatigued enough & in bad billet after eating a dish of steaks & onions. Slept most soundly.

20 November

Woke at 6 & roused with my bones full of pains & aches, marched over a charming country & good roads to [Calzada de] D[on] Diego 4 or 5 leagues & got a most miserable hole indeed, however I slept well in it after drinking plenty of milk & carrying the Colours.

21 November
Marched at 7 this day over the most astonishing country I yet have seen, perfectly flat & cultivated roads, excellent indeed & day lovely. A vast deal of cultivation in this part, we were to reach old Salamanca this day & about 12 had a view of that most renowned & famous city, so extolled in the books of Gil Blas & Don Quixote. It appeared about a league off, something like Canterbury only much finer; however when I entered it we billeted the men in a convent where they got good beds & mess. Sir J[ohn] M[oore] was here, we found & our 2nd Battalion, the 28th, Queen's [2nd Foot] & in fact most of General Beresford's Division & General Paget's. Breakfasted with the 2nd who I was very glad to see. They all had good billets. Salamanca I liked very much, it is a pretty, clean & large town. There is an opera & coffee houses, a very famous & gaudy college which holds about 13 of our Irishmen who came here to study. There are also a vast number of convents, good houses & buildings, the people mad for their cause & glad to see us I firmly believe. There is an amazing good square in Salamanca of excellent houses similar to Lisbon, though for my part what of S[alamanca] I have seen I like it much better & think it far superior in every point, it is at present very full of troops. Divers reports of the enemy, some say they are at Valladolid, others retreating to Burgos & some which are most credible, is Blake being finely licked & routed. Sir D[avid] Baird is expected daily with the artillery, they are to halt one day at Madrid.

22 November
Spent this day chiefly in getting a map, shoes &c &c & looking about the place. The large square affords a deal of commerce, in it there are several good shops of jewellery & linen, drapery, also some remarkable good houses. A proclamation made to save the milk for the British troops by the corregidor & our regiment to be inspected by Sir J[ohn] M[oore] on Thursday. Reports of our being the Reserve.

23 November
Bought some pencils, knife, castanets &c. Asked Champagny [Champagne] to dinner, ordered a sketch & journal book. Also gave my padrona cash to purchase me a vocabulary. Weather very fine. Report of General Blake having licked the enemy & divers other things, saw Major

Hull of the 43rd[351] Regiment by the university, which I intended this day to see but many things hindered me. A man of the 6th Regiment hung a few days back for theft. Sergeant Major Winterbotham made Adjutant.[352]

24 November
Mustered this morning at ¼ before 8, weather very cold indeed; spent this day in writing letters to England & drawing. 200 carts of ammunition arrived & several artillery, no couriers arrived yet.

25 November
Wrote letters to England all this day from 12 to 3; drilled & marched in line before Major General Paget. The 50th Regiment arrived; weath[er] very cold.

26 November
Wrote to Mrs Young & Mrs Miller this day. Drilled in the morning, dined with Captain Murray[353] yesterday & today, no news particulars.

27 November
Orderly officer this day, all night, wrote to Colonel Robinson[354] & Stapleton.[355] Was asked to dine with Seward of the 9th Regiment tomorrow.[356] Heard from a Staff officer, the enemy had 170,000 men & that Napoleon was actually in Spain. Saw a convent this day, the top of which was crammed with nuns looking through wooden blinds. Poor girls they waved their handkerchiefs & hands to me. Long orders given out by Sir J[ohn] Moore, concerning the loss of the ammunition.

28 November
Dined with Seward this day & had an excellent dinner at Colegio De Santa Maria Magdalena. Gave my coat to be turned.

29 November
Took a long walk in the country this day, which affords a vast number of beautiful rides &c, attempted to take a sketch of the town but the fog prevented me. Went out to drill this morning before breakfast, my head

351 Major Edward Hull, 43rd Foot.

352 Ensign John Winterbottom, 52nd Foot.

353 Probably Captain John Murray, 20th Foot.

354 It is unclear who this officer was.

355 The most likely candidate is Lieutenant Colonel the Honourable George Stapylton, 6th Foot.

356 Ensign William Seward, 9th Foot.

ached very much from drinking too much Malaga wine the preceding night. Orders for the sick to march all to Almeida. The 91st & 28th to form part of the reserve with ourselves. Various reports concerning the enemy. Mail from England arrived & went, no letters for me. Asked to dine tomorrow with Champagny [Champagne] of the 20th Regiment. Took a long walk over Salamanca this evening, saw some beautiful & superb architecture on one of the cathedrals.

30 November
The Rifle Corps had orders to march this day at 12 o'clock, which they did. Heard of the enemy being at Toro and an officer the other day having fallen up with their outlier pickets. The 20th had orders to march tomorrow also at 12 o'clock. An express came from Sir John Hope's army, contents to me unknown. Dined this day, myself & Dick[357] with the 20th Regiment was made a present of a snuff box. Looked out to get some stockings changed, but could not find the house. Took a pleasant walk. Reports of the enemy being at Burgos, Toro, Pamplona & in fact all over the country. Toro lies north from this town 12 leagues; certain it is however we had orders this day to hold ourselves in readiness to turn out & not to be without sound of the bugle. An alarm last night at the magazine & drum beat to arms, no mischief whatever.

1 December
Parade this morning at ½ past 6 o'clock for punishment. Two men flogged for making away with their necessaries punished this morning & formed hollow squares against cavalry. The 20th marched, so that we were in the brigade now by ourselves; a change taken place in the brigades & divisions. Report of a very decisive engagement having taken place between Sir D[avid] Baird & the enemy in which Sir D[avid] lost his left arm & he took 15 pieces of cannon & 4,000 prisoners, together with many killed & wounded. The English lost 1,800 men.[358] Several deserters arrived from the Spanish army; also two French prisoners who told us the Spaniards said to the French, that as soon as we had eat all up we could get, we should take to our shipping & be off. The Junta has I heard, been petitioned by several noblemen to yield to the French yoke. Heard of Lord Holland having been in Spain & returned not well satisfied with the Spanish patriots.[359] Settled my accounts with Butler & gave him a draft for £40 on Morland at

357 Lieutenant James Dick, 52nd Foot.

358 A false rumour.

359 Henry Vassall-Fox, 3rd Baron Holland MP, travelled to Spain with his wife and toured the country.

ten days after sight; found £12 10s the of my bat & forage money was coming to me. Got my short stockings changed. Walked a deal this day in the square. Got my razor ground & at last my coat to be turned; resolved to get some segars [sic] &c.

2 December
Did not march today as expected; heard of the Spaniards having licked very much the French near Saragossa, the report not quite confirmed.[360] Met with a very entertaining signora. General Hope is expected tomorrow for certain. Lent old Dobbs 10 dollars & young Dobbs 1 dollar; the former for the mess the latter for segars. Old Rowan is expected every day. Turned off my washing woman Mrs Greenwood & got Mother Sutcliff. Taylor [sic] sent in his bill, a d[amne]d rascal. Weather much finer than usual & more mild.

3 December
Reports this day of the Spaniards having been completely routed & beaten, they all seem much displeased; though I hear several petitions have been sent in from the first families to yield to the common enemy. I went with Dundas to see the cathedral which is an [sic] high, handsome building, with a vast number of smaller steeples, somewhat resembling Westminster Abbey. The outside is famed for the amazing beautiful architecture which cut in the most minute manner representing our saviour's birth & the wise men; the flight into Egypt & other similar things. The inside is also excessively beautiful, being amazing high pillars of stone & beautiful painted glass. The wainscots are made chiefly of different saints carved in marble & relics of saints. There is an excessive handsome room on the right side of nearly 20 large lookup glasses & an immense table of marble in the centre. Out of this there is another small closet, which has in it our saviour on the cross carved in the most elegant & tasteful manner. There is also in it several glass cases filled with the relics of saints, St Paul & various others. I also saw yesterday a beautiful library of various books at the convent on the right of the nunnery, which also I visited the day before. Heard nothing of marching. Got my coat turned &c. Paid John Jack 2 dollars for shoes & mending.[361] Mr Brawdy[362] dined with us, who had been to Madrid, through Segovia & the Kingdom of Murcia, he gave a very flattering account of the people in Madrid, that they were all boasting

---

[360] Another false claim.

[361] Private John Jack. His photograph as an old man is included in this volume.

[362] The identification of Brawdy is unclear, there was no officer of this name in the army.

of the number of Frenchmen they had killed & the theatres represented, the siege of Saragossa, with the various stratagems they practised of destroying the French in that place. They were nearly attacked on their march several times & laid one night out in a thick wood to avoid the enemy's cavalry formed at the same time in a hollow square; the baggage &c being placed in the centre. A courier arrived which brought certain information of the defeat of the Spanish army. The 9th, 2nd, 52nd Regiments & the 43rd had orders to march tomorrow to Ledesma a town to the north west of Salamanca. Bought some segars & saw Major Hull of the 43rd.

4 December
Walked out with Lord James Hay[363] to see a brigade of artillery arrive. Sir John Moore also rode out of the town to meet General Hope. Intended to have finished my sketch of Salamanca in my new book, but had not time sufficient to finish more than the bridge, which has hung over the pass 'The head of a Traitor.' Various reports concerning the Spaniards & of our facilitating a retreat. Appearances give such a report very good credit at this time.

5 December
Slept at the convent last night on picket, myself, Snodgrass[364] & Ferguson[365] came off this evening. Went out in the morning for a field day marched about 2 leagues & advanced in line nearly 2 miles & got to Salamanca about 2 o'clock, when I made a second breakfast. Our 2nd Battalion marched to Ledesma this day at 5 o'clock. Reports of the Spaniards having been more thrashed; some general arrived to consult, Sir J[ohn] on the subject. The 60th countermanded marching.

6 December
A courier arrived this day, which brought the intelligence of the French having entered Madrid on the first of December at the gate of Santa Barbara and that the Spaniards blew up a mine, which put to death 12,000 men & finally ended in their defeat and added that the people from the balconies flung out iron gratings, which fitted to the feet of the cavalry & thereby threw their riders, indeed the enemy were repulsed with great slaughter; but Joseph Buonaparte assured his army that he would be crowned king, the 24th of the month at the same time. But the inhabitants of Madrid assert they would sooner

363 Lieutenant Lord James Hay, 52nd Foot.
364 Lieutenant Kenneth Snodgrass, 52nd Foot.
365 Lieutenant Dugald Ferguson, 52nd Foot.

all be buried in the ruins.[366] The 20th & 95th Regiments arrived & we hear the retreat of the artillery is countermanded and that a courier had been sent to Sir D[avid] Baird to countermand his ordered retreat; some say we shall march for Madrid immediately & various opinions on the subject. The inhabitants here did not seem much pleased about it; indeed its province has been remarked to send less men for soldiers than any other; so much so, that a proclamation was this day stuck up concerning it. I see daily at least a thousand idle fellows, young men doing nothing. We were mustered this evening at 3 o'clock as the paymaster had arrived. Bought some segars this day & some cloth for gaiters also paid my taylor [sic] washwoman & shoemaker. A mail from England arrived & papers up to the 15th ultimo. The retreat the army was about to perform is now put a stop to by this circumstance.

7 December
Took a sketch this day of the cathedral & Salamanca, which I was unable to equal. Punishment this morning at ½ past 7. Heard for certain we were now going to advance. There was a meeting of general officers this day, viz a Council of War & it is believed they determined on the advancement of the army. Two or three couriers arrived from the Spanish army. Various reports in circulation. Napoleon undoubtedly is in Spain. The 95th arrived.

8 December
Had a field day & came home about 11 o'clock, nothing particular happened except various reports concerning the enemy. Went to the cathedral with Love[367] & afterwards to my lodgings, expected to march shortly.

9 December
Orders to march in the morning tomorrow at length arrived after staying at Salamanca 3 weeks, but towards evening the order was countermanded & we were not to march till the day after, with the 20th, 95th & 91st Regiments supposed towards Toro where report says there are 6,000 French. Had a field day this morning under General Paget, saw Sir John [Moore] who looked very well & in good spirits. Took Brawdy into our mess. Orders given out for a mail for England to be closed tomorrow, wrote to William this night. Bought a bottle of rum, some worsted gloves & sent my servant out to look for a Toledo

366 The defence of Madrid was almost non-existent when the French entered the city.
367 Lieutenant James Love, 52nd Foot.

blade having broken my own. Weather excessively cold indeed. Report of the junta having written to Sir John [Moore] to say he had either advanced or quit the kingdom; heard they had retired to Badajoz; no good sign. Also heard of Lord Holland having returned to England describing the patriots.

[The journal finishes at the list of distances marched shown below, however a new journal entitled 'Journal from Salamanca' starts from the 10th. The entries from the new journal for these few duplicated days are printed here in *italics*.]

10 December
Rested at Salamanca & got several little necessaries, a blanket, mat &c. *Halted at Salamanca.*

11 December
Marched at last to Villa del Rey where I got a tolerable billet alone, 6 leagues this day heard of an action with the 18th Dragoons in which there were 25 French & 12 English,15 of the former were taken & 5 killed & the other escaped by the swiftness of their horses. *Stopped at Salamanca & got some things washed.*

12 December
Arrived at Toro. *Marched to Fuente de Pena, 6 leagues. An action took place between some of our dragoons, who behaved in a most gallant manner, the 18th [Hussars] I believe.*

Portugal	**Leagues**
Estremoz	
Monforte	4
Arronches	3
Spain Estramadura	
Albuquerque	5½
Aliseda	7
Brozas	4
Alcantara	3
Zarza [la] Mayor	3
Moraleja	4

Perales [del Puerto]	2
Salamanca	
Peniparda	4
[Fuente]Guinaldo	3
Ciudad Rodrigo	4
San Munoz	7½
Calzada de Don Diego	5
Salamanca	6
Fuentelapena	6
Toro	6
Pedrosa del Rey	4
Tiedra	3
Valderas	4
Santervas [de Campos]	5
Grajal de Campos	7

13 December
Marched to Toro, 6 leagues from the latter place, it is a large town, situated on an immense cliff on the Douro. Got a billet on a tobacco shop. Walked with John Wallace[368] to an adjoining village.

14 December
Walked with Major Wallace[369] to an adjoining village. Another action equally gallant took place with our dragoons. [Joseph] Bonaparte in this town three days before the British entered had been proclaimed king.

15 December
Marched to Pedrosa del Rey 5 leagues, country as yet from Salamanca particularly flat & every day the Spaniards seem to wear off in civility to the English.

16 December
Marched this morning towards Tordesillas when suddenly we changed our route to Tiedra, reason unknown to me, marched 2 leagues.

368 Actually Lieutenant John Wallis, 52nd Foot.
369 Probably Major William Wallace, 20th Foot.

17 December
Halted here & spent the day with Wallace [Wallis] in shooting nightingales, I had a large pistol & he a Frenchman's gun, sport excellent.

18 December
Marched 6 or 7 leagues to Prau [Prado], a dirty little hole, where every kind of incivility was shown us, Our left wing rested at an adjoining villa; got in about 8 o'clock at night.

19 December
Marched back a league to Villalpando.

20 December
Marched to Valderas, 6 leagues, it is a tolerable town, got coffee & sweets. Myself & Powys[370] billeted together. Got a good straw mattress. Another action took place between our dragoons who with much inferior numbers conquered.

21 December
Marched about 3 leagues to Santervas [de Campos] & got a most vile hole, a little smoky closet for 9 of us; our mule & horse as yet kept up well.

22 December
Marched to Grajal de Campos, 2 or 3 leagues. Heard of the French being in a strong position, under Marshal Soult & waited our attack.

23 December
Halted at Graja de Campos & shot pigeons but the enemy being near, our sport was stopped by order of General Paget. A deal of snow on the ground. Got some pistols & a letter from my brother John by a Mr Adey,[371] he breakfasted with me today & set to join the 2nd Battalion, but as he could not walk, the ground being so very slippy. Orders to get under arms at 6 o'clock, which was done, when we marched off intending to attack the enemy at break of day. The whole army was in motion, when at 12 o'clock at night we faced to the right about & took up our old quarter. The reason I knew not, some say he was reinforced, others he quitted his position. The night was very cold. Two or three false alarms a few days ago had been given to us.

[370] Lieutenant the Honourable Henry Powys, 52nd Foot.
[371] Ensign Capel Adey, 52nd Foot.

24 December
Came off picket from sickness this night, being very chilly & ill, but better towards morning. Shot off my pistols. Orders to march tomorrow & now begins our dreadful retreat from Sahagun.

25 December
The weather was damp & rainy & the road ankle deep in mud from the snow, marched to Mayorga 6 leagues from this, 3 leagues in deep mud & ploughed fields & for the last two leagues it rained incessantly, got a kind of a billet & messed with Captain P Campbell's[372] company. Also a hock steak & a little native wine. I had charge except a blanket & therefore my clothes dried on me.

26 December
Baggage guard this day. Marched by Valderas to Fuentes de Ropel 7 good leagues. Valderas scarcely was inhabited as myself & Dundas went in, lent him 3s 6d to buy sugar with; it rained all this day; very chilly & weak. Sheddon[373] on picket, Dobbs[374] & me slept in a bed. Several soldiers in the house, no charge.

27 December
Marched at 6, a league. Orders to keep close together as we expected to be attacked hourly by cavalry, road more muddy & unpleasant. At 6 o'clock took possession of the pass at Benavente, with some of the Germans & 3 pieces of cannon; stood to our arms all day & relieved at 5 o'clock at night by our 2nd Battalion & the 43rd Regiment. A gallant action taken place between Lord Paget & the enemy, we as usual victorious. Slept at Benavente this night, dined with Dobson.[375]

28 December
Halted at Benavente, a false alarm given got under arms & the whole army took up their position, rained dreadfully & returned wet to the skin. The bridge was blown up here though not effectively. Billeted with Colonel Elley.[376]

---

372 Captain Patrick Campbell, 52nd Foot.
373 Lieutenant John Sheddon, 52nd Foot.
374 Ensign John Dobbs, 52nd Foot.
375 Ensign George Dobson, 43rd Foot.
376 Lieutenant General John Elley, Royal Horse Guards, Assistant Adjutant General.

29 December
Marched to La Baneza 8 leagues. Roads strewed with ammunition, dead horses & sacks. Got the opthalmia [ophthalmia]. General Lefebvre taken in the action of today & the Imperial Guards quite defeated, he forded the river & behaved well, but our hussars better, 40 prisoners taken. Very wet today indeed & knee deep in mud. Gaiters, boots & all destroyed, arrived excessively fatigued indeed.

30 December
Arrived at Astorga & also Romana's army from Leon, all peasants & mob, though fine pieces of cannon, in 3 days the whole army deserted & the cannon was by chance dragged on to Lugo & there fell into the enemy's hands. Knee deep in mud this march, several men fell out from fatigue & all were captured by the enemy, also our sick. Billeted in a convent ankle deep in bullock's blood & men's [mess?]. Met Mein,[377] got a pair of good English shoes.

31 December
Marched 5 miles to a small village; most dreadfully frosty & mountainous, which is the entrance of Galicia, till now being perfectly flat. Got some straw & broke open the door of a convent to sleep in. Romana's army flying elsewhere. Marched at 10 o'clock at night, through a most mountainous country, indeed we went 8 leagues uphill nearly. It was most bitter cold & falls of snow in the night. The road was covered with clothing, cartridges, dead horses & men. All sorts arrived at Bembibre at 11 o'clock on the 1 January.

1 January
Orders to march at 5 tonight but contradicted, got some straw in an old house with the men.

2 January
Marched from Bembibre to Cacabelos 4 leagues, excessively muddy, mountainous & cold. Got some ham here at 2 dollars each, also good wine but no bread could be met with. We had an excellent billet.

3 January
Three men were sentenced to be hung but reprieved by General Paget, the French being at hand. Was under arms all this day; in the evening engaged the enemy, who had two large columns but no artillery. Poor

377 Captain William Mein, 52nd Foot.

Captain Bennett of the 95th killed[378] & two others wounded. Marched through Villafranca [del Bierzo], about 8 o'clock at night raining much, bridge not effectively blown up. Very muddy, men fell down asleep. Rocky & a river by the road.

4 January
At 8 o'clock arrived at a village, slept here a little,

5 January
Marched to a village 6 leagues over a most mountainous country, got a billet with the men & some salt pork.

6 January
Marched six leagues to a small villa, billeted with the men.

7 January
Marched and attacked by the French, quitted it & took our position for the night. Dollars 90,000 lost.

8 January
Marched all night after lighting our fires 10 leagues & arrived at 12 o'clock a league beyond Lugo, billeted in a pigstie [sic] 3 young men joined, heard from John[379] & the joyful news of the *Ville de Paris*[380] at Vigo.

9 January
Very rainy. My servant lost me a pistol; a sock, a map & a pair of shoes & I was now destitute of everything except a dirty shirt, a knapsack & white waistcoat which I picked up from the spoils of the road. An alarm given, all turned out while it rained a deluge & obliged to leave behind some apple dumplings in the camp kettle. Wet march to Lugo & out, staying till dark in the rain. The Guards were slightly engaged. Quartered in a convent this night, wet to the skin & no change whatever as our baggage was sent on to Corunna, laid me down in my wet things but could not sleep much. Orders for the men each to have 70 rounds of ammunition.

10 January
Marched off at 5 o'clock am to offer the French battle, took our position opposite the enemy on a furzy plain; progged, got a few turnips & a live pig made me a dish of soup, each cooked now & kept himself from

---

378 Captain L Bennett, 95th Rifles, died of his wounds, 14 January 1809.

379 His brother, Lieutenant John Paget, Royal Navy.

380 HMS *Ville de Paris* of 110 guns.

starving. My shirt was worse than all being visited by vermin, but many were eat up by them. Marched off at 8 o'clock & were (shameful to say) 3 hours in which [we] reached Lugo.

11 January
Kept marching & halted at 2 o'clock to cook. Myself & Mr Maling fell asleep in a hovel & nearly taken by the enemy kept marching all night.

12 January
Kept marching on, report of a French picket being seen, took our position for the event, saw them round up the fatigued stragglers, which troubled us not a little; marched on & took up our position this side of Betanzos & slept amongst the straw under a hedge, got a blanket, some rum given to the troops.

13 January
Marched on to Corunna, I went on before as I now had walked my shoes & stockings off my feet & was badly blistered. Arrived there at 2 o'clock, got a bed at a taylor's shop for ½ a dollar but alas! Saw no shipping to carry us off.

14 January
Got some shoes &c & some stockings, heard the regiment was near the bridge.

15 January
Joined my regiment. Sent on fatigue with a sergeant & corporal of the rifle corps to receive my orders from the Adjutant General. I did so & it was to pick up all stragglers, found none. Asked to dinner by an officer of the 23rd Fusileers [sic].

16 January
Reported myself to the Adjutant General & to the colonel, about some stragglers of our 2nd Battalion, ordered me to repair to the Convent of St Francisco & collect the convalescent men & see them embarked towards 3 or 4 o'clock. I heard there was skirmishing & at last turned to a general action. I wished to join myself but the order I received prevented me. Slept aboard the *Ville de Paris.*

17 January
Went ashore & embarked several sick & straggling men. Found my regiment embarked last night & was but slightly engaged; embarked

on board the *Ville de Paris* for good, but without leave, it being a perfect scramble & my brother was on board her. Got a cot strung for me, some cold meat, English wine & butter, also a clean shirt, stockings from John &c. The French batteries opened on us, but the transports getting under weigh, did not do us much injury. We had 12 sail of the line here under Sir Sam[uel] Hood[381] & Admiral de Courcy.[382] I was now, thank God, rid of Spain. Three transports run foul of each other got ashore & were burnt by the boats of the fleet.

18 January, Wednesday
Sailed from Corunna with a fine breeze at south-west with the *Resolution 74; Tonnant 80,* Admiral de Courcy; *Barfleur* 98 Sir Samuel Hood; *Ville de Paris* 110, *Victory* 100, *Elizabeth* 74, *Plantagenet* 74, *Zealous* 74, *Norge* 74, *Implacable* 74, *Audacious* 74, *Endymion* [40], *Minerva* [38], *Serapis* [44] *& Unicorn* [32] frigates, some cutters, brigs & schooners.

19 January
Wind fair. Had 900 troops on board & 70 officers including wounded, also Sir D[avid] Baird & Staff. An officer sent home with the dispatches from General Hope.

20 January
Fine weather, but calm during the night. Some men flogged on board, found ourselves by observations to be latitude 47 [degrees] 12 [minutes] North; hazy weather, fleet much scattered.

21 January
Received permission [via] telegraph from the *Tonnant* to proceed to Portsmouth for the benefit of the general. Hazy weather, light winds, all possible sail set.

22 January
Strong gale from the eastward. Saw land, Lizard Point.

23 January
In the morning quite calm, came on a fresh breeze from the southward. Made all sail up channel. At noon Portland lighthouse NE by E 2 or 3 leagues distant.

381 Admiral Sir Samuel Hood.
382 Vice Admiral Michael de Courcy.

24 January
Blowing hard from the westward, thick hazy weather. Beating off & on the back of the Isle of Wight, weather too thick to allow our entering St Helens. Saw an Indiaman homeward bound, signal of distress flying, having lost her main top mast, blew too hard to send a boat on board.

25 January
Fresh breezes & clear. Made in for the land. Saw the Isle of Wight & St Helens; 3 line of battleships & a frigate coming out of Spithead, anchored at 3 o'clock at Spithead. A few officers went ashore, found a great number of men of war at Spithead.

26 January
Heard of General Brownrigg[383] being at Portsmouth. Orders to land sick & wounded. Strong gales from the westward with rain.

27 January
Went ashore & bought boots, pantaloons &c. Play in the evening. Met my old friend Cole,[384] dined at the Blue Post.[385] 82nd disembarked.

28 January
Came aboard the *Ville de Paris* again, after giving John's things to be washed ashore. John had a letter from William. The 32nd & other regiments disembarked. Heard we were to go to Deal Barracks & General Oakes[386] to have the regiment. In short after a few days I quitted the *Ville de Paris* & went on board a transport to Ramsgate where on the 17th of February, we disembarked & marched to Deal & once more got comfortably settled in Old England.

Return of men embarked on the 16 & 17 January [1809]

16 – Embarked 16 men of the 91st Regiment & 1 of the 28th, also 8 men of the 1st Battalion [52nd].
17 – Embarked 10 men of the 1st Battalion who lost their regiment in the night, three or four men of the 91st & Campbell[387] & a wounded man of the 1st Battalion. Found several men of the 91st, 28th & 52nd in the Franciscan Convent at the citadel.

---

383 General Sir Robert Brownrigg.
384 Lieutenant John Cole, 45th Foot.
385 The *Old Blue Post*, 38 Broad Street, Portsmouth.
386 Lieutenant General Sir Hildebrand Oakes became colonel of the 52nd Foot.
387 Captain Robert Campbell, 52nd Foot, was severely wounded at Corunna.

Walcheren

17 July
Marched from Shorncliffe at 3 o'clock am & embarked the same day on board the *Circe* frigate Captain Woolcombe,[388] the officers very uncivil. Went over to Ramsgate to visit with my brother & charge on board the *Serapis* Captain Lloyd.[389] About 300 sails in the Downs reaching from Dover nearly opposite Dymchurch Bay.

The fleet sailed on the 28th, wind fair, anchored during the night.

29 July
Got underweigh at 6 o'clock, saw land at 9 supposed [to be] Walcheren. Fresh breezes. Anchor at 4 o'clock off Cadzand.

30 July
Got under weigh at 6 o'clock, saw Lord Gardner's[390] fleet my brother came on board, anchored again at 12 o'clock. Saw a fire on shore & a shot or two from the ships.

31 July
John went off again after breakfast, hears of Shoven [Schouwen] being taken, saw some firing on shore as to appearance our line advancing & the other retreating. The hook in sight, Lord Gardner's fleet got under weigh.

1 August
John came on board last night, after seeing the siege of Casmue[391] & walking over the island saw the great cleanliness of the Dutch. Went off this morning before breakfast again. Casmue [Veere] Surrendered & heard distinctly the bombardment of Flushing. Colonel Ross went ashore, where there was a report of 15,000 men being entrenched up to their teeth in a little pass leading to Antwerp. Peace between Austria & France confirmed; 400 prisoners taken, 2 gunboats sunk. A Dutch officer told us had it not been for the peace between Austria & France, they would have received us with open arms.

---

388 HMS *Circe*, of 32 guns, Captain Edward Woolcombe.

389 HMS *Serapis* of 44 guns.

390 Admiral Alan Gardner had commanded the Channel Fleet, but he had died on 1 January 1809. The fleet was commanded by Sir Richard Strachan.

391 It is clear that he refers to the siege of Veere, which surrendered on 1 August.

2 August
Almost the whole of the transports got under weigh this morning with several men of war, supposed to go round the back of the island for Flushing.[392] The *Imperieuse*[393] & other frigates went round the other side. Got under weigh but anchored three times on account of no wind.

3 August
Anchored this morning again, the wind being quite against us, we have orders to proceed up the Scheldt; brought to opposite Casmere [Veere]. Heard of the French entering Flushing, a reinforcement. Saw several divisions ashore. Heard nothing of John this day. At night saw the bombardment of Flushing.

4 August
Several officers went on shore; saw a great smoke over Flushing & heard several guns fired ashore. Asked Colonel Ross's leave to go ashore & got it.

5 August
Went ashore at 6 o'clock this morning & took my dirty things with me to get them washed. Breakfasted at the English hotel at Casmere [Veere]. The room where we breakfasted had several shot through it. Paid 1s 6d for an excellent breakfast a head, observed particularly the extreme cleanliness of the people & sheets. Milk, butter, cheese, &c very cheap, walked to Middleburg after breakfast, the high road all paved & extremely neat & clean, a most beautiful walk in this gentleman's seat, far superior, fitted out to any in England or elsewhere. The grounds are cultivated & most beautifully overspread with green fields, streams &c. Got to Middleburgh at 11 o'clock, saw my brother John, bought several things, fur gloves, astrakhans, pipes, snuffboxes &c &c & it was Middleburgh fair & the gayest time in the Netherlands. Dined at the Rotterdam Hotel off Goose, mutton, roast beef, soups, salad, vegetables, puddings, beer, champaign, claret, port, madeira & various other wines for 7 s[hillings]. Met Robertson[394] of the *Venerable*.[395] Went to Arnemuiden after dinner, in a chaise drawn by 2 horses drawn very quick & got aboard again at 9 o'clock. Highly pleased with my day's pleasure, batteries not yet

392 Modern day Vlissingen.
393 HMS *Imperieuse*, a 38-gun frigate.
394 There are too many Robertsons in the Navy to be certain who this is.
395 HMS *Venerable* was a 74.

opened in Flushing. Went to the lace shop & [linen] shop, saw most elegant dresses.

6 August
Wrote 3 letters to England. Various reports of the French fleet, the army &c, got milk from the shore & my things on board, sent by John, *was obliged to use mercury.*[396]

7 August
An order for no more officers to go ashore; Lord Huntly's Division[397], came in yesterday from Cadsand [Kadsand], having failed in the attempt of landing. Heard of our 1st Battalion having been cut up in Spain. John dined onboard with us & Captain Sandys[398] & Cox[399] went to England.

8 August
Moved on board transports this evening, the regiment supposed for the purpose of going up the Scheldt. Various reports ashore.

9 August
Dropped down to Chamour [?] & anchored, went a foraging ashore, observed several beautiful farmhouses, from which we got milk. The women wear a curious kind of metal to keep their sheets in. Picked up a feather in the garden which the men threw away with great contempt. Their cleanliness very great & neat. The coat platted round with straw. Found much inconvenience from walking about. Got my things from on board the *Aire,* found I had got my old disease again. Got lots of milk &c. The country beautiful & neat. Hay, beans &c similar to ours & the manner of making the former. A great similitude in their language to ours.

10 August
Went up the Scheldt & landed on S[outh] Beveland; the regiment marched to Goes, I was obliged to ride on one of the cars. The country very beautiful & very much cultivated. Roads very good. A few men fell out. Arrived at Goes about 8 o'clock, got a billet but being a bad one & not being able to walk about I was obliged to put up at the hotel where I got a 4 bedded room to myself. The people here understand French as well as Dutch.

---

396 Mercury was commonly used as a treatment for syphilis.

397 General George Gordon, Marquess of Huntly.

398 Probably Captain Edwin Sandys, 11th Foot.

399 Lieutenant Thomas Cox, 51st Foot.

11 August
Stopped in the whole of this day. I regretted much not being able to walk about to make observations on the country. Various reports of Flushing & the Russians being at war with France. Goes a very clean town though not so good as Middleburgh.

12 August
Took a little walk out with Jones & made a sketch of the town. Endeavoured to buy a poodle dog & was just doing so, but the man told me he would bring a better tomorrow for a higher price & was the same dog with his hair cut off. Almost the whole of people dirty but clean in their houses.

13 August
Amused myself this day with writing & drawing for I had but one book which I'd read through at least twenty times. Went up at night on the great church to see the bombardment of Flushing which began this day. Could make out the rockets & shells, distinctly heard it the whole of the night.

14 August Monday
Went up during the night to see the bombardment from a person's house. Distinguished it perfectly well, rockets &c &c.

15 August
Flushing surrendered being almost as they said here, beaten to pieces, the soldiers are all prisoners of war. Lord Chatham issued out proclamations to say if any Frenchmen did not give himself up in three days, he would be considered a prisoner of war. Took a small walk out with the doctor & I here saw too forcibly the mischief of ill health; not being able to walk about, it is impossible to make observations.

16 August
Felt much the same today as yesterday, amused myself this day by learning & writing as much French as I was able, for here they speak it as well as Dutch. Newspapers came from England to Mr Hayward the clergyman,[400] in them we heard of Sir A[rthur] W[ellesley] being at Madrid & having defeated 40,000 men with 20,000 but with the loss of the 4th part of his army. Curious verses about the

400 This must refer to Chaplain John Hayward.

war in the newspapers. The peace with Austria & France they state to have taken place. Doubts whether we go up the Scheldt or not. Considering all things, the time passes tolerably well as about 5 or 6 my brother officers come & sit with me every day. Lord Harrington[401] is appointed Commander in Chief, General Stuart[402] spoke to the officers about the knapsacks & his orders not being obeyed. Reported that some of the army is to go to Spain. Caution in general. Orders about eating unripe fruit which is remarkably cheap here, sugar is the dearest thing I know here, about 4 shillings a lb. Butter, milk & eggs are cheap. An officer bought a double-barrelled gun & a very good one for 3 guineas & the man assured him before the English came, it sold for about 7 shillings. Tried for a poodle dog but could not walk about to look for one.

17 August
Expected from this day to advance up the country, various reports about Antwerp &c 5,400 prisoners laid down their arms at Flushing. It is said here Monnet is an Irishman.[403] Captain Rowan[404] & Snodgrass[405] left us this morning at 4 o'clock.

18 August
Amused myself this day with making a case for my pistols! Did not hear anything concerning my brother John. An English ship passed a fort & a shot struck a magazine, by which [it] was blown up. Read of poor Beaufoy's death in Spain.[406]

19 August
Nearly finished my pistol case & paid my bill at the inn, which came to 2 guineas having at night, 2 beds, one for my servant & one for myself; I had an excellent dinner every day & breakfast & tea in the evening, the account was made up for 9 days. Almost got through the *Spectator*[407] which I regret, as not a million would purchase an English book here. The women have a curious dress, being a large straw bonnet resembling an umbrella, two earrings in the centre of the cheeks, a long waist, a hoop & very short petticoats & they wear slippers not shoes.

[401] General Charles, Earl Harrington.
[402] Major General William Stewart.
[403] General Louis Claude Monnet de Lorbeau was certainly French, having been born in Mougon.
[404] Captain William Rowan, 52nd Foot.
[405] Captain Kenneth Snodgrass, 52nd Foot.
[406] Lieutenant John Beaufoy, 7th Foot, was killed at the Battle of Talavera.
[407] The *Spectator* was a daily periodical.

The weather here very uncertain raining & being fine the whole of the day. Bought some cloth to make a little waistcoat, being ¾ of a yard, for which they charged 5 shillings. My finances begin to get rather low. John arrived today from Middleburg in time for dinner with Captain Gubbins of the 3rd Dragoons.[408]

20 August
The regiment went to church this morning, John & Captain Gubbins went out to walk. Read the Gazette of Sir A[rthur] Wellesley's action. An order for the regiment to march tomorrow, was obliged to stay behind & without my servant.

21 August
The regiment marched this morning into cantonments about 11 miles from this. John & me went to the Burgomaster at the States General house & got a billet where I removed all my things to & slept this night. Met Ogilvie[409] & Robinson of the *Venerable* dined with them & Captain Evans [at 6] o'clock & eat at the Ship Inn. John & Captain Gubbins went to Batz in a cart with Robertson,[410] a Marine officer & several others. The *Venerable* is in sight of the French fleet, Robertson told us Sir H[ome] Popham has gone to reconnoitre the French Fleet. Various reports concerning the advance of the army. Wrote letters to England, one to Bess, the other to William, some say we are going to Spain & others that there (Mein won laurels for Vimiera) is no probability of it.

22 August
Put myself under the care of Mr Gordon, Surgeon to the Forces,[411] he seems a clever man. Slept in my billet last night & on the whole was tolerably comfortable. Book lent me the 2nd volume of R[obinson] Crusoe. Expected John back today, as he left Thomas & his goods at the Ship. Gave him my things to take to England with him.

23 August
John not yet arrived, several officers came over to see me, saw Jackson[412] of the 50th. Weather bad.

---

[408] Captain James Gubbins, 3rd Dragoons.
[409] 2nd Lieutenant Conyngham Ogilvie, 95th Foot.
[410] Probably 1st Lieutenant William Robertson, 95th Foot.
[411] Staff Surgeon William Gordon, No. 2455 in Johnstone.
[412] Lieutenant Edward Jackson, 50th Foot.

24 August
A vast number of the troops taken ill with the fever, amused myself by taking a sketch of a barn & writing letters to England.

25 August
Peach[413] gave me a call with Captain Ewart,[414] breakfasted with some officers of the 9th Dragoons in the square, wrote more letters to England it being a very rainy day. John came back with Captain Gubbins & intended had they found Thomas, to set off immediately for Middleburg & then apply to Captain Paget for a pass for England. Rained hard. Dined with John, Captain Gubbins & an officer of the 9th Dragoons in the square. Report of a Council of War sitting to determine the advance or retreat of the army. My throat gets worse, gave John all my letters to take with him, wherein I determined to enter the dragoons.

26 August
John and Captain Gubbins set off this morning for the square. Met Colonel Ross & some other officers. Wrote to Captain Fuller[415] by him to ask the colonel's permission for my servant to remain with me. Felt very ill the whole of the day & my throat went worse, the doctor having neglected to send me the gargle. Drank an immense basin of broth from the Ship Inn. Paid my bill, which amounted to about 13 florins, equal to £1 9s 0d for a week's living. Went to bed early being very weak & sickly.

27 August Sunday
Very rainy the whole of the day, I was therefore obliged to stop in doors. Endeavoured to get a man of the 68th Regiment to attend me. Got all my medicines safe from the doctor. Sent Holford[416] my mattress, which I bought [for] 10 shillings at Deal. Found my warm flannel night cap was missing & could not find it. I unluckily sent my clothes to the wash without an inventory. Dreadful rainy day. My doctor told me that out of 16,000 men, who were in this island, in the course of one Friday to another, he had taken in the hospital 1,600 men, so prevalent is the fever from the water.

---

413 Surgeon George Peach had been in the 52nd Foot until June 1809, when he transferred into the 9th Light Dragoons.

414 Captain John Ewart, 52nd Foot.

415 Captain Thomas Fuller, 52nd Foot.

416 Ensign James Holford, 52nd Foot.

28 August
Received Fuller's note concerning my servant, wherein the colonel refused his remaining with me, but told me to get a certificate to return to England, as the retreat of the army was now resolved upon. Holford, Murray[417] & some other officers came to see me. Wrote to Mr Gordon, Surgeon of the Forces, concerning the certificate & he said he would send it to me.

29 August
Called on Mr Gordon who was sick with the fever, he had drawn out the certificate but was informed since, it was to be done by the surgeon of the regiment. I accordingly wrote a note to Maling, begging him to do it & send it over. Headquarters established at this place today. Found myself very weak from the nursing. Captain Smith[418] behaved very civil to me & allowed his servant to drawing rations for two days, which was 4 turnips, 2lb of meat, 1 loaf, half a pint of rum. I accordingly got Sunnecliffe to make some broth for me & bring it to my billet. Hired a man of the 85th to do some few things for me, but he went off & I never saw him more. Sent Captain Smith an epaulette & 2 volumes of the Spectator. York[419] told me of Sir A[rthur] W[ellesley] being obliged to retreat & leave his sick & wounded behind.

30 August
Very fine weather, Maling came over with Chalmers[420] & made a great row & behaved in a most unmannerly way about the certificate & swore he would not make one out. McNeil[421] came in & declared [that] the regiment embarked this evening & got orders to march at 4 o'clock. I would hardly credit it. I enquired, found it the case, but knew not what steps to take.

31 August
Dined with Mr Maling, who told me the officers were aboard the *Superb* & all expect to sail for England. Agreed with Mr Gordon to go tomorrow with him on board an hospital ship for England.

1 September
Left Goes at 12 o'clock, having paid my lodgings &c then things fetched from the Old Ship Inn. McNeil slept at my billet last night, told

417 Possibly Captain John Murray, 20th Foot.
418 This is most likely to be Captain James Webber-Smith, Royal Artillery.
419 Lieutenant Charles Yorke, 52nd Foot.
420 Captain William Chalmers, 52nd Foot.
421 Ensign Roderick McNeil, 52nd Foot.

him to tell Ross I had gone aboard, an hospital surgeon Mr Bartain [?] went with us to the Ship in a cart, after that we got out another to take us to Middleburg, where after having some soup we went to the *Rotterdam,* spoke to Mr Webb[422] (Gordon's aid) & set off to Flushing the same night, where we drove about the streets for a long time looking for quarters. At last we went to a private house & promised the man payment. The town is a good deal battered, met with two French officer[s], exchanged some Dutch money for French. They had been in Spain, Portugal, Martinique &c &c. Got a bed but full of fleas.

2 September
Employed the whole of the day in looking for a passage, myself & Gordon fagged ourselves to death. He endeavoured to find out General Graham[423] but went to Captain Paget & General Picton,[424] who told us Admiral Otway[425] was the proper person & he could do nothing for us. Went aboard the Agent, he promised us one, but we doubted how long we should be detained. Looked out for a Deal boat but they were employed under government. Got some cider & porter; soap &c. This agent told us tomorrow or this evening we could most likely get onboard the *Appollonia* as she was going to England for water. Went almost the whole of the day to Ramaborg [Rammakens?] for a Deal boat, but they not having posted with their cargo, could not go.

3 September
Gordon got up at 6 o'clock this morning & most immediately heard a person call out for the *Appollonia* boat, he agreed with the captain to take us for 8 or 10 guineas, paid our bill, went aboard & thank God, once more got under weigh at 8 o'clock, wind rather south & very little of it, fine clear day. Got things tolerably comfortable aboard & made three sketches in the morning.

4 September Monday
Discovered the N[orth] Foreland towards evening, with a water gate. Landed once more at Ramsgate thank God & I am now more & more convinced that none is equal to incomparable England, for trade, commerce &c for the modesty & beauty of our women, the bravery, health & comfort of our men. Post chaise at Ramsgate & slept

422 Surgeon Sir John Webb, No. 1429 in Johnstone.
423 General Sir Thomas Graham.
424 General Sir Thomas Picton.
425 Admiral Sir Robert Otway.

at Canterbury. Arrived in London the next day & Leith, [put] up at Woods Hotel, Portman Square. 99 Mount Street [to] 127 Mount Street.

Paget did not serve abroad again until promoted from the 52nd Foot to captain in the Royal York Rangers, when he served at Nivelle and the Nive. Unfortunately any journal from this period has not been found.

Copies of Orders issued out to the troops previous to their embarkation AD 1809 July.

Major General [William] Stuart [Stewart] appointed to the brigade of the 95th, 43rd, 52nd (5 companies) in a letter dated 5 July. Adjutant General.

Officers desired to bring packs or knapsacks!! Besides a portmanteau weighing 25 lbs.

Earl of Chatham appointed Commander in Chief in a letter dated Horse Guards 9 July & Sir Eyre Coote second in command! All women to be left behind!!

Lieutenant General [John Pitt] Earl of Chatham, Commander of the Forces, Sir Eyre Coote 2nd in command. [Lieutenant Generals] Sir John Craddock, The Earl of Rosslyn, The Marquis of Huntly, Sir John Hope, Mackenzie Fraser, Lord Paget, General [Sir Robert] Brownrigg, Major General von Linsingen, [Sir Thomas] Graham, Earl of Dalhousie, Dyott, Leith, Picton, Stewart, Sir William Erskine.

Brigadier Generals Houston, Disney, Montresor, Acland, Sontag, Rottenburg, Browne,

Colonel Thomas Mahon, as Colonel on the Staff & Brigadier, Alten as ditto.

Quarter Master General's Department

General Brownrigg, Lieutenant Colonel Buck, Deputy Quarter Master General; Lieutenant Colonel [H] Perponcher Assistant Quarter Master General [William] Offeney KGL; Sir N Douglas, Honourable Upton; Majors Mackay; Buller, Nisbett, Dixon, Montelambert, Honourable E Blacquire, Honourable Cathcart.

Deputy Assistant Quarter Master General

Captain McLouth

Captain White

Captain Dickens

Captain Pierrepoint

Captain Harris

Captain French

Captain Owen.

17. SURGEON JOHN GIBSON JOURNAL 1811 TO 1814[426]

John Gibson had originally been appointed an assistant surgeon in the 20th Light Dragoons in September 1808 but was promoted surgeon in the 52nd Foot on 20 December 1810. He joined the 2nd Battalion in March 1811 and was in the peninsula for a year before leaving from April 1812 to April 1813 and then returned for the final year of the conflict. He saw service with the battalion at Sabugal, *Fuentes de Oñoro,* Ciudad Rodrigo, Vitoria, the Pyrenees, Bidassoa, Nivelle, Nive, Orthez and Toulouse.

1811

On the 25th of March, the 2nd Battalion joined the Light Division at Navazinies [Nabainhos] (having embarked at Portsmouth January 26th) and landed at Lisbon on the 6th of March. The division marched to Celorico [da Beira] on the 26th, halted on the 27th and the next day marched upon Sabugal.

Affair at Sabugal

3 April. The division crossed the Coa at a ford two or three miles above the town of Sabugal with the intention of getting round the enemy's left flank, whilst two divisions were to attack him in front, but in consequence of the very hazy state of the atmosphere, the movement of the Light Division was not sufficiently extended and instead of getting in rear of the enemy's left flank, it came in full contact with it, before the other two divisions had arrived at their point of attack. Colonel Beckwith's Brigade led the march of the division and became first engaged and whilst opposed to such a superior force, a vigorous charge of cavalry compelled him to resist the efforts of the enemy until

426 A typescript copy of this journal is held at the Museum of the Oxfordshire Soldier, reference SOFO 6388.

the arrival of the 2nd Brigade, when after some resistance the French troops fled in the greatest disorder. In this affair the Light Division was opposed to General Reynier's entire corps. After the action, the French army hastened across the Agueda and the regiment marched from Sabugal and Quadracies [Quadrazais], on the 4th, to Forcalhos, on the 5th, to Albergaria [Albergueria de Argañán] on the 6th and went into cantonments at Gallegos [Gallegos de Argañán] on the 9th.

23 April. An affair of picquets at the Bridge of Marialva.

27 April. Battle of Fuentes d'Onoro

The precipitate retreat of the French Army after the affair at Sabugal, left Almeida to its own resources and the forward movement of the British effectually blockaded the place, which was then but indifferently provisioned. Marshal Massena crossed the Agueda on the 2 May with a large convoy of military stores for its relief and the Light Division fell back the same day from Gallegos [de Argañán] and bivouacked on the skirts of the wood between Almeida and Fuentes d'Onoro. On the morning of the 3rd the division passed through Fuentes and marched to the high ground behind Alameda [La Alameda de Gardón], while the French army were concentrating in great force in its front, the British line extended along the left bank of the Duas Casas, from Fort Conception [Concepción] to some distance beyond Fuentes. The enemy's attack of the village of Fuentes on the 3rd having failed, the French columns were observed moving to their left on the afternoon of the 4th and General Houston's[427] Division made a corresponding movement and occupied Pasabelho [Poco Velho] with two battalions. Early on the morning of the 5th, the Light Division moved to the extreme right of the line to support General Houston. It had scarcely arrived upon its ground when the British cavalry fell back upon the line closely pursued by the French. Squares of battalions were instantly formed, and the division retired in the most perfect order for nearly two miles in the face of General Montbrun's[428] cavalry and a numerous artillery which played upon the squares during their retreat. In the course of the evening the regiment moved forward to the enclosures in rear of the village of Fuentes, entrenching itself during the night, and at daylight next morning this part of the position, which was originally the weakest, had become almost inaccessible. Both armies remained inactive on the 6th and on the morning of the 7th the French army fell back from Fuentes towards the Agueda, followed by the Light Division

427 Major General William Houston commanded the 7th Division.

428 General Louis Pierre Montbrun commanded the cavalry.

to Espeja, and next day marched to Gallegos [de Argañán] where the regiment halted until the 6 June. In consequence of the French army of the North being in march to relieve Badajoz, the divisions of the army which were cantoned between the Agueda and the Coa under the command of Sir Brent Spencer, hastened to join Lord Wellington, who was personally superintending the siege. On the 6 June the regiment marched from Gallegos [de Argañán] to Naver de Haver and pursued its route by Penamacor, Niza, Portalegre and arrived at Arronches on the 22nd. On the 23rd encamped at Monte Reguingo [Reguengo] on the banks of the Carja [Caia], ready to move to the position which was selected for the British Army on the heights behind Campo Major [Campo Maior].

On the 19 July Marshal Marmont's army retraced its steps to Salamanca and the Light Division returned to the banks of the Agueda. The regiment marched from Reguingo [Reguengo] to Portalegre on the 21 July, arrived at Castelo de Vide on the 23rd and halted there until the morning of the 29th when the march was resumed by Niza [Nisa], Vilha Velho [Vila Velha de Ródão], Castel Branco, Escalos de Cima, Bienposta [Bemposta], Memoa [Meimao], Sabugal, Quadracies [Quadrazais], Aldea de Ponte [Aldeia da Ponte] and arrived at [Fuente] Guinaldo on the 9th of August. On the 11th the Light Division crossed the Agueda and the 52nd cantoned at Sauga [El Sahugo] until the 23rd of September. The French army commanded by Marshal Marmont arrived at Tamames on the 22nd of September with a large convoy of military stores for the relief of Ciudad Rodrigo; the main body of the British army was stationed at Fuenteguinaldo and Picton's Division at El Bodon. On the 23rd the regiment marched to Martiago and on the 24th in camp near La Herquera. On the morning of the 25th a great force of the enemy's cavalry, supported by a body of infantry attacked General Picton's Division at El Bodon which fell back to [Fuente] Guinaldo. The enemy's attitude now made it very doubtful whether the Light Division could by passing the Agueda at Robleda, effect a junction with Lord Wellington at [Fuente]Guinaldo, therefore it was intended to march into Portugal by crossing the Sierra de Gata and on the evening of the 25th the regiment marched from La Herquera for this purpose, the baggage preceding the column, but it was soon discovered that the enemy was in possession of the Pass of Perales which rendered this line of retreat impracticable. The column immediately countermarched and moved rapidly upon Robleda and just arrived in time to cross the river without molestation, a little distance above the town, and about 3 pm on the 25th the Light Division joined the army in position at [Fuente]Guinaldo. At 10 o'clock the same night the army retired upon the Coa covered by the Light Division and a small body of cavalry. The regiment reached Casillas de Flores at daylight next morning and after a few minutes halt the division proceeded towards Alfaiates retiring slowly before the enemy. On the afternoon of the 27th the Light Division took up a position at Alfaiates, the enemy occupied a contiguous range of hills in the front and afterwards the close of the evening made one or two demonstrations of attack, but the picquets only were engaged, the regiment was not permitted to light fires and the men lay by their arms until midnight when the division began to fall back upon Soito, when the army took up a position, the left resting upon Rendo and the right upon Soito, here the enemy discontinued his operations and retired upon Salamanca, the army went into cantonments the following day (30th). The 52nd marched to Casillas de Flores and remained there until the 13 October, when the battalion marched to Robleda.

17 October. Marched to Robleda to Tamara.

14 December. Changed its quarters to Los Agallos [Agallas], where the men were employed until the 6th of January in making fascines and gabions for the intended siege of Rodrigo.

1812 Siege of Rodrigo

8 January. The Light Division crossed the Agueda and invested Rodrigo, the other divisions having closed up, occupied the adjacent villages on the left bank of the river. About 10 pm a detachment from the regiments of the Light Division commanded by Lieutenant Colonel Colborne, stormed and gallantly carried the advanced redoubt, which was destroyed during the night and on its site, the first point of attack was securely established at daylight next morning. At this season of the year it was considered necessary to keep the men under cover as much as possible and one division of the army at a time was thought sufficient to carry on the operations in the trenches while the others were quartered in the contiguous villages. Therefore, the siege was prosecuted by the daily relief of divisions in regular succession. The 52nd Regiment occupied El Bodon on the days it was not employed in the trenches.

19 January Two breaches being deemed practicable, the Light Division was formed at 9pm and carried the lesser breach in gallant style. 57 killed and wounded.

On the afternoon of the 20th the 52nd returned to their quarters at El Bodon, and marched from thence to [Fuente]Guinaldo on the 31 January.

25 February The skeleton of the 2nd Battalion marched for Lisbon on its way to England.

1813

20 May The regiment marched from [Fuente]Guinaldo to take the field and encamped near Carpio.

21 May Crossed the Agueda and occupied San Felices [Saelices] el Chico, from thence it moved on Salamanca, by Sancti Espiritus [Spiritus], San Munoz, Coco de Robles [Robliza de Cojos] and on the 26th encamped on the Tormes about two leagues from Salamanca.

28 May Forded the Tormes and marched to Aldea Nova [?]. The Light Division arrived on the Douro on the 2 June and encamped below Toro, on the 3rd crossed the Douro by the broken bridge at Toro and marched to Tagarabuena.

The five divisions under Sir Thomas Graham, that had passed the Douro at Lamego and pursued their route by Braganza [Braganca], Cavagales [Carbajales de Alba] and Zamora, had now united with the rest of the army at Toro and the whole moved upon Burgos.

4 June Marched to Convento de Espinar [El Espinar], Tamara [de Campos], Pina [de Campos], Lantadillo, Villa Sandine [Villasandino] and arrived at Hornillos [del Camino] on the 12th, during the whole of this day the Light Division was occupied in supporting the light cavalry and artillery in harassing the French rearguard.

13 June At five o'clock am the castle of Burgos was blown up and the regiment marched to Tovar [Tobar].

14 June Marched to Quinta Maguar [?]

15 June Marched to Puente Arenas.

16 June Crossed the Ebro at Puente Arenas and marched to Medina de Pomar.

17 June Marched to Rio Lozo [Rio Losa]

Affair at San Millan

18 June The 2nd Brigade of the Light Division unexpectedly fell in with one of the enemy's small corps of observation near to San Millan [de San Zadornil] (on the left bank of the Ebro, three or four leagues from Frias) The enemy had quitted the high road and was moving along a small ridge of hills to the right of the road, hoping to escape unperceived. The Rifle Corps commenced a fire upon the rear while the 52nd pushed on in double quick time along the flank of the column and attacked it; 300 of the enemy surrendered themselves prisoners, and a great quantity of baggage fell into the hands of the brigade. After the skirmish, the regiment encamped near Estrigon [Espejo].

19 June The Light Division arrived at [Subijana-]Morrillas about five miles from Vitoria.

20 June The other divisions closed up and were encamped chiefly between the River Bayas and the Zadorrra, high ridges of hills intercepted the view, both of Vitoria and the enemy's position in its front.

Battle of Vitoria

21 June At four o'clock am the Light Division marched from its encampment to share in the operations of the day. The principal part of the enemy's line extended along the left bank of the Zadorra, his left was covered by the village of Subijana de Alava and his right rested upon the heights in advance of the village of Albechuco [Abetxuko] on the right bank of the river. The attacking columns moved in three divisions, Sir Rowland Hill's corps formed the right and advanced by the high road from Miranda, Sir Thomas Graham's corps formed the left and by making a detour, advanced by the Bilboa road against the enemy's right. The centre was composed of the Light, 3rd, 4th and 7th Divisions, forming two columns behind the bridges of Nanclares [de la Oca] and Trespuentes, waiting only for the progress of Sir R[owland] Hill's attack to enable three divisions to force the bridges.

The 52nd crossed the bridge without loss and formed on the face of a hill opposite to the principal height, near the centre of the enemy's position, as soon as arrangements were completed for attacking this important eminence, the 52nd, covered by the skirmishers of the Rifle Corps, led the column of attack. General Picton's Division made a simultaneous movement along the base of the hill and the enemy, after firing a few shots, did not wait to receive the shock and fell back at all points towards Vitoria.

From the difficulties of the road, Sir T[homas] Graham's Corps did not arrive at the point of attack so early as was expected, however at this period of the action he had driven back the enemy from the heights of Albechuco [Abetxuko] across the Zadorra, but his opponents still commanded the bridge near this village, in order to force back this point, the 2nd Brigade of the Light Division made a movement to its left under a heavy fire of artillery. The efforts of six guns at a short range were directed solely against the 52nd and such was the admirable steadiness of the battalion that when the companies were ordered to wheel into line (being an open column of companies) the pivots took up the dressing under the direction of Major Mein[429] with the same coolness as if on a common parade. As soon as the line was formed, it advanced against the heights where the French artillery was

[429] Brevet Major William Mein, 52nd Foot.

posted and in a few minutes afterwards the guns were in possession of the regiment. On arriving at the summit of the hill, Captain Currie's[430] company (which was covering the advance of the regiment) forced back the enemy's skirmishers rapidly through a wood, and found himself at once close up to a French battalion in column and just as it was moving off, he charged with his company and unfortunately fell in executing this gallant enterprise. The brigade continued to sweep along the left bank of the river in front of Sir Thomas Graham's Corps and the victory being now complete, the regiment marched without intermission until eleven o'clock that night and bivouacked two leagues beyond Vitoria on the Salvatierra[431] road.

The men were so much fatigued after the Battle of Vitoria that it was nearly noon on the *22nd* before the division marched in pursuit of the enemy towards Pamplona and halted for the night within a league of Salvatierra. 23 killed and wounded.

23 June The division came up with the enemy near Iturmendi and after a slight skirmish their rearguard fell back along a straight line of road, which afforded Captain Ross's Troop of Horse Artillery an opportunity of firing with great effect upon the broken troops, who in their impatience to escape accidentally overturned a howitzer and a gun on the road, thus leaving the entire French army in possession of only one piece of artillery.

24 June Arrived within one league of Pamplona.

25 June Marched to Arre from whence the division was detached on a very harassing march to Sanguesa, for the purpose of intercepting the retreat of Clausel's Army.

26 June To Olonez [Oloriz]

27 June To Olite

28 June To Cassida [Caseda]

30 June To Sanguesa, but not having fallen in with the enemy, the division marched on the 2 July to Tiebas [-Muruarte de Reta].

3 July To Villaba [Villava].

4 July To Ostiz

6 July St Estevan [Doneztebe-Santesteban]. From thence on the 11th to Oronoza [Otietza].

14 July To Sumbilla [Sunbilla]

15 July To Vera [Bera]. The brigade took up its position in bivouac on the high ground behind the town, and the French were posted on the very formidable heights in its front, having their advanced sentries

430 Captain James Currie, 52nd Foot.

431 Now known as Agurain.

pushed forward to the steep brow which overlooks the streets where the Light Division picquets were established.

20 July Marched from Vera [Bera] to Lezaca [Lesaka].

Battle of the Pyrenees

On the 25 July Sir Thomas Graham made an unsuccessful attack upon San Sebastian and the same day Count d'Erlon and Marshal Soult respectively attacked the passes of Maya and Roncesvalles. On the evening of the 25 July the Light Division fell back from Lezaca [Lesaka] to near Sumbilla [Sunbilla] and continued to retrograde slowly towards Pamplona.

27 July To Subeite [Zibiete]

29 July To Lucumben [Lekunberri]

31 July To Delisape [Saldias?] The enemy's project for relieving Pamplona having failed, the Light Division countermarched and again arrived at Sumbilla [Sunbilla] on the 1st of August and reoccupied Vera [Bera] on the 2nd.

Affair at Lezaca [Lesaka] Bridge

At daybreak on 30 August, a considerable French force was assembled on their position above Vera, with a view of drawing off the garrison of San Sebastian by forcing through the covering army of Spaniards, which were posted on the heights of San Marcial. The columns soon began to descend the hill and the Light Division picquets having been driven out of the town, the enemy passed the Bidassoa, at a ford a little lower down where the river forms a kind of elbow. Its course at the bridge leading to Lezaca [Lesaka] being nearly at a right angle with the ford which the enemy passed. The uncertain result of the operations rendered it expedient to destroy the Lezaca [Lesaka] bridge, but to secure the brigade from sudden attack during the night, this bridge was partially blocked up with large sacks filled with stones, leaving only a narrow passage for a man. The attack of the Spaniards on the heights of San Marcial on the 31st having failed, the enemy returned the same night to regain their former position above Vera, but the heavy fall of rain rendered the ford which the enemy passed on the 30th now impracticable, his only resource was to force the Lezaca [Lesaka] Bridge and favoured by the dark tempestuous night, he succeeded in disposing of the double sentry of the Rifle Corps which was posted on it and the column commenced passing over as rapidly as the circumstances would permit.

As soon as the enemy's object was ascertained, some companies of the 52nd joined the Rifle Corps in a heavy fire upon the fugitives and at daylight 300 dead bodies were found near the bridge, besides great numbers were drowned in endeavouring to swim across the river.

Assault of San Sebastian

The assault of San Sebastian was to take place on the 31st and with a view of creating a fresh spirit and emulation amongst the assailants, a detachment from the Light Division was sent there as stormers, the proportionate quota to be given by the 52nd one captain, one subaltern and 35 rank and file. As soon as the order was communicated to the regiment, entire companies volunteered and the captains had now a difficult task in detecting the most fit men for such an undertaking without hurting the feelings of others. The party gallantly maintained the high reputation of the Light Division. The assault took place precisely at noon and after a severe contest of two hours, the enemy were driven out of the town and took refuge in the castle which surrendered a few days afterwards. 20 killed and wounded.

Capture of the heights of Vera [Bera]

7 October During the seven or eight weeks the French occupied the heights above Vera [Bera], they were actively employed in constructing redoubts on the projecting points in advance of their line and the position had become very formidable. On the evening of the 6th the plan of attack was communicated to the officers commanding companies; the redoubts were to be carried by the repeated charges of the 52nd in close column, while the other two regiments of the brigade (the Rifle corps and Portuguese Cacadores[432]) were to act as tirailleurs, every inequality of the hill where the charging column might find shelter to breathe between their attacks was distinctly pointed out to the officers. The men took a highly creditable interest in the success of the operations, by requesting permission to leave their knapsacks behind them in the bivouac.

At eight o'clock am of the 7th the two brigades made a simultaneous attack, the right commanded by Major General Kempt advanced by the Puerto to the right of the town of Vera, the left brigade commanded by Colonel Colborne skirted the left, a deep rugged ravine, which ran down the face of the hill prevented all communication between the brigades and each had to fight its way independently to the summit of the enemy's position. There were five redoubts surmounting each other on the part of the hill which the left brigade was to attack. The Rifle Corps and cacadores spread themselves across the brow of the

[432] 1st Caçadores.

hill to protect the formation of the 52nd column previous to its attack on the first redoubt. The difficult ascent compelled the men to scramble up singly and whilst the column was forming up in this manner, the enemy rushed out of the redoubt to charge it (five companies had just completed their formation and the sixth was in progress); the shock was parried without hesitation by a counter charge of these five companies led by Colonel Colborne, the enemy gave way and the redoubt was carried. The assailants having now established a footing at the bottom of the range of hills, a very few minutes were allowed for the men to breathe, after which the attack was prosecuted according to the original plan and each redoubt was captured in succession. On arriving at the last which formed the enemy's centre, an ineffectual resistance was made by his line, which soon fled, leaving three small pieces of artillery in the hands of the brigade, but not contented with this extraordinary success the pursuit was continued down the reverse of the hill and 22 officers and nearly 400 men surrendered themselves prisoners to a part of the regiment led on by Colonel Colborne. Thus ended the most brilliant achievement that perhaps was ever performed by a regiment. 84 killed and wounded.[433]

On the 9th of October, the regiment encamped to the right of the road leading through the pass of Vera and in a few days afterwards the regiment moved up to the heights of La Rhune, but nothing particular occurred till the 10th of November.

Passage of the Nivelle

On the night of the 9 November the regiment moved from its camp on La Rhune, and silently approached within 300 yards of the advanced point of the enemy's fortified height of La Petite Rhune. The signal of attack was made at daybreak on the morning of the 10th. A narrow ravine ran parallel to the head of the column forming nearly a right angle with the enemy's line of defence on the left side of the hill. Two companies of the 52nd and some cacadores were pushed across to protect the passage of the column. This being effected, the 52nd moved with great rapidity along the enemy's front, without firing a shot until it arrived at the redoubts on the right of this line; in the meantime the right brigade, having moved round the right of the hill, the enemy abandoned his redoubts after a slight resistance and the Light Division formed on the summit of La Petit Rhune, waiting the appointed time to take its share in the future operations of the day. As soon as the enemy

433 The actual figures were twelve men killed and six officers and sixty-six men wounded.

was driven out of the village of Sarre, the whole army moved forward to attack his entrenched line. The 2nd Brigade of the Light Division advanced against a strongly fortified part of the enemy's position, the flanks of it were covered by impracticable ravines, and it could only be approached in front over a very narrow low neck, exposed to the fire of two redoubts and of trenches cut in the hill half way down the slope; seeing however that shelter could be obtained under a bank on the opposite side, the 52nd headed by Colonel Colborne, crossed the ridge in single file, regardless of the fire from the defences. When collected under the bank the bugles sounded the advance, and the men ran up the slope with cheers, which had the effect of inducing the enemy to abandon his lines and the redoubt which supported them.

In following up this success the regiment advanced against a very strong irregular star fort and under a heavy fire from its garrison, formed columns of wings and instantly charged up to the ditch, but the enemy's fire was too powerful and a trifling inequality on the slope of the glacis, afforded the men sufficient protection to keep up a fire against the garrison, and in a few minutes afterwards a second effort was made. Upon a preconcerted signal both wings cheered and rushed forward, some men of the leading companies leaped into the ditch, but their efforts were unavailing, the scarp being 12 feet high, it was impossible to ascend it without ladders and the regiment was withdrawn a short distance out of the enemy's fire by the companies falling back in regular succession commencing with the rear. The success of General Beresford's operations left no hope for the garrison to escape and 560 men surrendered themselves prisoners laying down their arms on the glacis. 240 killed and wounded.

After the action the regiment halted for the night near St Pe [Saint-Pée-sur-Nivelle] and next day encamped near Arbonne, and on the 19th went into quarters in the village.

The enemy made a reconnaissance on the 20th and in this affair of picquets the 52nd had three rank and file wounded. A defensive line of posts being appointed for the different divisions of the army (stretching from the sea to Arcangues), the Light Division changed its quarters on the 24th and the 52nd occupied the Chateau of Castleneur and some farmhouses in the neighbourhood of Arcangues.

Passage of the Nive

On 9 December Sir John Hope's Corps reconnoitred Bayonne closely and the Light Division drove in the enemy's outposts in front of Arcangues in order to make a diversion in favour of Sir Rowland Hill's Corps which passed the Nive at Cambo [les-Bains] on this day and took up a position with its right upon the Adour and its left at Ville Franche [Villefranque].

Early on the morning of the 10th of December the Light Division picquets at Arcangues were very vigorously attacked and the enemy's columns pressed on so rapidly on the flanks that the picquets had an opportunity of making a serious stand, until they arrived at the abbatis, near the Chateau of Castleneur behind which Captain Douglas[434] formed up his company and made a very gallant resistance against the enemy's overwhelming force, but unfortunately he received a musquet shot in the head, of which he died a few days (16) afterwards. As soon as the picquets were driven back, the enemy occupied the range of hills at Castleneur and the Light Division was posted on a parallel ridge in their front, having converted a farmhouse which stood in the centre of the position into a post of defence. Skirmishing was continued throughout the day and in the evening the enemy's columns got under arms and made a demonstration of attack, which was not pressed beyond the picquet houses in the small valley which separated the positions of the two armies. On both the 10th and 11th the efforts of the enemy were directed against Sir John Hope's Corps which formed the left of the British line, on the road to St Jean de Luz, and having failed in his attempts against this part of the position, on the 13th he attacked Sir Rowland Hill's on the right of the line with no little success. On the night of the 12th two battalions of Nassau troops came over to the allies and were received by the picquets of the Light Division. 29 killed and wounded.

The enemy having retired towards Bayonne on the evening of the 13th, the Light Division went into cantonments on the 14th and the 52nd returned to nearly the same quarters that it occupied previous to the attack on the 10th.

1814

On the 4 January the regiment marched to Anainz [Arrauntz?], on the 5th to Ustaritz, and went into cantonments at Sala [?] on the 8th. It broke up from its cantonments on the 16 February and marched to Mobzao [?], La Bastide [-Clairance], St Martin [d'Arberoue], S[ain]t-Palais, Etcharry and arrived near Orthez on the 24 February.

434 Captain John Douglas, 52nd Foot, was severely wounded at the Nive and died of his wounds on 24 December 1813.

Battle of Orthez

On 25 February the Light Division arrived close to Orthez, halted upon the heights above the bridge; as soon as a close examination of the loopholed houses which defended its passage was effected, the division retired into the low ground and encamped for the night. On the 26th the division moved to its right, with the intention of passing the river at a ford above the town, but in the course of the evening the column countermarched and halted for the night near the village of Bereu [Baure]. Early on the morning of the 27th the regiment crossed the Gave de Pau by a pontoon bridge, which was laid a little lower down the river.

The left of the French position rested upon Orthez and from thence the line was continued along a range of hills in the direction of Dax, the right terminated on a commanding height behind the village of S[ain]t Boes. The 4th and 7th Divisions attacked the enemy's right, the 3rd and 6th Divisions attacked the centre and left of the position and the left brigade of the Light Division was standing in reserve near S[ain]t Boes. In consequence of the difficult approach to the enemy's right flank, the attack did not succeed at that point, neither was the centre making any progress when the left brigade of the Light Division was ordered to attack the left flank of the heights which the enemy's right occupied. The Rifle Corps and Cacadores were thrown out in front to cover the advance of the 52nd Regiment in line. The retrogression of the divisions both on the right and left placed the 52nd in a very critical situation and the importance of the movement was known to every individual. The regiment advanced up the hill under a heavy fire, preserving a most perfect formation and without returning a shot until within a few yards of the enemy's line, when a steady volley was given which was instantly followed by a determined charge, which drove the enemy off the hill and the success of the day was no longer doubtful. 93 killed and wounded.

The regiment halted at Bonnegarde after the Battle of Orthez on the 27th and marched next day to near Montaut.

On the 1st of March the regiment arrived at Mont de Marsan and marched the next day in the direction of S[ain]t Maurice [-sur-Adour] where the regiment arrived on the 3rd and went into cantonments at Barcelone [Barcelonne-du-Gers] on the 9th.

Affair at Tarbes

The regiment marched to Plaisance on the 19th, to Haget on the 20th and on the 21st attacked the enemy near Tarbes. 4 killed and wounded.

During the night of the 21st the French army retired upon Toulouse and on the 22nd the regiment marched to Lannemezan and pursued the route by Sanon [Saman?], Agacen [Agassac?], Soisever, [Seysses-Saves?] Plaisance [-du-Touch], Cugneaux [Cugnaux] and arrived at St Simon and Portet [sur-Garonne] on the 29th of March. The division moved to Selle [Seilh] on the 4th of April.

Battle of Toulouse

On the morning of the 10th, the Light division crossed the Garonne by a pontoon bridge near the village of Ausonne [Aussonne] and the whole army moved forward to the attack; the Light Division approached Toulouse by the Montauban road and subsequently moved to its left to the support of General Freire's Spanish Army, which was destined to attack the heights of La Pujade. The Spaniards having failed in their attack fell back in the greatest disorder, abandoning the bridge of Croix d'Aurade, but by a forward movement of the 2nd Brigade of the Light Division, the enemy were checked in their pursuit and the communication over the River Ers was preserved.

In the course of the afternoon the divisions of Sir Lowry Cole and Clinton attacked the redoubts of La Pujade on the Calvinet side, whilst the 52nd and 95th advanced on the opposite side, and after a very determined resistance the enemy abandoned all their works about five o'clock in the evening and the allied army formed upon the heights overlooking the town. The French army retired from Toulouse during the night of the 12th and the 52nd Regiment entered the suburbs of the town at daylight on the morning of the 13 April. In the course of the day couriers arrived at Toulouse announcing the decree of the French Senate of the 2nd of April; and on the 18th a convention was agreed upon for the suspension of hostilities between the Marquess of Wellington and Marshal Soult. The line of demarcation having been arranged the 52nd went into cantonments at Castel Sarrasin [Sarrazin] on the 22nd and remained there until arrangements were made for evacuating the south of France.

On the 3rd of June the regiment marched from Castel Sarrasin [Sarrazin] and proceeded to Bordeaux, where it arrived on the 14th of June and was received by the Duke of Wellington on taking leave of the army previous to its return to England.

17 June. Embarked at Pauillac on board His Majesty's Ship *Dublin* and landed at Plymouth on the 28th.

28 June. Marched from Plymouth to Tavistock.

11 July. Marched from Tavistock.

2 August. Arrived at Hythe Barracks.

31 August. Marched from Hythe Barracks.
2 September. Arrived at Chatham.
27 December. Marched from Chatham to embark for America.

Having tried to sail for America twice and forced into Cork for shelter, they received orders to proceed to Belgium to take part in the Waterloo campaign.

His later journal for Waterloo has been published elsewhere.[435]

[435] *52nd (Light Infantry) Eyewitness Accounts of the Waterloo Campaign*. Published by Ken Trotman Publishing 2020.

18. PRIVATE ELI GILL
NARRATIVE OF LIFE AND ADVENTURES[436]

Eli Gill, the subject of the following history, was born in Arkingarthdale [Arkengarthdale], near Richmond, on 23 August 1777.

Being born of poor parents at a time when learning was considered by the miners as a matter of comparatively trivial importance, his education was neither liberal nor extensive. Happy however, for himself and for all those who feel themselves interested in a circumstantial narration of the most important circumstances of his life, he was taught to read and write. Having received instruction in these two branches of useful learning, he was qualified to keep a journal of his services while in His Majesty's army.

In his juvenile years nothing occurred of so material and interesting a character as to deserve the attention of the reader; yet it may not be improper to observe that he was employed in the mining business by the agents of Sir C Turner,[437] Lord of the manor, from the 10th year of his age until he left the place of his nativity. Feeling much dissatisfaction with this low and humble employment, his mind restless and unfurnished with that *wisdom that cometh from above*, and unsubdued by divine grace, at the age of 25 he hired at Berwick [Borwick] near Lancaster, as a substitute for Mr William Gardiner, into the 1st Royal Lancashire Militia on the 13th of January 1802. On the 2nd of May, in the same year, he was embodied with the regiment at Lancaster and continued there nine months; in which time they were practised in the different evolutions of the army, in order to obtain skill in military discipline.

436 Originally published at Barnard Castle in 1826.

437 Sir Charles Turner of Kirkleatham Hall.

On the 14th of July [1802], the regiment was marched, according to orders from Lancaster to Chelmsford, the county town of Essex. They performed their march in 21 days and in their route went through Preston, Chorley, Manchester and Macclesfield. Three weeks after the arrival of the regiment at Macclesfield, it was divided into cantonments, when Eli, with that detachment unto which he belonged, went to Brentwood and completed their knowledge of the divers turns, motions and figures, made by soldiers, whether by way of exercise or during an engagement. The time of their practical inuration being expired, they marched from Danbury to camp, where the different cantonments, or detachments, were embodied in November 1802. Soon after, they marched to Maldon New Barracks and continued there under the command of Major General Beckwith[438] [for] 12 months. The purposes of their destination being accomplished, the major marched them from Maldon Barracks to Tilbury Fort, situate on the Thames, opposite to Gravesend, where they crossed the river and landed at the last-named place.

When they had arrived at Gravesend, Major General Nightingale[439] took the command and marched them to Braburn [Brabourne] Lees Barracks, where they abode 12 months; in which time they were twice reviewed by his present majesty, then Prince of Wales and His Royal Highness, Duke of York, commander in chief of His Majesty's forces. On the 10th of April 1805, at Braburn [Brabourne] Lees in Kent, Eli took the King's bounty and immediately entered into the 52nd Regiment of light infantry, commanded by Lieutenant General Moore, commander of the forces in Kent.

He remained in Kent under this general from the 10th of April 1805, until the 2nd of May 1807. The 52nd Regiment of light infantry, to which Eli belonged, joined the expedition, and embarked for Denmark on the 2nd of May 1807. The expedition arrived at Elsinor, a sea-port of Denmark, seated on the Sound, in the Isle of Zealand, anchored there the 13th and disembarked on the following morning at two o'clock. The British flag was carried by Captain Euit [Ewart][440] of the 52nd Regiment.

When the expedition had disembarked at Elsinor, the soldiers were told into brigades; the brigade with which Eli was embodied, consisted of the 43rd and 52nd Regiments of infantry, the 1st and 2nd Battalion of the 95th Rifle corps and the 79th light infantry, under the command of Sir Arthur Wellesley, the present Duke of Wellington. On the 15th

---

438 Major General John Beckwith, the father of Sir Thomas Sydney Beckwith.

439 Major General Miles Nightingall.

440 Captain John Ewart, 52nd Foot.

they marched towards Copenhagen and on the day after demolished some powder mills at Crosshillerow [Frederiksvaerk], belonging to the Danes. On the 17th the brigade retreated to Kioge [Køge] and was divided into cantonments. They continued in this state, observing the movements and operations of the enemy until the 10th of August.

On the 11th they attacked a part of the Danish army stationed in that place [Køge] with six pieces of cannon, small arms &c before one o'clock, their fortification wall was broken down; the 43rd and 52nd Regiments, with their commander, Sir A Wellesley at their head, entered the town. After a smart engagement, the Danes retreated from the town at the west end. But while Sir A Wellesley with these two regiments were engaging the Danish soldiers in the town, the other part of the English forces marched round to the west end thereof and fired upon the Danes as they were retreating. Upon the plain before the town, the two divisions were united and after they had pursued the enemy across the plain, took 1 general, some officers, 740 privates, 9 pieces of cannon, a quantity of small arms, and some ammunition waggons. In this battle, Sir A Wellesley was slightly wounded in the right shoulder, by a musket ball from the Danes.[441] After the termination of the action, the English soldiers marched west from the town to take up their quarters and when they had accomplished their object, the 43rd and 52nd Regiments returned to plunder it.

At the commencement of this battle, a circumstance of a very singular nature occurred. Two brothers, who were natives of Scotland, belonging to the 79th Regiment,[442] commanded by Colonel Cameron,[443] requested the colonel to permit them to cover each other from the enemies' fire. The colonel, being a person of a benevolent, humane disposition, on observing the tender affection and earnest concern, which the two brothers manifested towards each other, acceded to their request. Being placed side by side according to their desire, the first cannon ball that came from the enemy killed them both.

The day after the battle, the brigade lay in quarters and in the evening received an express from Lord Cathcart, commander in chief, to march for Copenhagen, to assist in the bombardment of that city. On the 15th they arrived at the Windmill Battery about two miles from Copenhagen, and until the morning of the 21st were employed in throwing up breastworks and fortifications against the enemy. In the 21st, the city was taken, having sustained the previous calamity

441 This was a false rumour, he was not wounded.

442 The 79th Foot were not at Køge. It is likely that he has confused them for the 92nd who were there.

443 Lieutenant Colonel Philips Cameron 79th Foot.

of three days embarking. From the 21st of August, until the 6th of September, the soldiers were employed in embarking the Danish stores and destroying their arsenals and batteries. Eli with five companies of the 52nd Regiment went onboard the repeating frigate *Lizabelak.*[444] Everything being properly adjusted, the expedition weighed anchor and about nine o'clock sailed for England, with the prize ships and stores. However, not more than two hours after their departure from Copenhagen, one of the prize ships, in which were five companies of the 79th Regiment struck on a sandbank. In consequence of this misfortune the repeating frigate, whose duty it was to observe the situation of every ship in the fleet, was under the necessity of taking the men and stores from the prize ship and landing them at Scarlet Island,[445] on the coast of Sweden. After this affair, which detained them about three weeks, they sailed to Gottenburg [Gothenburg] where the commander obtained provision for the crew and immediately sailed for home. In about 48 hours they were safely landed in Yarmouth roads and early the next morning, by telegraphic communication informed Admiral Duncan.[446]

The admiral soon after ordered them to sail to the Little Nore and disembark the troops; immediately on their disembarkation, they marched for Canterbury and ultimately for Ramsgate in Kent, where they laid in barracks until an expedition was formed under the command of Sir Hew Dalrymple[447] for Portugal, on the 24th of June 1808.

After a slow and tedious passage, the expedition landed at Vimiera, on the 13th of August, and encamped there until the 21st, when they advanced against the French under General Junot, engaged and defeated them.

The village stands in a lovely valley, about three miles from the sea and is screened from the breezes by the mountains through which the little River Maceira winds its way. The greater part of the infantry were posted in these mountains with eight pieces of cannon; the attack commenced with the usual impetuosity of the French and was sustained with that firmness and intrepidity, which are peculiar to the English soldiery. General Ferguson's Division[448] received the enemy

444 I have been unable to identify this vessel.

445 The Danish ship *Neptunus* ran onto a sand bank and the soldiers of the 92nd onboard were landed on Hewan Island (not Scarlet Island).

446 Admiral Adam Duncan.

447 General Hew Dalrymple was given overall command of the expedition to Portugal but he was Governor of Gibraltar and was delayed in joining the expedition until after the Battle of Vimeiro.

448 Major General Ronald Ferguson.

with a tremendous volley and brought them to close action. The French though disciplined, brave and accustomed to victory, could not withstand the charge of the British bayonet. In one moment, after they came to close action, their foremost rank fell like a line of grass, before the scythes of the mowers. The French immediately gave way and in their retreat, sustained the loss of six pieces of cannon.

A French general named Bernier [Brennier][449] was wounded in the Battle of Vimiera and was in danger of being killed by these into whose hands he had fallen, when Mackay,[450] a highland corporal of the 31st [71st] Regiment came up, had compassion on him and rescued him. Bernier [Brennier] feeling grateful for his preservation and deliverance from a premature death, offered for the acceptance of his deliverer, his watch and purse; these Mackay positively refused to accept. When he had delivered his prisoner safely to Colonel Pack, the French general exclaimed 'What sort of man can this be? He has just done me the greatest service and refuses to take the only reward I can at present offer!' Colonel Pack replied 'We are British soldiers sir, and not plunderers.' In reward of this noble, disinterested conduct, by the express desire of Sir Arthur Wellesley, he was directly made a sergeant; and the Highland Society, at their next meeting, voted that a gold medal, with a suitable device and inscription, should be presented to him, as expressive of their approbation of his meritorious conduct.

Another circumstance took place at the same time worthy of record. A piper to the grenadier company of the name of Stewart, early in the action received a dangerous wound in the thigh and rendered incapable of following his regiment. He refused to be carried off the field, but sat down where his companions might hear him and with a truly admirable and heroic spirit, continued playing warlike airs till the conclusion of the engagement. His country's society voted to him a fine stand of highland pipes, containing an inscription in commemoration of the manner in which he had rendered himself worthy of the donation.

The total loss of the enemy in the action, was about 3,000 in killed and wounded, 13 pieces of artillery and 23 ammunition waggons, that of the English 720. The decisive victory, which the English here obtained over the French, was owing to the superiority of their skill and valour, rather than the equality of their numbers; for the French were superior, both in cavalry and artillery, all of which were engaged, while one half of the English was unengaged.

449 French General Antoine Brennier was wounded and captured.

450 Corporal John Mackay, 71st Foot.

From the 21st of August to the 29th of December 1808, nothing of an interesting nature transpired, except an unimportant contest, between the English and French at Coimbra, a town in Portugal, which stands on a mountain, by the side of the River Mondego, in a very pleasant part of the country, abounding in vineyards, olive yards and fruits. After marching from one place to another, according to the orders they received, the situation of the enemy and the various purposes intended to be accomplished by their movements; Sir John Moore, with one division of the British army reached Benavente, a town in Spain, seated on the River Esla. Immediately after the rear of the army had marched into the town, on the 28th of December, an alarm was circulated that the enemy were on the opposite heights; in an instant the soldiers poured out at the gates, and every man with alacrity hastened to his proper post, the French observing from the heights their alertness and resolution immediately retired. The following morning the French again made their appearance, crossed the river with some of their cavalry at a ford 300 yards below the bridge. The 10th Hussars, with the picquets of the night, were placed under General Stewart;[451] and when they charged upon them, the enemy gave way and repassed the ford more precipitately than they had crossed it. About 100 of the French were killed, and 69 prisoners taken, exclusive of Lefebvre,[452] the commander of the Imperial Guard of cavalry. The Light Brigade were among the picquets.

After this engagement, two brigades were dispatched by way of Orouse [Ourense] to Vigo, under General Crawford [Craufurd], to which port Sir John Moore had ordered empty transports to be sent, supposing it to be the best point for embarkation. In their melancholy retreat, mountains covered with heavy clouds and the roads knee deep in snow, were the objects that powerfully arrested their attention and excited feelings of discontent, anxiety and despair.

The horses of the retreating army began to fail principally for want of shoes. As soon as these noble animals foundered, they were shot lest the enemy should profit by them. The rain continued to pour, the baggage was to be dragged and the men were to wade through half melted snow, the feet of the men as well as the beasts began to fail, more waggons were left behind, more ammunition destroyed on the way and when they were at Villafranca [del Bierzo], they were in such a state, that several experienced officers predicted that, if this march were persevered in, a fourth part of the army would be left in the

451 Colonel Charles Stewart (later Vane) commanded a cavalry brigade.

452 General de Division Charles Comte Lefebvre-Desnouettes.

ditches, before it was accomplished. More magazines and carriages were (2nd January) here destroyed. Some of the men abandoned themselves, knowing that if they proceeded, they must die of cold, hunger and weariness, penetrated into the wine cellars, and giving way to desperate excess, were found dead, when the French entered the town. When the general marched with the reserve from Bembibre, he left a detachment to cover the town, while parties were sent to warn the stragglers of their danger, and drive them out of the houses, for the place was filled with them; near 1,000 men of the preceding divisions, having remained there all abandoned to despair and most of them to drunkenness. A few were prevailed upon to march on, but the greater number were deaf to threats and insensible to danger, till the rear-guard was compelled to march. A small detachment of cavalry still covered them and did not quit the town till the enemy approached and then the road was filled with the stragglers, Spanish and British, armed and unarmed, mules, carts, women and children. Four or five squadrons of French cavalry, compelled the detachment in the rear to retire and pursued them closely for several miles, till General Paget,[453] with the reserve repulsed them. As the French dragoons galloped through the long line of these stragglers, they slashed them with their swords to the right and left, the men being so insensible from liquor, that they neither attempted to resist, nor retire from the road.

However, a more prudent, cautious and temperate conduct preserved Eli from so dreadful a catastrophe, the consequences of which do not terminate in this world. So great were the sufferings of the British soldiers in their retreat, that 2,000 of them were picked up by the French between Astorga and Lugo. As they proceeded, the places through which the army had to pass, were covered with snow. There was neither provision to sustain nature, nor shelter from the rain and snow, nor fuel for fire to keep the vital heat from extinction, nor place in which the weary could recruit their strength; that everything tended to augment their already almost intolerable burden. What added horror to the scene, was that women and children attended this wretchedly situated army. Some were frozen to death in the baggage waggons; some died of fatigue and cold, while their helpless infants were pulling at the empty breast. When the horses arrived at Lugo, many of them through fatigue, fell down dead in the streets; others were shot. Near 400 dead bodies were laying in the street, swelling with the rain and infecting the atmosphere.

---

[453] Major General Sir Edward Paget.

On the sixth and seventh, the French made two attacks upon them, which were received with a strength and courage that again rendered the English victorious. From Lugo, they had 11 leagues to march before they could reach Corunna, the place of their embarkation. When they left Lugo, many of the men were so exhausted that they could not keep ranks. However, such as were able to continue in their ranks, reached Corunna, without further molestation from the enemy.

On the 15th of January, the two divisions of the army that separated at Lugo, were reunited at Corunna, Sir John ordered the transport ships to meet the army at Vigo, when the impropriety of this measure was discovered, it was countermanded; but not so soon as to give the transport ships time to arrive at Corunna, to receive the English soldiers on the day of their arrival. Therefore, to the grief and sorrow of the British army they perceived the impossibility of escaping without engaging the enemy; and winning a battle.

In the evening of the 14th, the transports hove in sight and the sick and dismounted cavalry were sent on board with all possible expedition. All the preparations for embarking were completed on the morning of the 16th, when the general gave notice, that if the French did not move, he intended to begin embarking the reserve at four o'clock in the afternoon. However, before that time, the French were seen pouring down the hill, on the right wing of the British and a part of their soldiers were beginning to fire at them. Five companies of the 52nd, five of the 43rd and [an]other five of the 95th corps; were selected from the rest of the army, to cover the retreat, at the distance of four paces. Eli was among the five companies from the 52nd and though thus exposed to the continual fire of the enemy, which brought numbers to a premature and instantaneous death, yet providence permitted him not to fall by the devastating hand of war. The number of killed and wounded in his own regiment were: 1 captain, 1 lieutenant, 1 sergeant and 31 rank and file. In this battle, the commander, Sir John Moore, was killed by a cannonball, which carried away his left shoulder, and part of his collar bone, leaving the arm hanging by the flesh. But soon after he expired without a struggle.

After Sir John's death, the command devolved upon General Hope,[454] who passed the whole night in embarking the troops. By ten o'clock, the ensuing morning, he ordered the soldiers to march by brigades from the field, leaving strong piquets as guards, and to give notice if the enemy advanced. Almost all the army were embarked in the night; the piquets were withdrawn, and embarked also before day, so

---

[454] Lieutenant General Sir John Hope.

that scarcely any remained on shore at daylight, except the rear guard and the reserve. When the French saw this, their light infantry were immediately pushed to the heights of St Lucia, which command the harbour; they placed some cannon on a rising ground and fired at the transports. All things relating to the embarkation of the army being finished, the rear guard retired to the boats, no attempt being made to hinder them. Early the following morning, the French opened their batteries upon them, when they were obliged to cut their cables and put to sea.

Nothing material happened to Eli, on his return from Spain, the passage was pleasant, except the striking of the ship against a rock off the Land's End. On the 25th of February, the 52nd Regiment arrived at Ramsgate harbour in Kent, disembarked the following day and immediately marched for Deal Barracks, where they laid until called to join another expedition to Portugal.

On the 24th of May 1809, Eli, with the 52nd Regiment, joined a second expedition for Portugal, and that day sailed for Lisbon. After experiencing many casualties on the first of July, they discovered Cape Clear, a promontory of a little island on the south of Ireland. Here on the same day, they fell in with a French privateer, with an American vessel in tow; they were required after a proper signal, to hoist their colours, when the Frenchman showed French colours and the American, American colours. The captain of the American ship informed them that she had been captured by the French 14 days before; the English captain immediately replied 'You are my prize'. They took the vessel to Lisbon and sent her to England by the first convoy.

On the 4th of July they disembarked at this noted city; and on the 29th joined the grand army under Sir A[rthur] Wellesley at Talavera, a town in Spain, in New Castille, the day after the French had been defeated at that place; having made a forced march of 14 Spanish leagues, in twenty-four hours.

After reaching Talavera, they marched towards Las Casses del Pererquo[?], where they arrived on the 1st of August and for nineteen days received only 3½ lbs of bread each, for their subsistence. After obtaining a supply of provisions, and improving their condition, they marched towards Campo Maior, a town in Portugal, 100 miles east of Lisbon, where their numbers were increased by receiving from the battalion of detachments 120 men, who were left in Spain in their retreat the preceding year.

On the 14th of December, they marched from Campo Maior, towards Pinhel, the capital of a territory named Tras os Montes, seated at the confluence of the Rivers Coa and Pinhel. This territory abounds with game, is peculiar for its wine and fruits and contains a great number of cattle. They reached Pinhel on the 7th of January 1810, and abode there observing the operations of the French until the 14th of March; when they marched towards Almeida, a fortified town near the River Coa, and had an unimportant contest with the French on the 24th of July.[455] The 52nd Regiment had 1 [rank & file] killed, 1 major, 1 captain, and 16 men wounded.[456]

From the 24th of July unto the 25th of September, they laid in cantonments and were employed in observing the state, movements and policy of the enemy. On the 25th it was observed that the whole of the 6th and 2nd Corps, of the French crossed the Criz. When General Pack and Craufurd retired with their divisions to that position, which Lord Wellington determined the army to occupy on the top of the Sierra de Busaco. This place, that was chosen by His Lordship for the allied army to make a stand, is a high ridge which extends from the Mondego, in a northerly direction, about eight miles. At the summit of the ridge about two miles from its termination, are the convent and garden of Busaco.

The whole of the allied army, with the exception of some soldiers under General Hill, was collected on the Sierra de Busaco, with the British cavalry watching the plain in the rear of their left, and the road leading through the mountainous tract from Mortagao [Mortagua] to Oporto. On the 26th of September, the light troops were engaged through the line, yet nothing singular or important happened. Early the following morning, the French made two impetuous attacks on their position, the one on the right, and the other on the left. That part of the ridge which was occupied by the Third Division of infantry, was desperately assailed by two divisions of the Second Corps of the French. So great were the spirit and ardour of the French, that one division of their infantry arrived at the top of the ridge, where it was met in the most courageous manner by the 88th and 45th Regiments and the 8th Portuguese under Lieutenant Colonel Douglas.[457] These three corps advanced with the bayonet, and compelled the French to retreat from the advantageous ground they had obtained. The other division, that made an attack near to the right, was repulsed by Lieutenant Colonel Trench[458] and a brigade of Portuguese infantry

455 A strange description of the Action on the Coa.

456 These are low casualty figures in comparison with the other regiments at the Coa.

457 Lieutenant Colonel Douglas was not colonel of the 8th Portuguese Line Battalion until 1812.

458 Lieutenant Colonel Robert le Poer Trench, commanding 74th Foot.

under the command of Colonel Mackinnon[459], before it could reach the top of the hill. On the left, three divisions of French infantry, belonging to the Sixth Corps, advanced up that part of the ground occupied by the left division, commanded by General Craufurd and the Brigade of Portuguese infantry, under General [Denis] Pack. One division of the French approached to the top of the hill, when they were instantly charged by the bayonet, by General Craufurd with the 48th [43rd], 52nd and 95th Regiments, together with the 3rd Portuguese Cacadores and driven down with great loss.

Here Eli was called to witness a shocking effusion of human blood, occasioned by the jealousy, pride and insatiate thirst after power and glory, which too often inhabit, actuate and influence the minds of men. In the battle described above, not less than 2,000 Frenchmen were left dead in the field.

After the battle, the French received such considerable reinforcements and became so much superior to the allied forces in point of number, that it became expedient for the English to retreat towards Lisbon, hoping that famine would weaken and discourage the French troops. They arrived at Arieda [Arruda dos Vinhos] in the lines before Lisbon on the 14th of October.

On the 24th of January 1811, they were divided into cantonments at Valle, where they continued in a state of inactivity till the 6th of March, when they marched after the French under Massena. This general, in his retreat, displayed great military talents, the glory of which was tarnished by the personal cruelties which were perpetrated by his sanction. The conduct of the French under Massena, through this retreat, was marked by a barbarity seldom equalled and never exceeded. Even in the towns of Torres Novas, Thomar [Tomar] and Pernes, in which the headquarters of some of the corps had been for four months, and in which the inhabitants had been induced to remain by promises of good treatment, they were plundered, and many of their houses destroyed, on the night, the enemy withdrew from their position; and they afterwards burnt every town and village through which they passed. They rendered their retreat more rapid, by abandoning their wounded, and destroying part of their baggage. They advanced up the country and after occupying several strong positions, remained in force at Guarda, a town fortified both by nature and art, till the close of March, when upon the advance of the allied main army, they retired and occupied a new position at Sabugal on the River Coa.

---

459 Colonel Henry Mackinnon commanded 1st Brigade of 3rd Division.

At Sabugal the French were attacked on the 3rd of April by the allied troops, in several divisions and repulsed with the loss of 200 killed and 300 prisoners. The 52nd Regiment in this action, had 3 killed; Captain P[atrick] Campbell severely wounded,[460] together with a lieutenant[461] and 17 privates.[462] The French entered Spain on the following day, and continued their retreat across the Agueda. The enemy made two unsuccessful attempts upon the British picquets, in one of which 2 sergeants and 3 privates, belonging to the 52nd were wounded.

On the 2nd of May, the whole French army, consisting of the 2nd, 6th and 8th Corps, with all the cavalry that could be raised in the provinces of Castile and Leon, recrossed the Agueda at Ciudad Rodrigo and immediately advanced towards the allied army. The allied army, with the Light Division to which Eli belonged, were ranked along the River Duas Casas and when the enemy advanced, the Light Division, with the British cavalry, fell back upon Fuentes d'Onoro, where three other divisions were posted.

On the afternoon of the 3rd, the French, with a large force, made an attack upon the village of Fuentes d'Onoro, which was very gallantly defended by Lieutenant Colonel Williams,[463] at the head of some battalions of light infantry. The French by repeated efforts, gained a momentary possession of a small part of the village, but were soon dispossessed by a charge of the 71st Regiment.

On the morning of the 6th [5th], the various French corps, with the cavalry, made a lively attempt to cross the River Duas Casa and succeeded in taking possession of Fuente d'Onoro. On this day, after a number of partial actions and operations that were directed with great skill and executed with facility and courage by the troops, and which in different quarters continued till the evening, the assailants were ultimately repulsed at all parts. At this place, it is said, that the whole loss of the British and their allies on these two days, was not much short of 1,700 in killed, wounded and missing of all descriptions. That of the French, not precisely known,[464] must have been very considerable; besides a number of prisoners taken from them, they left 400 men dead in the village of Fuentes d'Onoro, against which their principal efforts had been directed. After the French were defeated,

460 Captain Patrick Campbell, 52nd Foot, was wounded.

461 Lieutenant John Gurwood, 52nd Foot.

462 And one sergeant.

463 Lieutenant Colonel William Williams, 5th Battalion, 60th Foot, commanded twenty-eight light companies from the regiments of the First and Third Divisions apart from the Guards.

464 The British and Portuguese losses were around 1,500 killed and wounded. The French lost about 2,200 killed and wounded.

they fell back towards a town in Spain, on the River Agueda, called Ciudad Rodrigo leaving picquets at El Bodon.

On the 23rd of September, the French made their appearance very near Ciudad Rodrigo and on the 24th made a general attack on the posts of the allied army, on the heights of El Bodon, which after much skirmishing, terminated in an orderly retreat of the allies to a more favourable position.

In the autumn, Lord Wellington continued his troops on the frontiers of Portugal, in the most healthy parts of the vicinity of the Agueda. Eli, with the Light Division, laid at El Bodon from about the 25th of September 1811, until early in January 1812, when the allied army crossed the river into Spain, and invested the fortress of Ciudad Rodrigo. The siege of this place was carried on with uncommon and extraordinary success. The place was considerably strengthened by a redoubt which the French had constructed on the hill of San Francisco, that communicated with the three fortified convents in the suburbs. Yet in the night of the same day on which the siege was begun, a detachment of the division under Lieutenant Colonel Colborne of the 52nd, stormed and carried the redoubt on the hill, took some prisoners and put their associates to the sword. Eli was among the volunteer stormers of the redoubt of Francisco.

Among the various preparations and works that it was necessary to execute previous to the taking of the town Eli, with the Light Division was cantoned at El Bodon, on the opposite side of the river, which they had to cross morning and evening.

The success that attended their operations against the redoubt of San Francisco, enabled them to break ground near their works. On the 14th towards evening, a fire was opened from the first parallel, with 22 pieces of cannon, and three batteries; and the same evening the besiegers were established in the second parallel, that was within 120 yards of the place. In ten days after the opening of the siege, the approaches were completed, several breaches were also made in the wall, when they came to an immediate resolution to carry the works by storm. Lord Wellington, finding it inconvenient to advance his approaches very near the town, as was usual on former occasions, it called for the greatest efforts of bravery, to succeed in the assault. The storming parties, in five separate columns, made up of the Third and Light Divisions of the army and of General Pack's Brigade, were commanded to advance. Two officers of distinguished talents, Picton and Major General Craufurd took an eminent part in the operations, and to their great satisfaction, the efforts of the various columns, were followed with success.

Here a circumstance occurred, which from its singularity and importance in estimating English valour, ought to be inserted. That party of soldiers under General Pack, was ordered to make a false attack; but such was the ardour and impetuosity of the troops, that the false attack was converted into a real one; the enemy therefore was charged in a direction not originally intended, forced into their works, and speedily overcome.

The subject of this history was upon the Forlorn Hope, and not more than twenty minutes after they had entered the town, he received a wound in his left temple, while upon the ramparts. The second battalion of the 5th Regiment, under Major General Ridge,[465] with the 95th Regiment under Lieutenant Colonel Campbell,[466] with amazing valour, stormed the principal breach in the body of the place. Though the defence was well maintained by the French, yet every effort was unavailing. The troops bore down all resistance; yet as in all instances of war, while the English were proceeding to certain, complete victory, a heavy loss was sustained, by the death of Major General Mackinnon, who fell a victim to the enemy, at the head of his storming party.

The total loss of the British, in killed and wounded was 1,200; the battalion with which Eli was engaged had 1 captain and 9 men killed; Lieutenant Colonel Colborne severely wounded, Major Napier,[467] Captain Man [Mein][468] and Lieutenant Woodgate[469] were also wounded; Major Napier had his right arm amputated in consequence of the wound he had received in this affair.

After the storming of Ciudad Rodrigo, that was honourable to Lord Wellington, the commander of the army and the soldiery under his direction, his lordship moved part of his men towards Badajoz, a fortified town of Spain, the capital of Estremadura.

About the 17th of March the city was completely invested, the first parallel was formed within 200 yards of the outwork. On the 19th the garrison made a sortie against the British works, but were immediately repulsed with considerable loss. On the 26th the besiegers fired into the place from a distance of 200 yards and on the very same day carried Fort Picurina by storm and put the garrison to the sword. By the 6th of April, so unexampled was their success, that no less than three practicable breaches were effected when the storming of the city was immediately arranged. On the 6th, in the storming of the town,

465 Major Henry Ridge, 5th Foot.

466 An error by Eli, it was actually Major Alexander Cameron, 95th Foot.

467 Major George Napier, 52nd Foot.

468 Captain William Mein, 52nd Foot.

469 Lieutenant John Woodgate, 52nd Foot.

the resistance that the Light Division met with was of a very serious nature; having advanced to the covered way, they descended into the ditch and proceeded to storm the breach; but so numerous were the obstacles of all kinds which the ingenuity of the enemy had thrown in the way, that although the attack was often renewed, they could not establish themselves in the place. However, the besiegers being successful at every other part, the Light Division was withdrawn. During the operations of the siege, the 52nd Regiment had killed; 3 captains, 1 lieutenant, 1 ensign,[470] 4 sergeants and 66 privates.[471] The number of wounded was 320, including 1 lieutenant colonel, 4 captains, 9 lieutenants, 3 ensigns and 24 sergeants. The names of the captains that were killed, belonging to Eli's regiment, were Jones, Maddon [Madden] and Poole.[472, 473]Among the wounded were Lieutenant Colonel Gibbs,[474] Major Mein, Captain R[obert] Campbell, Lieutenants York, Davis, Barlow and Winterbottom.[475] The whole loss the British and Portuguese sustained was 809 killed and about 2,000 wounded.[476] The French garrison, which originally amounted to 5,000 men, lost in the previous operations 1,200 killed and wounded independent of those who perished in the assault.[477]

Not long after, Eli, with the 52nd Regiment, entered the town, and when in the grandstand securing the prisoners, he was wounded above the right temple by a musket ball from the French. On the evening of the 7th they marched from the town to their former encampments and on the following day were employed in burying the dead belonging [to] the British and French armies. They were thrown in heaps, around the works of Badajoz, without any distinction, English and French, making one undistinguishable mass.

From the 6th to the 22nd, they laid in camp at Badajoz, when they advanced to their former cantonments, on the frontiers of Portugal. About the 30th of April, the 52nd Regiment arrived at El Bodon, where they lay, until every necessary preparation was made for the advance of the whole British army into Spain.

470 Actually two lieutenants were killed, not ensigns.

471 These numbers vary from the original returns and probably reflect the final death toll.

472 Captains William Jones, William Madden & Clement Poole.

473 Mein had become a major in February 1812.

474 Lieutenant Colonel Edward Gibbs, 52nd Foot.

475 Lieutenants Charles Yorke, Francis Davies, George Barlow and John Winterbottom, 52nd Foot.

476 Total allied losses at the siege amounted to nearly 5,000 killed and wounded.

477 The French loss was nearer 1,500 killed and wounded and 3,500 prisoners.

On the 13th of June, they crossed the Agueda and on the 16th reached the city of Salamanca. On their arrival here, the French evacuated the town and recrossed the Tormes, when the allied army immediately entered the city. On the 22nd of July, a general engagement took place, in which the allies were completely victorious. The slaughter on the field of battle and in the pursuit, was amazing; and the proofs of the victory answered to its importance. Eleven pieces of cannon, two eagles, and six colours were taken; five generals, three colonels, 130 officers of different ranks and 7,000 soldiers were made prisoners.

The Light Division was on the reserve until evening, and then advanced to harass and cut off the enemy in their retreat. They pursued them until 12 o'clock pm and after resting upon their arms till ½ past two, attacked a part of the French, (ten miles before the rest of the allied army) and took from them 74 bullocks and 200 sheep. This capture was of considerable utility to the army in their advance towards the capital of Spain. In the whole affair of pursuing the enemy; and taking the bullocks and sheep, the 52nd Regiment had only two men wounded. The loss of the allies was small in proportion to the greatness of their success; 700 killed, and upwards of 4,000 wounded. After the Battle of Salamanca, the French continued their retreat towards Madrid and Lord Wellington with the main body of his army closely followed them. Joseph Buonaparte had under his command 20,000 men, yet when the British approached on the 12th of August, he hastily evacuated Madrid and retreated to Almanza.

Eli was in the city of Madrid for about six days, at the expiration of which he marched with the Light Division to Getaffe [Getafe], a village about seven miles south-east of the capital, a pleasant fertile part of the country, abounding in melons, pumpkins and grapes of different sorts, wine was so plentiful at this place, that he remembers he might have purchased any quantity at a penny-farthing per bottle.

From Getaffe [Getafe], the Light Division advanced to Alcantara, a small strong town, that had a magnificent bridge over the Tagus, built by Trajan,[478] that opened a communication between Madrid and the opposite country. The bridges on this river were destroyed in order to retard the progress of the French in their way back to Madrid and Salamanca. Eli was personally employed in destroying one of these bridges, which was effected in the following manner; planks were raised from the bottom of the river, on which three barrels of powder were placed near the stones of the arch; afterwards a train of powder

478 The bridge at Alcantara was built on the orders of Emperor Trajan between AD 104 and 106.

was laid to the distance of fifty yards. This preparatory work being executed, Eli mounted one of General Clinton's horses[479] kindled the match, and galloped off at full speed, until the powder exploded. This rendered the bridge completely impassable. The French received such a considerable reinforcement, that Lord Wellington, about the 27th of October, put his whole force in motion, and retired on Salamanca.

November the 15th, the Light Division retreated from Salamanca, and were so closely pursued by the French corps on the 16th & 17th, that on the latter day they were compelled to give them battle; in which Captain Dawson[480] and two men were killed; Captains Currie and Fuller,[481] 3 sergeants and 27 privates wounded, in the 52nd Regiment.[482] After this, the allies continued their retreat without interruption, being impeded only by the badness of the roads, till they reached the Portuguese frontier, where they were distributed into extensive cantonments, and allowed to enjoy a rest from the toils of war, that was indispensable to prepare them for the fatigues of another campaign.

They continued on the frontiers of Portugal, from the close of 1812, till the 20th of May 1813. After the Battle of Salamanca, reinforcements were sent to [the] amount of upwards of 20,000 men. So that in May, the number of troops disposable under Lord Wellington, was estimated at 80,000 British and Portuguese, with 40,000 or 50,000 Spanish regulars. On the 20th of May, they left their state of inactivity on the frontiers of Portugal and begun to march towards France, with the intention of passing through its interior. They continued their march until the 18th of June, when they arrived at San Millan, where the Light Division engaged a party of the French, in which the 52nd Regiment took several officers, 300 prisoners and a quantity of baggage.

On the 20th the two armies were in sight of each other, and the allied army halted before the town of Vitoria, capital of the province of Alaba [Alava]. On the 21st a general battle was fought, in which the French were completely defeated, with great loss. Lord Wellington himself made the following returns; 28 twelve pounder guns, 42 eight pounders, 43 four pounders, 3 eight-inch howitzers, 2 six inch mortars, all brass ordnance; together with 415 caissons of all sizes, both for guns and musketry, including 14,249 rounds of ammunition, for guns and howitzers, 1,973,400 musket ball cartridges, 40,668 pounds of

---

479 General Henry Clinton was then serving in the north around Burgos, so it is highly unlikely that his horses were at Madrid.

480 Captain Henry Dawson, 52nd Foot was killed.

481 Captain Thomas Fuller, 52nd Foot.

482 There was also twenty-one men missing.

gunpowder, 44 forge waggons and 56 forage waggons; including, in fact the whole 'materiel' of this boasted army.

During the various animated, strenuous and successful operations of the allied army, on the 21st the 52nd Regiment had Captain Currie[483] and 3 privates killed; Lieutenant Northy,[484] 1 sergeant and 16 privates wounded. The total loss sustained by the allied armies, was 740 killed and 4,170 wounded.

The day after the battle of Vitoria, the British and Portuguese soldiers continued to pursue the enemy in their retreat; and on the 24th the advanced guard pressed so closely upon their rear, as to be able to take from the French, the only gun they had saved. The enemy continued their retreat and the main body entered Pamplona, the capital of Upper Navarre, a considerable town, with a very strong citadel, with only one howitzer.

About the 24th of July, the Light and 7th Divisions occupied the heights of Santa Barbara and the town of Bera. They abode in their encampments until the 31st of August, when Eli, with a detachment from the 52nd and 95th Regiments, marched to San Sebastian.

An attack was made upon this town on the 31st and by the united persevering efforts of the troops that were employed, it ended in complete success. After the assault had continued two hours, under circumstances that occasioned much bloodshed, they obtained a firm footing in the town. Eli, with the detachment from the aforementioned regiments, was upon the Forlorn Hope; in the assault, the detachment lost Lieutenant Harvest[485] and 3 privates among the killed; Major Hunt,[486] Captain R[obert] Campbell, 2 sergeants and 16 men wounded. The whole loss was estimated at 2,300 killed and wounded. After the capture of this town, and while the French were making a quick retreat, a baggage waggon was abandoned, about a quarter of a mile from the scene of action, from which Eli obtained a prize of 848 Spanish dollars, about 4s 2d each in English money.[487] The detachment that assisted in the taking of San Sebastian joined the Light Division the day after the assault, at Vera, an episcopal town with a harbour.

On the 7th of October, the invasion of France by the allied army took place, by crossing the River Bidassoa, at the bridge leading to Anaye [Hendaye] a fortified town in France, in the department of Lower Pyrenees. After effecting with great spirit, a passage across the

483 Captain James Currie, 52nd Foot.

484 Lieutenant Edward Northey, 52nd Foot.

485 Lieutenant Augustus Harvey, 52nd Foot.

486 Actually Brevet Lieutenant Colonel John Hunt, 52nd Foot.

487 Worth about £12 each in modern terms.

Bidassoa, the Light Division under Major General Alten, supported by a Spanish division under Longa and Giron, attacked the French entrenchments and posts on a mountain, called La Rhune, which they carried. The 52nd Regiment here had 1 sergeant and 11 privates killed; 1 major, 3 captains, one lieutenant, 1 ensign, 2 sergeants and 62 privates wounded. Major Mein, Captain Douglas[488] and Lieutenant Hunter severely.[489]

Eli though engaged in these repeated contests for mastery, was more fortunate than many of his companions. While some of them were arrested by the King of Terrors, and others carried by their compassionate fellow soldiers, to seek an alleviation of their sufferings from a surgeon, rendered perhaps less tender and sympathetic by frequently performed operations, that many of his fellows; Eli, by that universal providence, was preserved in the midst of the greatest danger and saved from death and hell. The importance of his own salvation, was sometimes presented to his mind, arrayed in all the awfully interesting circumstances thereof, so as almost irresistibly to wring from his heart 'God be merciful to me a sinner!' Yet as in many other cases, those feelings were 'as the morning cloud and as the early dew that soon goeth away' he continued in a course of transgression and disobedience, living amidst the most imminent danger, 'without God and without hope in the world'.

The British with their allies laid in their encampment on the Bidassoa, near Anaye [Hendaye], until the 10th of November. On that day they made an attack upon the enemy in columns of divisions, each led by a general officer, and having its own reserve. Sir Rowland Hill directed the movements of the division on the right, and Marshal Beresford those of the centre. The operations began at daylight; but their number and variety was so great and the resistance made by the enemy was so stubborn, that the object contemplated by the commander, was not effected till nightfall. Then however they did gain the rear of the enemy's right; and on the morning pursued them across the Nivelle, which they had crossed during the preceding night, leaving all their works and posts in front of St Jean de Luz and on the following night they retired to an entrenched camp in front of Bayonne.

In the course of these operations the 52nd Regiment sustained a heavy loss. One captain and 30 privates were killed; 1 captain, 5 lieutenants, 7 sergeants, 3 buglers and 120 rank and file wounded. After the French

488 Captain James Douglas, 52nd Foot.

489 Lieutenant William Hunter, 52nd Foot.

retreated from the River Nivelle, they occupied a strong position in front of Bayonne.

It was the intention of Lord Wellington to have crossed the Nive immediately after the passage of the Nivelle, but a continued succession of heavy rain compelled him to continue his troops in cantonments until the 8th of December. On the 9th every necessary preparation was completed for crossing the river, and the right wing of the army under Sir Rowland Hill was ordered to pass at and in the neighbourhood of Cambo, while Marshal Beresford was to support and favour that operation by passing the 6th Division under General Clinton, at another point. In both these operations they were successful and the French were driven from the right bank of the river and retired towards Bayonne. The Light Division under Major General Alten moved forward and reconnoitred the enemy's entrenchments which were round Bayonne, but in the evening returned to the ground which they previously occupied. On the morning of the 10th, the enemy moved out of their entrenched camp with nearly their whole army and drove in the piquets of the Light Division. They next made a vehement attack upon the post of the Light Division, which was repulsed with the usual characteristic bravery of that division. In these conflicts the 52nd Regiment had 4 privates killed; 1 major, 1 captain, 2 sergeants and 12 rank and file wounded.

Nothing interesting that had any relation to the subject of our history transpired until the 27th of February, when as the 6th and Light Divisions crossed the Gave de Pau under the commander Lord Wellington, his lordship found the enemy's army in a strong position at Orthes. Lord Wellington in the battle moved forward the Light Division, to attack the left of the height on which the enemies right was posted. This attack was led with admirable gallantry by the 52nd regiment under Lieutenant Colonel Colborne and as well supported on their right by two brigades of the 3rd Division and by other attacks on the left by Anson's Brigade[490] of the 4th Division, and on the left by Sir Thomas Picton, with the remains of the 3rd Division. Here was a conflict of no common order; here depended the fate of the battle; here the valour and resolution of the troops must lead to victory, if victory be obtained; and here ultimately they discomfited the enemy, dislodged them from the almost inaccessible heights which they occupied; and here the allied arms were attended with certain and complete success. The pursuit of the vanquished army was continued until it was dark, when the army halted near Sault de Navailles during the night and

490 Major General William Anson.

prepared for the further operations intended for the next day. It was then utterly impossible to estimate the enemy's loss; so rapid was their flight that not more than 6 pieces of cannon were taken. The number of prisoners was considerable and those who deserted afterwards immense. On the morning after the battle, Eli distinctly remembers the awful and appalling scenes that were presented to their view: the whole country was literally covered with dead and dying and wounded French. The regiment in which Eli was, lost seven privates who were killed in the battle; Captains Yorke and March,[491] Lieutenants Nixon, Holford and Leaf,[492] together with 76 rank and file wounded.

On the 28th the English renewed the pursuit, following the receding enemy to St Sever [Saint Sever], in the Department of Landes, seated on the Adour. Here Lord Wellington fixed his headquarters, until the 1st of March, when he commanded his part of the army, to cross the river at that place. Having to make this advance, Sir William Beresford passed with the Light Brigade, proceeding onwards for Mont [de] Marsan, at which place he captured a large magazine of provisions.

After various movements, on the 20th of March, the Light Division engaged and dislodged a part of the French army on the heights above Oliex [Orliex] near Tarbes, a populous town of France, capital of the department of Upper Pyrenees, which contains an ancient castle and college. Soult, the French general, with his shattered and depressed army, retreated to Toulouse, one of the most ancient and celebrated cities of France.

Three days after the arrival of Soult at this place, Lord Wellington appeared with the whole of his army, which consisted of from 10,000 to 12,000 cavalry, and 40,000 to 50,000 infantry. On the 10th of April, a bridge was laid across the Garonne, on which Toulouse is situated, when the Spanish corps, under General Freire, moved round their left flank and having followed up their success, they soon compelled the whole corps to retire. The Light Division, which was immediately on their right, moved up to their assistance, when the Spanish corps rallied again, and the French were repulsed with great loss. The Spanish troops suffered so much in their retiring, that Eli remembers advancing on the same ground, when the battle took a more favourable turn, two or three inches deep in human blood. On the 12th they entered the city and continued three days in its suburbs. In the evening a messenger arrived from Paris to apprise Lord Wellington that a treaty of peace had been concluded and that the exiled family were restored.

491 Captain Charles Lennox, Earl of March, 52nd Foot.

492 Lieutenants William Nixon, James Holford & John Leaf, 52nd Foot.

An abandonment of the operations and animosities of war immediately followed; Eli and the rest of the British army marched back to Toulouse. On the 22nd they left the last mentioned city and continued their march towards Castle Jolous [Casteljaloux]. At this town the Light Division was cantoned until the 29th of May; when they proceeded on to Bordeaux, through a territory that is very fruitful, particularly in vines, chestnuts and fig trees. The adjacent country is exceedingly pleasant and during the season when peasants are all employed in the vintage, it forms one of the most delightful landscapes in the world. Here Eli and his fellow soldiers arrived on the 4th of June and were marched to a plain about two miles on the other side of the city, where they were reviewed by the King of France and the Duke of Wellington. After the review His Lordship ordered them to march for England. After a stay of 2 days, they marched towards the sea & on the 17th of June, embarked for England. The wind was low, which rendered their passage long and tedious.

On the 30th they landed at Plymouth and marched to Tavistock. On July the 8th they marched from Tavistock and in their route went through the populous and wealthy city of Exeter. On the 29th he reached Hythe Barracks and after laying there two days, continued their march to Chatham, one of the principal stations of the Royal Navy. Here they abode from 3rd of September until the 26th of December [1814] at which time the Light Division received orders to march for Portsmouth, a seaport in Hampshire, which has the most considerable harbour for men of war in England. It is the strongest fortified place in this country and its high importance renders it worthy of every attention. Many of the largest ships are always laid up here; it is the rendezvous of the Grand Channel Fleet. The docks, arsenals, storehouses, barracks &c are of amazing magnitude, and are always in the most perfect order . . .

Eli Gill's adventures at the Battle of Waterloo are published elsewhere.[493]

[493] Published in *Waterloo Archives*, volume XIII.